Extending Excel with Python and R

Unlock the potential of analytics languages for advanced data manipulation and visualization

Steven Sanderson

David Kun

Extending Excel with Python and R

Associate Group Product Manager: Kaustubh Manglurkar
Publishing Product Manager: Apeksha Shetty
Book Project Manager: Kirti Pisat
Senior Editor: Tiksha Lad
Technical Editor: Rahul Limbachiya
Copy Editor: Safis Editing
Proofreader: Safis Editing and Tiksha Lad
Indexer: Subalakshmi Govindhan
Production Designer: Shankar Kalbhor
Senior DevRel Marketing Coordinator: Nivedita Singh

First published: April 2024
Production reference: 1030424

Published by
Packt Publishing Ltd.
Grosvenor House
11 St Paul's Square
Birmingham
B3 1RB, UK.

ISBN 978-1-80461-069-5

www.packtpub.com

Contributors

About the authors

Steven Sanderson, MPH, is an applications manager for the patient accounts department at Stony Brook Medicine. He received his bachelor's degree in economics and his master's in public health from Stony Brook University. He has worked in healthcare in some capacity for just shy of 20 years. He is the author and maintainer of the healthyverse set of R packages. He likes to read material related to social and labor economics and has recently turned his efforts back to his guitar with the hope that his kids will follow suit as a hobby they can enjoy together.

I want to thank Packt for this opportunity and David, my co-author, for working on this with me. I also want to thank my family as this took a good deal of time to put together.

David Kun is a mathematician and actuary who has always worked in the gray zone between quantitative teams and ICT, aiming to build a bridge. He is a co-founder and director of Functional Analytics and the creator of the ownR Infinity platform. As a data scientist, he also uses ownR for his daily work. His projects include time series analysis for demand forecasting, computer vision for design automation, and visualization.

I extend my heartfelt gratitude to my partner, Ania, and my children for the encouragement throughout the journey of writing this, my inaugural book.

About the reviewers

Jesús Martín de la Sierra Silva is a dedicated R developer with an engineering background who has been involved in large IT projects transforming raw data into insightful actionable decisions. He provides decision-making capabilities based on a statistical approach, by exploring connections and patterns in data and producing valuable visualizations. Jesús also specializes in creating user-friendly applications that seamlessly integrate complex computations such as process mining, forecasting, network analysis, or machine learning predictive models. For years, he has promoted the transition from spreadsheet software to R to bring a powerful perspective on modern data analysis.

David Napoli holds a master's degree in aerospace engineering and *All but Dissertation* in Health Services Research/Biostatistics. David has 25 years of experience working with data, with extensive experience in quantitative development, including the development, maintenance, and governance of data repositories, risk adjustment methodologies, IBNR determination, and analytic platform innovation. David also has 25 years of experience in advanced data visualization, statistical modeling and evaluation, and survival analysis. David has applied his analytics proficiency in multiple roles, including director of strategic analytics and distinguished faculty instructor of data visualization, data analytics, and advanced analytics curriculums.

Mehmet Sinan İyisoy is a biostatistician with years of experience in medical statistics. He holds BSc and MSc degrees in mathematics and statistics. Starting out as a mathematician, his career transitioned through phases of programmer, system administrator, and biostatistician. Sinan has consistently shown a strong dedication to data and programming. He is an enthusiastic user of a wide array of technologies, predominantly consisting of open source components. He has accumulated experience across various institutions and diverse roles for which his profound expertise was central. With a passion for statistics, Sinan now continues to contribute to scientific literature and public knowledge while working at Necmettin Erbakan University.

Shane Alex Jose has a master's in statistics. His passion for coding stemmed from tutoring graduate-level Python courses – yet he claims he's more confident in R. Oddly, he relishes debugging and considers it very cathartic! Currently, Shane is working as an analyst programmer in EvoEnergy's data analytics team – enhancing models and building/testing internal R packages/shiny dashboards used across the company. Having worked across multiple sectors, Shane is fascinated by the variety of data used across various industries and the impact data can have (especially if incorrectly governed). He aims to become confident across multiple specializations to help identify gaps and develop unique solutions/insights that could potentially address these gaps.

Table of Contents

3

Executing VBA Code from R and Python   39

4

Automating Further – Task Scheduling and Email   55

Part 2: Making It Pretty – Formatting, Graphs, and More

5

6

10

Time Series Analysis: Statistics, Plots, and Forecasting   217

Part 4: The Other Way Around – Calling R and Python from Excel

11

Calling R/Python Locally from Excel Directly or via an API   257

Part 5: Data Analysis and Visualization with R and Python for Excel Data – A Case Study

12

Data Analysis and Visualization with R and Python in Excel – A Case Study — 285

Preface

Welcome to the world of *Extending Excel with Python and R*! In this book, we delve into the convergence of Excel with the powerful capabilities of Python and R, providing a comprehensive guide to leveraging these languages for data manipulation, analysis, visualization, and more.

Join us on this journey as we explore the intersection of Excel, R, and Python, empowering you to excel in today's data-driven landscape.

Who this book is for

This book is designed for intermediate or higher-level users of R and/or Python with some data analysis experience, as well as familiarity with Excel basics.

What this book covers

Chapter 1, Reading Excel Spreadsheets, delves into importing data from Excel into R/Python. You will begin by importing your first Excel sheet into R, navigating Excel file intricacies, and then conclude with a Python counterpart.

Chapter 2, Writing Excel Spreadsheets, explains how, after analyzing data in R/Python, it's essential to communicate findings effectively with Excel users. This chapter provides insights into creating Excel sheets from R/Python and exporting analysis results.

Chapter 3, Executing VBA Code from R and Python, explores how, next to writing the results out to Excel, you might want to add VBA macros and functions to the resulting Excel sheet to further empower the end users of the analysis results. We can do this in this chapter.

Chapter 4, Automating Further – Task Scheduling and Email, covers how we have R packages such as RDCOMClient, which will work with Outlook, and Blastula, which can help in automating the analysis and emailing of reports in R. In Python, the smtplib package serves the same purpose.

Chapter 5, Formatting Your Excel Sheet, discusses how packages can help with creating sheets and tables along with formatted data in Excel, and how to use them to create beautiful Excel reports.

Chapter 6, Inserting ggplot2/matplotlib Graphs, shows how to create graphics from ggplot2 and matplotlib. There are ggplot2 themes a user can use as well, along with others to create beautiful graphics in R/Python and place them in Excel.

Chapter 7, Pivot Tables and Summary Tables, explores the world of pivot tables in Excel using R and Python. Learn how to create and manipulate pivot tables directly from R/Python for seamless interaction with Excel.

Chapter 8, Exploratory Data Analysis with R and Python, explains how to pull data in from Excel and perform **Exploratory Data Analysis (EDA)** with various packages, such as `{skimr}` for R and `pandas` and `ppscore` for Python.

Chapter 9, Statistical Analysis: Linear and Logistic Regression, teaches you how to perform simple statistical analysis with linear and logistic regression in R and Python on Excel data.

Chapter 10, Time Series Analysis: Statistics, Plots, and Forecasting, explains how to perform simple time series analysis using the `forecast` package in R, and `kats` and **long short-term memory (LSTM)** in Python.

Chapter 11, Calling R/Python Locally from Excel Directly or via an API, calls R and Python from Excel locally and via an API. This chapter also covers the open source tools for calling a local R/Python installation from Excel using BERT and `xlwings`, as well as open source and commercial API solutions.

Chapter 12, Data Analysis and Visualization with R and Python in Excel – A Case Study, presents a case study of performing data visualization and machine learning in Excel by calling R or Python.

To get the most out of this book

Before diving into this book, it's helpful to have an intermediate understanding of either R or Python (or both), including intermediate-level proficiency in data manipulation and analysis using libraries such as pandas, NumPy, and the tidyverse. Familiarity with Excel basics, such as navigating spreadsheets and performing simple data manipulations, is also assumed. Additionally, a basic understanding of statistical concepts and data visualization techniques will be beneficial for following along with the examples and exercises presented throughout the book.

Software/hardware covered in the book	Operating system requirements
R	Windows (for the VBA parts), macOS, or Linux (for all content excluding VBA)
Python 3.11	
Excel (including VBA)	

An installation guide for the relevant packages and tools will be provided in each chapter.

If you are using the digital version of this book, we advise you to type the code yourself or access the code from the book's GitHub repository (a link is available in the next section). Doing so will help you avoid any potential errors related to the copying and pasting of code.

> **Disclaimer**
>
> The authors acknowledge the use of cutting-edge AI, such as ChatGPT, with the sole aim of enhancing the language and clarity within the book, thereby ensuring a smooth reading experience for readers. It's important to note that the content itself has been crafted by the authors and edited by a professional publishing team.

Download the example code files

You can download the example code files for this book from GitHub at `https://github.com/PacktPublishing/Extending-Excel-with-Python-and-R`. If there's an update to the code, it will be updated in the GitHub repository.

Conventions used

There are a number of text conventions used throughout this book.

`Code in text`: Indicates code words in text, database table names, folder names, filenames, file extensions, pathnames, dummy URLs, user input, and Twitter handles. Here is an example: "The `styledtables` package can only be installed from GitHub via the `devtools` package."

A block of code is set as follows:

```
install.packages("devtools")
# Install development version from GitHub
devtools::install_github(
'R-package/styledTables',
build_vignettes = TRUE
)
```

Any command-line input or output is written as follows:

```
python -m pip install pywin32==306
```

Bold: Indicates a new term, an important word, or words that you see onscreen. For instance, words in menus or dialog boxes appear in **bold**. Here is an example: "Before running this code, you can ensure that `iris_data.xlsm` has the macro by going to **Developer** | **Macros (or Visual Basic)** to see whether the macro exists."

> **Tips or important notes**
> Appear like this.

Get in touch

Feedback from our readers is always welcome.

General feedback: If you have questions about any aspect of this book, email us at customercare@ packtpub.com and mention the book title in the subject of your message.

Errata: Although we have taken every care to ensure the accuracy of our content, mistakes do happen. If you have found a mistake in this book, we would be grateful if you would report this to us. Please visit www.packtpub.com/support/errata and fill in the form.

Piracy: If you come across any illegal copies of our works in any form on the internet, we would be grateful if you would provide us with the location address or website name. Please contact us at copyright@packt.com with a link to the material.

If you are interested in becoming an author: If there is a topic that you have expertise in and you are interested in either writing or contributing to a book, please visit authors.packtpub.com.

Share Your Thoughts

Once you've read *Extending Excel with Python and R*, we'd love to hear your thoughts! Scan the QR code below to go straight to the Amazon review page for this book and share your feedback.

https://packt.link/r/1804610690

Your review is important to us and the tech community and will help us make sure we're delivering excellent quality content.

Download a free PDF copy of this book

Thanks for purchasing this book!

Do you like to read on the go but are unable to carry your print books everywhere?

Is your eBook purchase not compatible with the device of your choice?

Don't worry, now with every Packt book you get a DRM-free PDF version of that book at no cost.

Read anywhere, any place, on any device. Search, copy, and paste code from your favorite technical books directly into your application.

The perks don't stop there, you can get exclusive access to discounts, newsletters, and great free content in your inbox daily

Follow these simple steps to get the benefits:

1. Scan the QR code or visit the link below

https://packt.link/free-ebook/9781804610695

2. Submit your proof of purchase
3. That's it! We'll send your free PDF and other benefits to your email directly

Part 1:
The Basics – Reading
and Writing Excel Files
from R and Python

This introductory part lays the foundation for working with Excel files in both R and Python. The chapters cover essential tasks such as reading and writing Excel spreadsheets using popular libraries such as R and Python, enabling you to automate tasks and further enhance your Excel workflows using tools such as `RDCOMClient`, `blastula`, `schedule`, and `smtplib` for scheduling runs and sending `emails`. `readxl`, `openxlsx`, `xlsx`, `pandas`, and `openpyxl`. Additionally, you'll learn how to execute VBA code.

This part has the following chapters:

- *Chapter 1, Reading Excel Spreadsheets*

- *Chapter 2, Writing Excel Spreadsheets*

- *Chapter 3, Executing VBA Code from R and Python*

- *Chapter 4, Automating Further – Task Scheduling and Email*

1
Reading Excel Spreadsheets

In the deep and wide landscape of data analysis, Excel stands tall and by your side as a trusted warrior, simplifying the process of organizing, calculating, and presenting information. Its intuitive interface and widespread usage have cemented its position as a staple in the business world. However, as the volume and complexity of data continue to grow exponentially, Excel's capabilities may start to feel constrained. It is precisely at this point that the worlds of Excel, R, and Python converge. Extending Excel with R and Python invites you to embark on a truly transformative journey. This trip will show you the power of these programming languages as they synergize with Excel, expanding its horizons and empowering you to conquer data challenges with ease. In this book, we will delve into how to integrate Excel with R and Python, uncovering the hidden potential that lies beneath the surface and enabling you to extract valuable insights, automate processes, and unleash the true power of data analysis.

Microsoft Excel came to market in 1985 and has remained a popular spreadsheet software choice. Excel was originally known as MultiPlan. Microsoft Excel and databases in general share some similarities in terms of organizing and managing data, although they serve different purposes. Excel is a spreadsheet program that allows users to store and manipulate data in a tabular format. It consists of rows and columns, where each cell can contain text, numbers, or formulas. Similarly, a database is a structured collection of data stored in tables, consisting of rows and columns.

Both Excel and databases provide a way to store and retrieve data. In Excel, you can enter data, perform calculations, and create charts and graphs. Similarly, databases store and manage large amounts of structured data and enable querying, sorting, and filtering. Excel and databases also support the concept of relationships. In Excel, you can link cells or ranges across different sheets, creating connections between data. Databases use relationships to link tables based on common fields, allowing you to retrieve related data from multiple tables.

This chapter aims to familiarize you with reading Excel files into the R environment and performing some manipulation on them. Specifically, in this chapter, we're going to cover the following main topics:

- R packages for Excel manipulation
- Reading Excel files to manipulate with R
- Reading multiple Excel sheets with a custom R function
- Python packages for Excel manipulation
- Opening an Excel sheet from Python and reading the data

Technical requirements

At the time of writing, we are using the following:

- R 4.2.1
- The RStudio 2023.03.1+446 "Cherry Blossom" release for Windows

For this chapter, you will need to install the following packages:

- `readxl`
- `openxlsx`
- `xlsx`

To run the Python code in this chapter, we will be using the following:

- Python 3.11
- `pandas`
- `openpyxl`
- The `iris.xlsx` Excel file available in this book's GitHub repository

While setting up a Python environment is outside the scope of this book, this is easy to do. The necessary packages can be installed by running the following commands:

```
python -m pip install pandas==2.0.1
python -m pip install openpyxl==3.1.2
```

Note that these commands have to be run from a terminal and not from within a Python script. They need to be run in the folder where `requirements.txt` resides or a full path to the `requirements.txt` file has to be included.

This book's GitHub repository also contains a `requirements.txt` file that you can use to install all dependencies. You can do this by running the following command:

```
python -m pip install -r requirements.txt
```

This command installs all the packages that will be used in this chapter so that you don't have to install them one by one. It also guarantees that the whole dependency tree (including the dependencies of the dependencies) will be the same as what this book's authors have used.

Alternatively, when using Jupyter Notebooks, you can use the following magic commands:

```
%pip install pandas==2.0.1
%pip install openpyxl==3.1.2
```

There is a GitHub account for all of the code examples in this book located at this link: `https://github.com/PacktPublishing/Extending-Excel-with-Python-and-R`. Each chapter has it's own folder, with the current one as `Chapter01`.

> **Note**
>
> Technical requirements for Python throughout the book are conveniently compiled in the `requirements.txt` file, accessible on GitHub repository here, `https://github.com/PacktPublishing/Extending-Excel-with-Python-and-R/blob/main/requirements.txt`. Installing these dependencies will streamline your coding experience and ensure smooth progression through the book. Be sure to install them all before diving into the exercises.

Working with R packages for Excel manipulation

There are several packages available both on CRAN and on GitHub that allow for reading and manipulation of Excel files. In this section, we are specifically going to focus on the packages: `readxl`, `openxlsx`, and `xlsx` to read Excel files. These three packages all have their own functions to read Excel files. These functions are as follows:

- `readxl::read_excel()`
- `openxlsx::read.xlsx()`
- `xlsx::read.xlsx()`

Each function has a set of parameters and conventions to follow. Since `readxl` is part of the `tidyverse` collection of packages, it follows its conventions and returns a `tibble` object upon reading the file. If you do not know what a tibble is, it is a modern version of R's `data.frame`, a sort of spreadsheet in the R environment. It is the building block of most analyses. Moving on to `openxlsx` and `xlsx`, they both return a base R `data.frame` object, with the latter also able to return a `list` object. If you are wondering how this relates to manipulating an actual Excel file, I can explain. First, to manipulate something in R, the data must be in the R environment, so you cannot manipulate the file unless the data is read in. These packages have different functions for manipulating Excel or reading data in certain ways that allow for further analysis and or manipulation. It is important to note that `xlsx` does require Java to be installed.

As we transition from our exploration of R packages for Excel manipulation, we'll turn our attention to the crucial task of effectively reading Excel files into R, thereby unlocking even more possibilities for data analysis and manipulation.

Reading Excel files to R

In this section, we are going to read data from Excel with a few different R libraries. We need to do this before we can even consider performing any type of manipulation or analysis on the data contained in the sheets of the Excel files.

As mentioned in the Technical requirements section, we are going to be using the `readxl`, `openxlsx`, and `xlsx` packages to read data into R.

Installing and loading libraries

In this section, we are going to install and load the necessary libraries if you do not yet have them. We are going to use the `openxlsx`, `xlsx`, `readxl`, and `readxlsb` libraries. To install and load them, run the following code block:

```
pkgs <- c("openxlsx", "xlsx", "readxl")
install.packages(pkgs, dependencies = TRUE)
lapply(pkgs, library, character.only = TRUE)
```

The `lapply()` function in R is a versatile tool for applying a function to each element of a list, vector, or `DataFrame`. It takes two arguments, `x` and `FUN`, where `x` is the list and `FUN` is the function that is applied to the list object, `x`.

Now that the libraries have been installed, we can get to work. To do this, we are going to read a spreadsheet built from the Iris dataset that is built into base R. We are going to read the file with three different libraries, and then we are going to create a custom function to work with the `readxl` library that will read all the sheets of an Excel file. We will call this the `read_excel_sheets()` function.

Let's start reading the files. The first library we will use to open an Excel file is `openxlsx`. To read the Excel file we are working with, you can run the code in the `chapter1` folder of this book's GitHub repository called `ch1_create_iris_dataset.R` Refer to the following screenshot to see how to read the file into R.

You will notice a variable called `f_pat`. This is the path to where the Iris dataset was saved as an Excel file – for example, `C:/User/UserName/Documents/iris_data.xlsx`:

```
> # Use openxlsx
> openxlsx::read.xlsx(f_path) |> head(5)
  sepal_length sepal_width petal_length petal_width species
1          5.1         3.5          1.4         0.2  setosa
2          4.9         3.0          1.4         0.2  setosa
3          4.7         3.2          1.3         0.2  setosa
4          4.6         3.1          1.5         0.2  setosa
5          5.0         3.6          1.4         0.2  setosa
> openxlsx::read.xlsx(f_path, sheet = "iris")  |> head(5)
  sepal_length sepal_width petal_length petal_width species
1          5.1         3.5          1.4         0.2  setosa
2          4.9         3.0          1.4         0.2  setosa
3          4.7         3.2          1.3         0.2  setosa
4          4.6         3.1          1.5         0.2  setosa
5          5.0         3.6          1.4         0.2  setosa
```

Figure 1.1 – Using the openxlsx package to read the Excel file

The preceding screenshot shows how to read an Excel file. This example assumes that you have used the ch1_create_iris_datase.R file to create the example Excel file. In reality, you can read in any Excel file that you would like or need.

Now, we will perform the same type of operation, but this time with the xlsx library. Refer to the following screenshot, which uses the same methodology as with the openxlsx package:

```
> # Use xlsx
> xlsx::read.xlsx(file = f_path, sheetIndex = 1) |> head(5)
  sepal_length sepal_width petal_length petal_width species
1          5.1         3.5          1.4         0.2  setosa
2          4.9         3.0          1.4         0.2  setosa
3          4.7         3.2          1.3         0.2  setosa
4          4.6         3.1          1.5         0.2  setosa
5          5.0         3.6          1.4         0.2  setosa
> xlsx::read.xlsx(file = f_path, sheetName = "iris") |> head(5)
  sepal_length sepal_width petal_length petal_width species
1          5.1         3.5          1.4         0.2  setosa
2          4.9         3.0          1.4         0.2  setosa
3          4.7         3.2          1.3         0.2  setosa
4          4.6         3.1          1.5         0.2  setosa
5          5.0         3.6          1.4         0.2  setosa
```

Figure 1.2 – Using the xlsx library and the read.xlsx() function to open the Excel file we've created

Finally, we will use the `readxl` library, which is part of the tidyverse:

```
> # Use readxl
> readxl::read_excel(f_path) |> head(5)
# A tibble: 5 × 5
  sepal_length sepal_width petal_length petal_width species
         <dbl>       <dbl>        <dbl>       <dbl> <chr>
1          5.1         3.5          1.4         0.2 setosa
2          4.9         3            1.4         0.2 setosa
3          4.7         3.2          1.3         0.2 setosa
4          4.6         3.1          1.5         0.2 setosa
5          5           3.6          1.4         0.2 setosa
> readxl::read_excel(f_path, "iris") |> head(5)
# A tibble: 5 × 5
  sepal_length sepal_width petal_length petal_width species
         <dbl>       <dbl>        <dbl>       <dbl> <chr>
1          5.1         3.5          1.4         0.2 setosa
2          4.9         3            1.4         0.2 setosa
3          4.7         3.2          1.3         0.2 setosa
4          4.6         3.1          1.5         0.2 setosa
5          5           3.6          1.4         0.2 setosa
```

Figure 1.3 – Using the readxl library and the read_excel() function to read the Excel file into memory

In this section, we learned how to read in an Excel file with a few different packages. While these packages can do more than simply read in an Excel file, that is what we needed to focus on in this section. You should now be familiar with how to use the `readxl::read_excel()`, `xlsx::read.xlsx()`, and `openxlsx::read.xlsx()` functions.

Building upon our expertise in reading Excel files into R, we'll now embark on the next phase of our journey: unraveling the secrets of efficiently extracting data from multiple sheets within an Excel file.

Reading multiple sheets with readxl and a custom function

In Excel, we often encounter workbooks that have multiple sheets in them. These could be stats for different months of the year, table data that follows a specific format month over month, or some other period. The point is that we may want to read all the sheets in a file for one reason or another, and we should not call the read function from a particular package for each sheet. Instead, we should use the power of R to loop through this with `purrr`.

Let's build a customized function. To do this, we are going to load the `readxl` function. If we have it already loaded, then this is not necessary; however, if it is already installed and you do not wish to load the library into memory, then you can call the `excel_sheets()` function by using `readxl::excel_sheets()`:

```
read_excel_sheets <- function(filename, single_tbl = FALSE) {
  sheets <- readxl::excel_sheets(filename)

  if (single_tbl){
    x <- purrr::map_df(sheets, readxl::read_excel, path = filename)
  } else {
    x <- purrr::map(sheets, ~ readxl::read_excel(filename, sheet = .x))
    purrr::set_names(x, sheets)
  }

  x
}
```

Figure 1.4 – Creating a function to read all the sheets into an Excel file at once – read_excel_sheets()

The new code can be broken down as follows:

```
read_excel_sheets <- function(filename, single_tbl) {
```

This line defines a function called `read_excel_sheets` that takes two arguments: `filename` (the name of the Excel file to be read) and `single_tbl` (a logical value indicating whether the function should return a single table or a list of tables).

Next, we have the following line:

```
sheets <- readxl::excel_sheets(filename)
```

This line uses the `readxl` package to extract the names of all the sheets in the Excel file specified by `filename`. The sheet names are stored in the `sheets` variable.

Here's the next line:

```
if (single_tbl) {
```

This line starts an `if` statement that checks the value of the `single_tbl` argument.

Now, we have the following:

```
x <- purrr::map_df(sheets, read_excel, path = filename)
```

If `single_tbl` is TRUE, this line uses the `purrr` package's `map_df` function to iterate over each sheet name in `sheets` and read the corresponding sheet using the `read_excel` function from the `readxl` package. The resulting `DataFrame` are combined into a single table, which is assigned to the `x` variable.

Now, we have the following line:

```
} else {
```

This line indicates the start of the `else` block of the `if` statement. If `single_tbl` is FALSE, the code in this block will be executed.

Here's the next line:

```
x <- purrr::map(sheets, ~ readxl::read_excel(filename, sheet = .x))
```

In this line, the `purrr` package's `map` function is used to iterate over each sheet name in `sheets`. For each sheet, the `read_excel` function from the `readxl` package is called to read the corresponding sheet from the Excel file specified by `filename`. The resulting `DataFrame` are stored in a list assigned to the `x` variable.

Now, we have the following:

```
purrr::set_names(x, sheets)
```

This line uses the `set_names` function from the `purrr` package to set the names of the elements in the `x` list to the sheet names in sheets.

Finally, we have the following line:

```
x
```

This line returns the value of `x` from the function, which will be either a single table (`data.frame`) if `single_tbl` is TRUE, or a list of tables (`data.frame`) if `single_tbl` is FALSE.

In summary, the `read_excel_sheets` function takes an Excel filename and a logical value indicating whether to return a single table or a list of tables. It uses the `readxl` package to extract the sheet names from the Excel file, and then reads the corresponding sheets either into a single table (if `single_tbl` is TRUE) or into a list of tables (if `single_tbl` is FALSE). The resulting data is returned as the output of the function. To see how this works, let's look at the following example.

We have a spreadsheet that has four tabs in it – one for each species in the famous Iris dataset and then one sheet called `iris`, which is the full dataset.

As shown in *Figure 1.5*, the `read_excel_sheets()` function has read all four sheets of the Excel file. We can also see that the function has imported the sheets as a list object and has named each item in the list after the name of the corresponding tab in the Excel file. It is also important to note that the sheets must all have the same column names and structure for this to work:

```
> read_excel_sheets(f, T)
# A tibble: 300 × 5
    sepal_length sepal_width petal_length petal_width species
           <dbl>       <dbl>        <dbl>       <dbl> <chr>
  1          5.1         3.5          1.4         0.2 setosa
  2          4.9         3            1.4         0.2 setosa

> read_excel_sheets(f, F)
[[1]]
# A tibble: 50 × 5
    sepal_length sepal_width petal_length petal_width species
           <dbl>       <dbl>        <dbl>       <dbl> <chr>
  1          5.1         3.5          1.4         0.2 setosa
  2          4.9         3            1.4         0.2 setosa

[[2]]
# A tibble: 50 × 5
    sepal_length sepal_width petal_length petal_width species
           <dbl>       <dbl>        <dbl>       <dbl> <chr>
  1          7           3.2          4.7         1.4 versicolor
  2          6.4         3.2          4.5         1.5 versicolor

[[3]]
# A tibble: 50 × 5
    sepal_length sepal_width petal_length petal_width species
           <dbl>       <dbl>        <dbl>       <dbl> <chr>
  1          6.3         3.3          6           2.5 virginica
  2          5.8         2.7          5.1         1.9 virginica

[[4]]
# A tibble: 150 × 5
    sepal_length sepal_width petal_length petal_width species
           <dbl>       <dbl>        <dbl>       <dbl> <chr>
  1          5.1         3.5          1.4         0.2 setosa
  2          4.9         3            1.4         0.2 setosa
```

Figure 1.5 – Excel file read by read_excel_sheets()

In this section, we learned how to write a function that will read all of the sheets in any Excel file. This function will also return them as a named item list, where the names are the names of the tabs in the file itself.

Now that we have learned how to read Excel sheets in R, in the next section, we will cover Python, where we will revisit the same concepts but from the perspective of the Python language.

Python packages for Excel manipulation

In this section, we will explore how to read Excel spreadsheets using Python. One of the key aspects of working with Excel files in Python is having the right set of packages that provide the necessary functionality. In this section, we will discuss some commonly used Python packages for Excel manipulation and highlight their advantages and considerations.

Python packages for Excel manipulation

When it comes to interacting with Excel files in Python, several packages offer a range of features and capabilities. These packages allow you to extract data from Excel files, manipulate the data, and write it back to Excel files. Let's take a look at some popular Python packages for Excel manipulation.

pandas

`pandas` is a powerful data manipulation library that can read Excel files using the `read_excel` function. The advantage of using `pandas` is that it provides a `DataFrame` object, which allows you to manipulate the data in a tabular form. This makes it easy to perform data analysis and manipulation. `pandas` excels in handling large datasets efficiently and provides flexible options for data filtering, transformation, and aggregation.

openpyxl

`openpyxl` is a widely used library specifically designed for working with Excel files. It provides a comprehensive set of features for reading and writing Excel spreadsheets, including support for various Excel file formats and compatibility with different versions of Excel. In addition, `openpyxl` allows fine-grained control over the structure and content of Excel files, enabling tasks such as accessing individual cells, creating new worksheets, and applying formatting.

xlrd and xlwt

`xlrd` and `xlwt` are older libraries that are still in use for reading and writing Excel files, particularly with legacy formats such as `.xls`. `xlrd` enables reading data from Excel files, while `xlwt` facilitates writing data to Excel files. These libraries are lightweight and straightforward to use, but they lack some of the advanced features provided by `pandas` and `openpyxl`.

Considerations

When choosing a Python package for Excel manipulation, it's essential to consider the specific requirements of your project. Here are a few factors to keep in mind:

- **Functionality**: Evaluate the package's capabilities and ensure it meets your needs for reading Excel files. Consider whether you require advanced data manipulation features or if a simpler package will suffice.

- **Performance**: If you're working with large datasets or need efficient processing, packages such as pandas, which have optimized algorithms, can offer significant performance advantages.

- **Compatibility**: Check the compatibility of the package with different Excel file formats and versions. Ensure that it supports the specific format you are working with to avoid any compatibility issues.

- **Learning curve**: Consider the learning curve associated with each package. Some packages, such as pandas, have a more extensive range of functionality, but they may require additional time and effort to master.

Each package offers unique features and has its strengths and weaknesses, allowing you to read Excel spreadsheets effectively in Python. For example, if you need to read and manipulate large amounts of data, pandas may be the better choice. However, if you need fine-grained control over the Excel file, openpyxl will likely fit your needs better.

Consider the specific requirements of your project, such as data size, functionality, and compatibility, to choose the most suitable package for your needs. In the following sections, we will delve deeper into how to utilize these packages to read and extract data from Excel files using Python.

Opening an Excel sheet from Python and reading the data

When working with Excel files in Python, it's common to need to open a specific sheet and read the data into Python for further analysis. This can be achieved using popular libraries such as pandas and openpyxl, as discussed in the previous section.

You can most likely use other Python and package versions, but the code in this section has not been tested with anything other than what we've stated here.

Using pandas

pandas is a powerful data manipulation library that simplifies the process of working with structured data, including Excel spreadsheets. To read an Excel sheet using pandas, you can use the read_excel function. Let's consider an example of using the iris_data.xlsx file with a sheet named setosa:

```
import pandas as pd
# Read the Excel file
df = pd.read_excel('iris_data.xlsx', sheet_name='setosa')

# Display the first few rows of the DataFrame
print(df.head())
```

You will need to run this code either with the Python working directory set to the location where the Excel file is located, or you will need to provide the full path to the file in the read_excel() command:

```
>>> import pandas as pd
>>> # Read the Excel file
>>>
>>> df = pd.read_excel('iris_data.xlsx', sheet_name='setosa')
>>> # Display the first few rows of the DataFrame
>>>
>>> print(df.head())
   sepal_length  sepal_width  petal_length  petal_width species
0           5.1          3.5           1.4          0.2  setosa
1           4.9          3.0           1.4          0.2  setosa
2           4.7          3.2           1.3          0.2  setosa
3           4.6          3.1           1.5          0.2  setosa
4           5.0          3.6           1.4          0.2  setosa
>>>
```

Figure 1.6 – Using the pandas package to read the Excel file

In the preceding code snippet, we imported the pandas library and utilized the read_excel function to read setosa from the iris_data.xlsx file. The resulting data is stored in a pandas DataFrame, which provides a tabular representation of the data. By calling head() on the DataFrame, we displayed the first few rows of the data, giving us a quick preview.

Using openpyxl

openpyxl is a powerful library for working with Excel files, offering more granular control over individual cells and sheets. To open an Excel sheet and access its data using openpyxl, we can utilize the load_workbook function. Please note that openpyxl cannot handle .xls files, only the more modern .xlsx and .xlsm versions.

Let's consider an example of using the iris_data.xlsx file with a sheet named versicolor:

```
import openpyxl
import pandas as pd

# Load the workbook
wb = openpyxl.load_workbook('iris_data.xlsx')

# Select the sheet
sheet = wb['versicolor']

# Extract the values (including header)
sheet_data_raw = sheet.values

# Separate the headers into a variable
header = next(sheet_data_raw)[0:]
```

```
# Create a DataFrame based on the second and subsequent lines of data
with the header as column names
sheet_data = pd.DataFrame(sheet_data_raw, columns=header)
print(sheet_data.head())
```

The preceding code results in the following output:

```
>>> import openpyxl
>>> import pandas as pd
>>> # Load the workbook
>>>
>>> wb = openpyxl.load_workbook('iris_data.xlsx')
>>> # Select the sheet
>>>
>>> sheet = wb['versicolor']
>>> # Extract the values (including header)
>>>
>>> sheet_data_raw = sheet.values
>>> # Separate the headers into a variable
>>>
>>> header = next(sheet_data_raw)[0:]
>>> # Create a DataFrame based on the second and subsequent lines of data with the header as column names
>>>
>>> sheet_data = pd.DataFrame(sheet_data_raw, columns=header)
>>> print(sheet_data.head())
   sepal_length  sepal_width  petal_length  petal_width    species
0          7.0          3.2           4.7          1.4  versicolor
1          6.4          3.2           4.5          1.5  versicolor
2          6.9          3.1           4.9          1.5  versicolor
3          5.5          2.3           4.0          1.3  versicolor
4          6.5          2.8           4.6          1.5  versicolor
>>> []
```

Figure 1.7 – Using the openpyxl package to read the Excel file

In this code snippet, we import the load_workbook function from the openpyxl library. Then, we load the workbook by providing the iris_data.xlsx filename. Next, we select the desired sheet by accessing it using its name – in this case, this is versicolor. Once we've done this, we read the raw data using the values property of the loaded sheet object. This is a generator and can be accessed via a for cycle or by converting it into a list or a DataFrame, for example. In this example, we have converted it into a pandas DataFrame because it is the format that is the most comfortable to work with later.

Both pandas and openpyxl offer valuable features for working with Excel files in Python. While pandas simplifies data manipulation with its DataFrame structure, openpyxl provides more fine-grained control over individual cells and sheets. Depending on your specific requirements, you can choose the library that best suits your needs.

By mastering the techniques of opening Excel sheets and reading data into Python, you will be able to extract valuable insights from your Excel data, perform various data transformations, and prepare it for further analysis or visualization. These skills are essential for anyone seeking to leverage the power of Python and Excel in their data-driven workflows.

Reading in multiple sheets with Python (openpyxl and custom functions)

In many Excel files, it's common to have multiple sheets containing different sets of data. Being able to read in multiple sheets and consolidate the data into a single data structure can be highly valuable for analysis and processing. In this section, we will explore how to achieve this using the `openpyxl` library and a custom function.

The importance of reading multiple sheets

When working with complex Excel files, it's not uncommon to encounter scenarios where related data is spread across different sheets. For example, you may have one sheet for sales data, another for customer information, and yet another for product inventory. By reading in multiple sheets and consolidating the data, you can gain a holistic view and perform a comprehensive analysis.

Let's start by examining the basic steps involved in reading in multiple sheets:

1. **Load the workbook**: Before accessing the sheets, we need to load the Excel workbook using the `load_workbook` function provided by `openpyxl`.

2. **Get the sheet names**: We can obtain the names of all the sheets in the workbook using the `sheetnames` attribute. This allows us to identify the sheets we want to read.

3. **Read data from each sheet**: By iterating over the sheet names, we can access each sheet individually and read the data. `Openpyxl` provides methods such as `iter_rows` or `iter_cols` to traverse the cells of each sheet and retrieve the desired data.

4. **Store the data**: To consolidate the data from multiple sheets, we can use a suitable data structure, such as a `pandas DataFrame` or a Python list. As we read the data from each sheet, we concatenate or merge it into the consolidated data structure:

   - If the data in all sheets follows the same format (as is the case in the example used in this chapter), we can simply concatenate the datasets

   - However, if the datasets have different structures because they describe different aspects of a dataset (for example, one sheet contains product information, the next contains customer data, and the third contains the sales of the products to the customers), then we can merge these datasets based on unique identifiers to create a comprehensive dataset

Using openpyxl to access sheets

`openpyxl` is a powerful library that allows us to interact with Excel files using Python. It provides a wide range of functionalities, including accessing and manipulating multiple sheets. Before we dive into the details, let's take a moment to understand why `openpyxl` is a popular choice for this task.

One of the primary advantages of openpyxl is its ability to handle various Excel file formats, such as .xlsx and .xlsm. This flexibility allows us to work with different versions of Excel files without compatibility issues. Additionally, openpyxl provides a straightforward and intuitive interface to access sheet data, making it easier for us to retrieve the desired information.

Reading data from each sheet

To begin reading in multiple sheets, we need to load the Excel workbook using the load_workbook function provided by openpyxl. This function takes the file path as input and returns a workbook object that represents the entire Excel file.

Once we have loaded the workbook, we can retrieve the names of all the sheets using the sheetnames attribute. This gives us a list of sheet names present in the Excel file. We can then iterate over these sheet names to read the data from each sheet individually.

Retrieving sheet data with openpyxl

openpyxl provides various methods to access the data within a sheet.

Two commonly used methods are iter_rows and iter_cols. These methods allow us to iterate over the rows or columns of a sheet and retrieve the cell values.

Let's have a look at how iter_rows can be used:

```
# Assuming you are working with the first sheet
sheet = wb['versicolor']

# Iterate over rows and print raw values
for row in sheet.iter_rows(min_row=1, max_row=5, values_only=True):
    print(row)
```

Similarly, iter_cols can be used like this:

```
# Iterate over columns and print raw values
for column in sheet.iter_cols(min_col=1, max_col=5, values_only=True):
    print(column)
```

When using iter_rows or iter_cols, we can specify whether we want to retrieve the cell values as raw values or as formatted values. Raw values give us the actual data stored in the cells, while formatted values include any formatting applied to the cells, such as date formatting or number formatting.

By iterating over the rows or columns of a sheet, we can retrieve the desired data and store it in a suitable data structure. One popular choice is to use pandas DataFrame, which provide a tabular representation of the data and offer convenient methods for data manipulation and analysis.

An alternative solution is using the `values` attribute of the sheet object. This provides a generator for all values in the sheet (much like `iter_rows` and `iter_cols` do for rows and columns, respectively). While generators cannot be used directly to access the data, they can be used in `for` cycles to iterate over each value. The `pandas` library's `DataFrame` function also allows direct conversion from a suitable generator object to a `DataFrame`.

Combining data from multiple sheets

As we read the data from each sheet, we can store it in a list or dictionary, depending on our needs. Once we have retrieved the data from all the sheets, we can combine it into a single consolidated data structure. This step is crucial for further analysis and processing.

To combine the data, we can use `pandas DataFrame`. By creating individual `DataFrame` for each sheet's data and then concatenating or merging them into a single `DataFrame`, we can obtain a comprehensive dataset that includes all the information from multiple sheets.

Custom function for reading multiple sheets

To simplify the process of reading in multiple sheets and consolidating the data, we can create custom functions tailored to our specific requirements. These functions encapsulate the necessary steps and allow us to reuse the code efficiently.

In our example, we define a function called `read_multiple_sheets` that takes the file path as input. Inside the function, we load the workbook using `load_workbook` and iterate over the sheet names retrieved with the sheets attribute.

For each sheet, we access it using the workbook object and retrieve the data using the custom read_single_sheet function. We then store the retrieved data in a list. Finally, we combine the data from all the sheets into a single `pandas DataFrame` using the appropriate concatenation method from `pandas`.

By using these custom functions, we can easily read in multiple sheets from an Excel file and obtain a consolidated dataset that's ready for analysis. The function provides a reusable and efficient solution, saving us time and effort in dealing with complex Excel files.

Customizing the code

The provided example is a starting point that you can customize based on your specific requirements. Here are a few considerations for customizing the code:

- **Filtering columns**: If you only need specific columns from each sheet, you can modify the code to extract only the desired columns during the data retrieval step. You can do this by using the `iter_cols` method instead of the `values` attribute and using a filtered list in a `for` cycle or by filtering the resulting `pandas DataFrame` object(s).

- **Handling missing data**: If the sheets contain missing data, you can incorporate appropriate handling techniques, such as filling in missing values or excluding incomplete rows.

- **Applying transformations**: Depending on the nature of your data, you might need to apply transformations or calculations to the consolidated dataset. The custom function can be expanded to accommodate these transformations.

Remember, the goal is to tailor the code to suit your unique needs and ensure it aligns with your data processing requirements.

By leveraging the power of openpyxl and creating custom functions, you can efficiently read in multiple sheets from Excel files, consolidate the data, and prepare it for further analysis. This capability enables you to unlock valuable insights from complex Excel files and leverage the full potential of your data.

Now, let's dive into an example that demonstrates this process:

```python
from openpyxl import load_workbook
import pandas as pd

def read_single_sheet(workbook, sheet_name):
    # Load the sheet from the workbook
    sheet = workbook[sheet_name]

    # Read out the raaw data including headers
    sheet_data_raw = sheet.values

    # Separate the headers into a variable
    columns = next(sheet_data_raw)[0:]

    # Create a DataFrame based on the second and subsequent lines of
data with the header as column names and return it
    return pd.DataFrame(sheet_data_raw, columns=columns)

def read_multiple_sheets(file_path):

    # Load the workbook
    workbook = load_workbook(file_path)

    # Get a list of all sheet names in the workbook
    sheet_names = workbook.sheetnames

    # Cycle through the sheet names, load the data for each and
concatenate them into a single DataFrame
    return pd.concat([read_single_sheet(workbook=workbook, sheet_
```

```
                                     name=sheet_name) for sheet_name in sheet_names], ignore_index=True)


# Define the file path and sheet names
file_path = 'iris_data.xlsx' # adjust the path as needed

# Read the data from multiple sheets
consolidated_data = read_multiple_sheets(file_path)

# Display the consolidated data
print(consolidated_data.head())
```

Let's have a look at the results:

```
>>> import openpyxl
>>> import pandas as pd
>>> # Load the workbook
>>>
>>> wb = openpyxl.load_workbook('iris_data.xlsx')
>>> # Select the sheet
>>>
>>> sheet = wb['versicolor']
>>> # Extract the values (including header)
>>>
>>> sheet_data_raw = sheet.values
>>> # Separate the headers into a variable
>>>
>>> header = next(sheet_data_raw)[0:]
>>> # Create a DataFrame based on the second and subsequent lines of data with the header as column names
>>>
>>> sheet_data = pd.DataFrame(sheet_data_raw, columns=header)
>>> print(sheet_data.head())
   sepal_length  sepal_width  petal_length  petal_width     species
0           7.0          3.2           4.7          1.4  versicolor
1           6.4          3.2           4.5          1.5  versicolor
2           6.9          3.1           4.9          1.5  versicolor
3           5.5          2.3           4.0          1.3  versicolor
4           6.5          2.8           4.6          1.5  versicolor
>>> from openpyxl import load_workbook
>>> import pandas as pd
>>> def read_single_sheet(workbook, sheet_name):
...     # Load the sheet from the workbook
...     sheet = workbook[sheet_name]
...     # Read out the raaw data including headers
...     sheet_data_raw = sheet.values
...     # Separate the headers into a variable
...     columns = next(sheet_data_raw)[0:]
...     # Create a DataFrame based on the second and subsequent lines of data with the header as column names and return it
...     return pd.DataFrame(sheet_data_raw, columns=columns)
...
>>> def read_multiple_sheets(file_path):
...     # Load the workbook
...     workbook = load_workbook(file_path)
...     # Get a list of all sheet names in the workbook
...     sheet_names = workbook.sheetnames
...     # Cycle through the sheet names, load the data for each and concatenate them into a single DataFrame
...     return pd.concat([read_single_sheet(workbook=workbook, sheet_name=sheet_name) for sheet_name in sheet_names], ignore_index=True)
... # Define the file path and sheet names
...
>>> file_path = 'iris_data.xlsx'
>>> # Read the data from multiple sheets
>>>
>>> consolidated_data = read_multiple_sheets(file_path)
>>> # Display the consolidated data
>>>
>>> print(consolidated_data.head())
   sepal_length  sepal_width  petal_length  petal_width species    1    2    3
0           5.1          3.5           1.4          0.2  setosa  NaN  NaN  NaN
1           4.9          3.0           1.4          0.2  setosa  NaN  NaN  NaN
2           4.7          3.2           1.3          0.2  setosa  NaN  NaN  NaN
3           4.6          3.1           1.5          0.2  setosa  NaN  NaN  NaN
4           5.0          3.6           1.4          0.2  setosa  NaN  NaN  NaN
>>> []
```

Figure 1.8 – Using the openxlsx package to read in the Excel file

In the preceding code, we define two functions:

- `read_single_sheet`: This reads the data from a single sheet into a pandas `DataFrame`
- `read_multiple_sheets`: This reads and concatenates the data from all sheets in the workbook

Within the `read_multiple_sheets` function, we load the workbook using `load_workbook` and iterate over the sheet names. For each sheet, we retrieve the data using the `read_single_sheet` helper function, which reads the data from a sheet and creates a pandas `DataFrame` for each sheet's data, with the header row used as column names. Finally, we use `pd.concat` to combine all the `DataFrame` into a single consolidated `DataFrame`.

By utilizing these custom functions, we can easily read in multiple sheets from an Excel file and obtain a consolidated dataset. This allows us to perform various data manipulations, analyses, or visualizations on the combined data.

Understanding how to handle multiple sheets efficiently enhances our ability to work with complex Excel files and extract valuable insights from diverse datasets.

Summary

In this chapter, we explored the process of importing data from Excel spreadsheets into our programming environments. For R users, we delved into the functionalities of libraries such as `readxl`, `xlsx`, and `openxlsx`, providing efficient solutions for extracting and manipulating data. We also introduced a custom function, `read_excel_sheets`, to streamline the process of extracting data from multiple sheets within Excel files. On the Python side, we discussed the essential `pandas` and `openpyxl` packages for Excel manipulation, demonstrating their features through practical examples. At this point, you should have a solid understanding of these tools and their capabilities for efficient Excel manipulation and data analysis.

In the next chapter, we will learn how to write the results to Excel.

2
Writing Excel Spreadsheets

This may sound contradictory to modern-day data science practices, but Excel has its place in the world of analysis and data storytelling. Exporting data from R and Python to Excel can be beneficial for several reasons, offering users the opportunity to leverage the strengths of both platforms. Excel is a widely used spreadsheet program known for its user-friendly interface, while R and Python is a powerful statistical programming language. By exporting data from R and Python to Excel, users can take advantage of Excel's familiar and versatile features to further analyze, visualize, and share data.

One significant advantage of exporting data from R and Python to Excel is the ability to harness Excel's extensive range of data manipulation and visualization capabilities. Excel provides a variety of tools, such as pivot tables, charts, and conditional formatting, which enable users to explore and present data more interactively and intuitively. These features allow for quick data exploration, identification of trends, and the creation of professional-looking reports or presentations.

Moreover, exporting data to Excel can facilitate collaboration with colleagues or stakeholders who may not be familiar with R and Python or statistical programming. Excel is a widely recognized and accessible tool that's often used for data analysis and reporting across various industries. By exporting data to Excel, users can share the data with others who may prefer working with spreadsheets, allowing for easier collaboration and knowledge exchange.

Another reason to export data from R and Python to Excel is to take advantage of Excel's extensive ecosystem of add-ins and extensions. Excel offers numerous specialized tools and add-ins that can enhance data analysis, such as Power Query, Power Pivot, and Solver. These tools provide additional functionalities for data cleaning, advanced calculations, and optimization, which may not be readily available or as user-friendly in R and Python. Exporting data to Excel allows users to leverage these tools and benefit from the broader Excel ecosystem.

In summary, exporting data from R and Python to Excel allows you to utilize Excel's user-friendly interface, powerful data manipulation and visualization capabilities, and compatibility with a wide range of users. By combining the strengths of both R and Excel, individuals can enhance their data analysis workflows, improve collaboration, and effectively communicate insights derived from statistical analyses.

In this chapter, we will cover the following main topics:

- Packages to write into Excel sheets
- Creating and manipulating Excel sheets using Python
- Keeping it simple – exporting data to Excel with `pandas`
- Advanced mode – `openpyxl` for Excel manipulation
- Choosing between `openpyxl` and `pandas`
- Other alternatives

Technical requirements

We are going to use the built-in `Iris` dataset in this chapter. This is a good dataset for demonstration purposes.

This chapter's code can be found in this book's GitHub repository: `https://github.com/PacktPublishing/Extending-Excel-with-Python-and-R/tree/main/Chapter2`.

Packages to write into Excel files

In this section, we are going to go over a few different libraries that we can use to write `data.frames/tibbles` to Excel files. We are going to use the `writexl`, `openxlsx`, and `xlsx` libraries.

In the following section, we are going to list each package, specify where you can find the function documentation that writes the data to Excel, and go over the functions' parameters.

writexl

The `writexl` package is part of the rOpenSci consortium and can be found here: `https://docs.ropensci.org/writexl/reference/write_xlsx.html`.

The library does not require Java or Excel to work.

The function that writes the data to Excel is `write_xlsx()`. Let's go over the different parameters of the function and look at a full pseudo function call.

First, let's look at the function call itself – that is, `write_xlsx()`:

```
write_xlsx(
  x,
  path = tempfile(fileext = ".xlsx"),
  col_names = TRUE,
  format_headers = TRUE,
  use_zip64 = FALSE
)
```

Now, let's look at each of the parameters in this code:

- `x`: This is the DataFrame or named list of DataFrames that will be sheets in the `.xlsx` file.

- `path`: A filename to write to. Here, you could type something such as `tempfile(fileext = .xlsx")col_names` to write column names at the top of the file.

- `format_headers`: Make `col_names` in the `.xlsx` file centered and bold.

- `use_zip64`: Use **ZIP64** (`https://en.wikipedia.org/wiki/Zip_(file_format)#ZIP64`) to enable support for 4 GB+ `.xlsx` files. Not all platforms can read this.

Let's see what a simple example of this function would look like in typical practice:

```
write_xlsx(list(mysheet = iris), path = "./iris_data_written.xlsx")
```

openxlsx

The `openxlsx` package can be found at `https://ycphs.github.io/openxlsx/`; the function that we are going to use to write to an Excel file is `write.xlsx()`. Again, we'll go over the full function call and the parameters that get passed to this function:

```
write.xlsx(
  x,
  file,
  asTable = FALSE,
  overwrite = TRUE,
  ...
)
```

Now, let's go over all of the parameters of the function:

- x: A DataFrame or a (named) list of objects that can be handled by `writeData()` or `writeDataTable()` to write to the file.

- `file`: A file path to save the `.xlsx` file.

- `asTable`: If TRUE, then it will use `writeDataTable()` rather than `writeData()` to write x to the file (the default value is FALSE).

- `overwrite`: Overwrite existing file (this defaults to TRUE, as with `write.table`).

- `...`: Additional arguments passed to `buildWorkbook();`. To see additional details, you can type `?openxlsx::buildWorkbook` into the R console.

Let's take a look at a short example of some code where we will write the Iris dataset to a file:

```
openxlsx::write.xlsx(
x = iris,
File = paste0(getwd(), "/iris.xlsx"
)
```

Next, we'll look at the last package, xlsx.

xlsx

The xlsx package can be found at https://github.com/colearendt/xlsx; the function that we are using to explore writing to an Excel file is write.xlsx(). Given that this function has the same name as the function from the openxlsx library, it is important to be aware of namespace collision. This takes place when there is a function from two or more separate packages that have the same name. Avoiding any possible namespace collision for users is easy but can be cumbersome. To do so, you can write xlsx::write.xlsx(). Again, let's go over the full function call and the parameters that get passed to this function:

```
write.xlsx(
  x,
  file,
  sheetName = "Sheet1",
  col.names = TRUE,
  row.names = TRUE,
  append = FALSE,
  showNA = TRUE,
  password = NULL
)
```

Now, let's go over the parameters of the function:

- x: A DataFrame to write to the workbook.
- file: The path to the output file.
- sheetName: A character string that contains the sheet's name.
- col.names: A logical value indicating whether the column names of x are to be written along with x to the file.
- row.names: A logical value indicating whether the row names of x are to be written along with x to the file.

- `append`: A logical value indicating whether x should be appended to an existing file. If TRUE, the file is read from disk. Otherwise, the file is created.

- `showNA`: A logical value. If set to FALSE, NA values will be left as empty cells.

- `password`: A string containing the password.

A simple function call would take the following form:

```
xlsx::write.xlsx(x = iris,
File = paste0(getwd(), "/iris.xlsx"
)
```

Now that we have gone over the three different functions, it is important to see how each one writes – that is, how long they take to write to disk and how large the output file is. To do this, we are going to use the rbenchmark library for speed testing. We will also bring in the dplyr library to arrange the results by their relative order of speed. After this, we will see which file has the smallest size output.

Here is the code for doing this:

```
library(rbenchmark)
library(xlsx)
library(writexl)
library(openxlsx)
library(dplyr)

n <- 5

benchmark(
  "writexl" = {
    writexl::write_xlsx(iris, tempfile())
  },
  "openxlsx" = {
    openxlsx::write.xlsx(iris, tempfile())
  },
  "xlsx" = {
    xlsx::write.xlsx(iris, paste0(tempfile(),".xlsx"))
  },
  replications = n,
  columns = c(
    "test","replications","elapsed","relative","user.self","sys.self")
) |>
  arrange(relative)
```

Figure 2.1 – File write benchmark

This R code is used to compare the performance of three different packages for writing DataFrames to Excel files: `writexl`, `openxlsx`, and `xlsx`. Here's a breakdown of what the code does:

1. The code starts by loading several libraries (`rbenchmark`, `xlsx`, `writexl`, `openxlsx`, and `dplyr`) using the `library()` function. These libraries provide functions that will be used later in the code. If you do not have them installed, you will need to use something such as `install.packaegs("package")` to do so.

2. The n variable is assigned a value of 5. This variable represents the number of times the code will be executed for each package to measure performance.

3. The `benchmark()` function is called to compare the performance of the three Excel-writing packages. It takes several arguments:

   • The first argument, `writexl`, is a name that's assigned to the first test. Inside the curly braces, the `write_xlsx()` function from the `writexl` package is called to write the `iris` dataset to a temporary Excel file.

   • The second argument, `openxlsx`, is a name that's assigned to the second test. Inside the curly braces, the `write.xlsx()` function from the `openxlsx` package is called to write the `iris` dataset to a temporary Excel file.

   • The third argument, `xlsx`, is a name that's assigned to the third test. Inside the curly braces, the `write.xlsx()` function from the `xlsx` package is called to write the `iris` dataset to a temporary Excel file with an `.xlsx` extension.

   • The `replications` argument is set to n, indicating the number of times each test should be repeated.

   • The `columns` argument specifies the columns to include in the output. It includes the names of the test, any replications, the elapsed time, relative performance, user time, and system time.

4. The resulting benchmark results are then piped (| >) to the `arrange()` function from the `dplyr` package. The `arrange()` function is used to sort the results based on the relative performance column, arranging them in ascending order.

   For the preceding benchmarking process, the results are as follows:

```
  test       replications elapsed relative  user.self  sys.self
1 writexl         5          0.03   1.000       0.01       0.00
2 openxlsx        5          0.32  10.667       0.01       0.00
3 xlsx            5          0.88  29.333       0.81       0.01
```

In summary, the preceding code loads the necessary libraries, performs benchmarks on three different Excel-writing packages (`writexl`, `openxlsx`, and `xlsx`), and sorts the results based on relative performance. The purpose is to compare the efficiency of these packages when writing the `iris` dataset to an Excel file. It is important to note that there are many factors at play here, such as the system and operating system, among others. Now, let's see how the sizes measure up:

```
writexl::write_xlsx(iris, tmp1 <- tempfile())
file.info(tmp1)$size
[1] 8497

openxlsx::write.xlsx(iris, tmp2 <- tempfile())
file.info(tmp2)$size
[1] 9628

xlsx::write.xlsx(iris, tmp3 <- paste0(tempfile(),".xlsx"))
file.info(tmp3)$size
[1] 7904
```

Figure 2.2 – File size comparison

This R code performs the following tasks using different packages to write the `iris` dataset to Excel files and then retrieves the sizes of those files, listed in bytes:

- The `write_xlsx()` function from the `writexl` package is called with two arguments: the `iris` dataset and a temporary file path generated using the `tempfile()` function. The `write_xlsx()` function writes the `iris` dataset to the temporary Excel file.

- The `file.info()` function is called with the temporary file path, (`tmp1`), as an argument. It retrieves information about the file, including its size. The `$size` attribute is used to extract the size of the file.

- The `write.xlsx()` function from the `openxlsx` package is called with two arguments: the `iris` dataset and another temporary file path generated using the `tempfile()` function. The `write.xlsx()` function writes the `iris` dataset to the temporary Excel file.

- Similar to *the second point*, the `file.info()` function is called with the temporary file path, (`tmp2`), as an argument to retrieve the size of the file.

- The `write.xlsx()` function from the `xlsx` package is called with two arguments: the `iris` dataset and a temporary file path generated using the combination of `tempfile()` and `paste0()` functions. The `write.xlsx()` function writes the `iris` dataset to the temporary Excel file with an `.xlsx` extension. For the `xlsx` package, we use `paste0()` and specify the file extension since this isn't done by default in the function, so the user must be careful and specify this accordingly.

- Again, the `file.info()` function is called with the temporary file path, (`tmp3`), as an argument to retrieve the size of the file.

In summary, this code uses different packages (`writexl`, `openxlsx`, and `xlsx`) to write the `iris` dataset into three separate Excel files. Then, it retrieves the sizes of those files using the `file.info()` function. Its purpose is to compare the sizes of the resulting Excel files when using these different packages. Again, many factors that are outside the scope of this book could be affecting file sizes, but you must be aware the different systems and configurations could have an impact on this.

A comprehensive recap and insights

In the previous section, we learned how to write `data.frame` to Excel using three different packages. We learned that with these three different packages come differences in the speed of writing in a file and differences in the size of the output file itself. It is important to run these benchmarks as we might be trying to achieve speed, a small file size, or some combination thereof.

When it comes to speed, there are a few reasons why it is good to run benchmarks in R:

- **Accuracy**: Benchmarks can be used to accurately measure the speed of different functions. This is important because it can help you choose the fastest function for your task.

- **Consistency**: Benchmarks can be used to consistently measure the speed of different functions over time. This is important because it can help you identify any changes in performance that may have occurred.

- **Reliability**: Benchmarks can be used to reliably measure the speed of different functions across different platforms. This is important because it can help you ensure that the results of your benchmarks are accurate and reproducible.

In addition to these advantages, benchmarks can also be used to identify bottlenecks in your code. This can help you improve the performance of your code as you can optimize the areas that are taking the most time to execute.

Here are some of the most popular R packages for benchmarking:

- `microbenchmark`: This package provides a simple and convenient way to benchmark R code

- `rbenchmark`: This package provides a more comprehensive set of benchmarking features than `microbenchmark`

- `rbenchmark2`: This package is a fork of `rbenchmark` that provides additional features, such as the ability to benchmark multiple cores

When choosing a benchmarking package, it is important to consider your needs and the available features. For example, if you need to benchmark a large amount of code, you may want to choose a package that supports *parallel benchmarking*.

Once you have chosen a benchmarking package, you can use it to compare the speed of different functions. To do this, you will need to create a benchmark object that contains the functions that you want to compare. You can then use the `benchmark` object to run the functions and measure their execution time.

The results of the benchmark can be used to identify the fastest function for your task. You can then use this information to improve the performance of your code.

In this section, we learned not only how to write data to an Excel file, but also how to do so with different R libraries. This is important as it helps you explore different methods of achieving the same goal. This exercise also illustrated the differences in implementations, which we saw by checking the output file size and by benchmarking the time it took to write our data to Excel with each package. Next, we will conduct similar exercises using Python.

Creating and manipulating Excel sheets using Python

In this section, we will explore how to create and manipulate Excel sheets using Python.

Exporting data to Excel is a common requirement in various data analysis and reporting scenarios. Excel provides a familiar and widely used interface for data visualization, sharing, and further analysis.

We'll cover various tasks in the sections ahead, including creating new workbooks, adding sheets to existing workbooks, deleting sheets, and manipulating data within an Excel workbook. Python provides several libraries that make these tasks straightforward and efficient. But first, let's understand why we need to export data to Excel.

Why export data to Excel?

Exporting data to Excel offers several benefits. Firstly, Excel provides a user-friendly environment for data exploration and visualization, allowing users to easily sort, filter, and analyze data. Additionally, Excel's rich formatting capabilities make it suitable for generating professional reports or sharing data with stakeholders who may not have programming knowledge. Furthermore, Excel supports various formulas and functions, enabling users to perform calculations on the exported data easily.

Let's see how we can export data to Excel with Python!

Keeping it simple – exporting data to Excel with pandas

`pandas` is a popular data manipulation library in Python that provides powerful tools for data analysis. It also offers excellent functionality for exporting data to Excel. Using `pandas`, you can effortlessly transform your data into Excel sheets or workbooks.

pandas provides the `DataFrame.to_excel()` method, allowing you to export data to an Excel file with just a few lines of code. Here's an example:

```python
import pandas as pd

# Create a DataFrame with sample data
data = {
    'Name': ['John', 'Jane', 'Mike'],
    'Age': [25, 30, 35],
    'City': ['New York', 'London', 'Sydney']
}
df = pd.DataFrame(data)

# Export the DataFrame to an Excel file
df.to_excel('data.xlsx', index=False)
```

The code doesn't return anything, but it does have a side effect – it creates the `data.xlsx` file with the exported data:

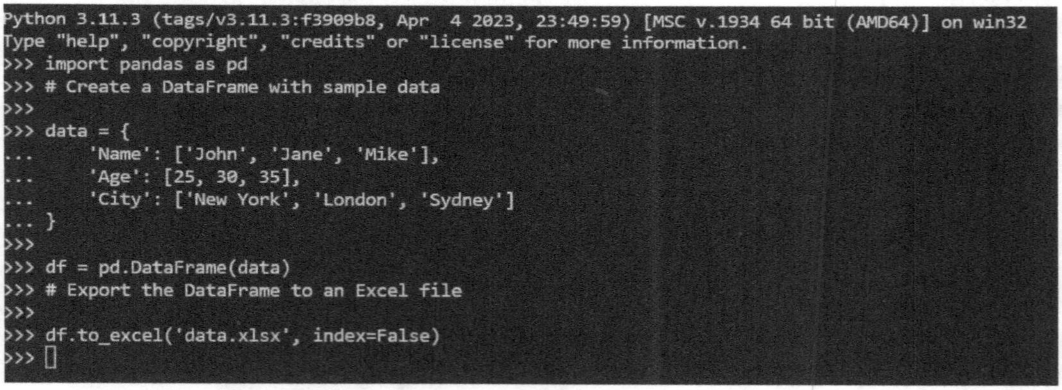

```
Python 3.11.3 (tags/v3.11.3:f3909b8, Apr  4 2023, 23:49:59) [MSC v.1934 64 bit (AMD64)] on win32
Type "help", "copyright", "credits" or "license" for more information.
>>> import pandas as pd
>>> # Create a DataFrame with sample data
>>>
>>> data = {
...     'Name': ['John', 'Jane', 'Mike'],
...     'Age': [25, 30, 35],
...     'City': ['New York', 'London', 'Sydney']
... }
>>>
>>> df = pd.DataFrame(data)
>>> # Export the DataFrame to an Excel file
>>>
>>> df.to_excel('data.xlsx', index=False)
>>> []
```

Figure 2.3 – Excel export with pandas

While `pandas` is good at simple data export, we may want to have more control over the Excel workbook. The next few subsections cover more advanced Excel manipulation using `openpyxl`. We will cover the capabilities of `openpyxl`, starting with the basics such as creating a new workbook by adding and deleting sheets up to and including manipulating data in an existing sheet.

Advanced mode – openpyxl for Excel manipulation

In this section, we will look at the `openpyxl` package, which allows for a more nuanced interaction with Excel when writing data.

Creating a new workbook

To start working with Excel sheets in Python, we need to create a new workbook. `openpyxl` provides an intuitive API to create, modify, and save Excel workbooks. Here's an example code snippet that demonstrates creating a new workbook:

```python
import openpyxl

# Create a new workbook
workbook = openpyxl.Workbook()
```

Once again, the preceding code snippet doesn't return anything but it does have a side effect – it creates the workbook:

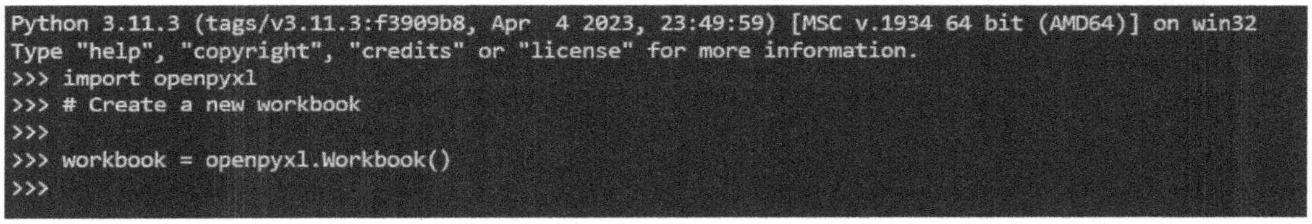

```
Python 3.11.3 (tags/v3.11.3:f3909b8, Apr  4 2023, 23:49:59) [MSC v.1934 64 bit (AMD64)] on win32
Type "help", "copyright", "credits" or "license" for more information.
>>> import openpyxl
>>> # Create a new workbook
>>>
>>> workbook = openpyxl.Workbook()
>>>
```

Figure 2.4 – Creating a workbook with openpyxl

Adding sheets to the workbook

Once we have a workbook, we can add sheets to it. Adding sheets allows us to organize data into separate sections or categories. `openpyxl` provides a simple method, `create_sheet()`, to add sheets to a workbook. Let's see an example:

```python
import openpyxl

# Create a new workbook
workbook = openpyxl.Workbook()

# Add a new sheet
workbook.create_sheet(title="Sheet2")

# Save the changes
workbook.save("example.xlsx")
```

The result is an `openpyxl` worksheet object we can use going forward. The resulting workbook can then be saved for future use.

The preceding example attempts to save the workbook you are working with. If the workbook is open in Excel, the attempt will fail, with a hard-to-decipher error message about the COM systems. Make sure you close your Excel instance before attempting to save your work from the Python side! This warning will remain applicable to most of this book, so keep it in mind for later chapters as well.

Deleting a sheet

At times, we may need to remove a sheet from a workbook. The `remove()` method in `openpyxl` allows us to delete a sheet by its name. The following is an example of how you can delete a sheet from a workbook. Please note that we will not save the result, so the stored version of the file remains unchanged:

```
import openpyxl

# Load an existing workbook
workbook = openpyxl.load_workbook("example.xlsx")

# Delete a sheet
sheet_name = "Sheet2"
sheet = workbook[sheet_name]
workbook.remove(sheet)
```

As before, the code has a side effect (the deleted sheet) but no return value:

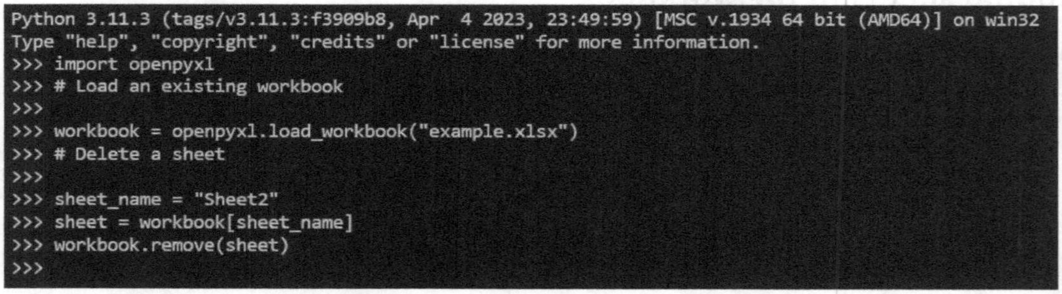

```
Python 3.11.3 (tags/v3.11.3:f3909b8, Apr  4 2023, 23:49:59) [MSC v.1934 64 bit (AMD64)] on win32
Type "help", "copyright", "credits" or "license" for more information.
>>> import openpyxl
>>> # Load an existing workbook
>>>
>>> workbook = openpyxl.load_workbook("example.xlsx")
>>> # Delete a sheet
>>>
>>> sheet_name = "Sheet2"
>>> sheet = workbook[sheet_name]
>>> workbook.remove(sheet)
>>>
```

Figure 2.5 – Deleting a sheet with openpyxl

In this example, we used the sheet we created previously. The `load_workbook()` method from `openpyxl` is used to load the existing workbook, after which the `remove()` method is used to delete a sheet specified by name.

Manipulating an existing workbook

Python libraries such as openpyxl provide powerful methods to manipulate existing Excel workbooks. We can modify cells, apply formatting, insert formulas, and more. Let's look at an example of how to update a cell value in an existing workbook:

```python
import openpyxl

# Load an existing workbook
workbook = openpyxl.load_workbook("example.xlsx")

# Add a new sheet
workbook.create_sheet(title="Sheet1")

# Select a sheet
sheet_name = "Sheet1"

sheet = workbook[sheet_name]

# Update a cell value
sheet["A1"] = "Hello, World!"

# Save the changes
workbook.save("example.xlsx")
```

This code snippet will directly change the value of a cell in the Excel sheet:

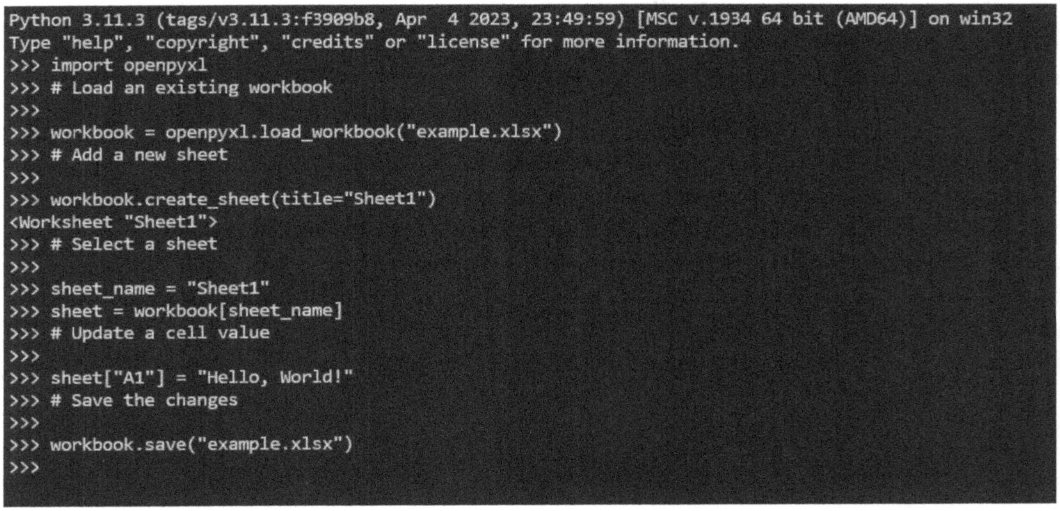

```
Python 3.11.3 (tags/v3.11.3:f3909b8, Apr  4 2023, 23:49:59) [MSC v.1934 64 bit (AMD64)] on win32
Type "help", "copyright", "credits" or "license" for more information.
>>> import openpyxl
>>> # Load an existing workbook
>>>
>>> workbook = openpyxl.load_workbook("example.xlsx")
>>> # Add a new sheet
>>>
>>> workbook.create_sheet(title="Sheet1")
<Worksheet "Sheet1">
>>> # Select a sheet
>>>
>>> sheet_name = "Sheet1"
>>> sheet = workbook[sheet_name]
>>> # Update a cell value
>>>
>>> sheet["A1"] = "Hello, World!"
>>> # Save the changes
>>>
>>> workbook.save("example.xlsx")
>>>
```

Figure 2.6 – Updating the value of a cell with openpyxl

The result is as we expect (keep in mind that the process of deleting the sheet was not saved):

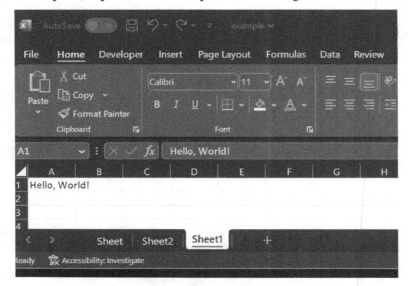

Figure 2.7 – The fruit of our efforts – Hello, World! in A1, Sheet1

Choosing between openpyxl and pandas

When it comes to exporting data to Excel, both openpyxl and pandas are excellent choices. openpyxl is a dedicated library for working with Excel files as it provides extensive functionality for creating, modifying, and saving Excel workbooks. On the other hand, pandas offers a high-level data manipulation interface with convenient methods for exporting data to Excel, which is ideal when a simple data dump is all you need.

If you require fine-grained control over the Excel file's structure, such as adding formatting, formulas, or charts, openpyxl is a suitable option. It allows you to work directly with the underlying Excel objects, providing more flexibility. On the other hand, if you primarily focus on data manipulation and want a simpler way to export DataFrames to Excel without worrying about Excel-specific features, pandas is a convenient choice. It abstracts away some of the lower-level details and provides a more straightforward interface for exporting data. While openpyxl provides a simple abstracted way of manipulating and controlling sheets, R also has this in packages such as openxlsx and xlsx, both of which provide their own form of these types of functionalities.

Other alternatives

Apart from `pandas` and `openpyxl`, there are other libraries available for exporting data to Excel from Python. Some popular alternatives include `XlsxWriter`, `xlrd`, and `xlwt`. These libraries offer different features and capabilities, and the choice depends on your specific requirements. `XlsxWriter`, for example, emphasizes performance and supports advanced Excel features, while `xlrd` and `xlwt` provide functionality for reading and writing older Excel file formats (`.xls`).

In this section, we explored the benefits of exporting data to Excel, demonstrated how to do so using `pandas`, went through the process of creating and manipulating Excel sheets using `openpyxl`, discussed the reasons for choosing `openpyxl` or `pandas` based on your needs, and mentioned other alternatives available. By leveraging the power of these libraries, you can seamlessly export your data from Python to Excel, enabling efficient analysis, reporting, and collaboration.

Summary

In *Chapter 2*, we explored the process of writing data to Excel using different R and Python libraries and benchmarking their performance. We also discussed creating and manipulating Excel sheets from Python using `pandas` and `openpyxl`. By comparing their features and exploring alternatives, you have gained insights into the capabilities of both R and Python for Excel tasks.

In the next chapter, we will learn how to execute VBA code with R and Python.

3
Executing VBA Code from R and Python

Integrating different programming languages can unlock powerful capabilities and streamline workflows. When it comes to working with Excel files, **Visual Basic for Applications (VBA)** is a popular choice for automating tasks. However, there are scenarios where you may want to execute VBA code from within R or Python, harnessing the strengths of these languages for data manipulation, analysis, and visualization.

Executing VBA code from an Excel file through R or Python provides a flexible approach to leverage existing VBA macros or extend the functionalities of Excel. This integration enables data scientists, analysts, and developers to seamlessly incorporate Excel files into their workflows, combining the strengths of VBA with the analytical capabilities of R or Python.

By executing VBA code from R or Python, you can automate complex processes, perform data manipulations, generate reports, and interact with Excel's features programmatically. This capability empowers users to handle large datasets, implement advanced data processing techniques, and produce customized outputs.

There are several libraries and packages available in R and Python that facilitate the execution of VBA code from an Excel file. These tools provide APIs and functions to communicate with Excel and execute VBA macros directly from your scripts, eliminating the need for manual intervention.

In this chapter, we will explore different approaches to executing VBA code from an Excel file using R and Python. We will delve into practical examples, showcasing how to integrate these languages with Excel and leverage the combined power to automate tasks and enhance data analysis workflows.

By unlocking the potential of VBA execution in conjunction with R or Python, users can take their Excel-based projects to the next level, driving efficiency, accuracy, and productivity. Stay tuned to learn more about this exciting integration and its wide-ranging applications.

In this chapter, we're going to cover the following main topics:

- Installing and explaining the R package, RDCOMClient
- Executing sample VBA code with RDCOMClient
- Python for VBA integration with `pywin32`

Technical requirements

In this section, we will need to install one R library and one for Python:

- The `RDCOMClient` R library
- The `pywin32` Python library

All relevant code for this chapter can be found in the GitHub repository here:

`https://github.com/PacktPublishing/Extending-Excel-with-Python-and-R/main/chapter3`

Installing and explaining the RDCOMClient R library

`RDCOMClient` is an R package that provides a bridge between R and Microsoft's **component object model (COM)** architecture, enabling users to interact with COM objects from within R. With RDCOMClient, users can harness the power of COM-based applications, such as Microsoft Excel, Word, PowerPoint, and Outlook, to automate tasks, manipulate data, and integrate R with other software systems.

Before diving into RDCOMClient, it's important to grasp the concept of COM objects. COM is a binary interface standard that allows different software components to interact and share functionality across various programming languages and platforms. In the context of RDCOMClient, COM objects refer to the application-specific objects exposed by COM-based applications that can be accessed and manipulated programmatically.

RDCOMClient provides a set of functions and methods to interact with COM objects, making it easier to automate tasks and extract data from COM-based applications. Here are some key features:

- **Object creation and connection**: `RDCOMClient` allows users to create and connect to COM objects, establishing a communication channel between R and the target application. For instance, you can create an Excel application object and access its functionalities directly from R.
- **Accessing methods and properties**: Once connected to a COM object, `RDCOMClient` enables you to invoke methods and retrieve or modify object properties. This functionality allows you to automate complex tasks, manipulate data, and customize application behavior.

- **Working with collections and worksheets**: With RDCOMClient, you can access collections within COM objects, such as workbooks, worksheets, or ranges in Excel. This capability facilitates data extraction, manipulation, and analysis directly from R, leveraging the power of Excel's built-in features.

- **Event handling**: RDCOMClient supports event handling, allowing users to respond to events triggered by COM objects. For example, you can write R code that executes whenever a specific event occurs in Excel, such as a cell value change or a worksheet activation.

- **Error handling and memory management**: RDCOMClient provides mechanisms for handling errors that may occur during COM object interactions, ensuring robustness in your code. It also manages memory allocation and cleanup, preventing memory leaks and optimizing resource utilization.

The versatility of RDCOMClient opens up a wide range of applications. Here are a few examples:

- **Excel automation**: RDCOMClient enables users to automate repetitive tasks in Excel, such as data extraction, formatting, chart creation, and report generation. This can significantly enhance productivity and accuracy in data analysis workflows.

- **Word document manipulation**: With RDCOMClient, you can programmatically create, modify, and extract content from Word documents, allowing for automated document generation, formatting, and data integration.

- **Outlook integration**: RDCOMClient facilitates integration with Outlook, enabling users to automate email management, calendar scheduling, and contact synchronization, among other functionalities.

- **PowerPoint presentations**: Users can leverage RDCOMClient to create and modify PowerPoint presentations dynamically, automating the generation of slides, formatting, and embedding charts or tables based on data analysis results.

RDCOMClient serves as a powerful tool for integrating R with COM-based applications, offering extensive capabilities for automation, data manipulation, and system integration. By bridging the gap between R and the COM architecture, RDCOMClient empowers users to leverage the strengths of both R and various COM applications, opening endless possibilities for enhanced productivity, data analysis, and task automation.

Now that we have discussed what we can do with RDCOMClient, let's go through the installation process.

Installing RDCOMClient

To install packages in R, you would usually type in the command prompt something like `install.packages("dplyr")` if you wanted to install the `dplyr` library.

For the `RDCOMClient` library, this is going to change a little bit. Typically, if you are using RStudio—your default repository from where you are going to get packages—it is going to default to the Global (CDN) RStudio repository, but for this package, we are going to give some special instructions to the installation command.

> **Note**
>
> RDCOMClient is only available on Windows.

Here is how the command will look:

```
install.packages(
"RDCOMClient",
repos = "http://www.omegahat.net/R",
type = "win.binary"
)
```

Now that we have installed `RDCOMClient`, we can move on to doing something with it. In the next section, we will go over some examples of how to use it. This library installation can be clunky and, for some, the following will work better:

```
Install.packages("devtools")
Library(devtools)
Install_github("omegahat/RDCOMClient")
```

Executing sample VBA with RDCOMClient

For this execution, the first thing we will need is a new workbook. Let's call it `mult_by_rand_ch3`.

On **Sheet1**, we can create two columns, one called `Record` and the other called `Value`. These columns will simply be the numbers 1 through 10. When that is done, we will need to go ahead and create a simple VBA script to execute from the `RDCOMClient` library.

We are going to write a macro that will take the `Value` column and then multiply the number by a random number using the `RAND()` function.

Let's go over the steps to make the macro and describe how it works. First, take a look at the following VBA code:

```
Sub MultiplyByRandom()
    Dim rng As Range
    Dim cell As Range
    ' Set the range to the desired range on Sheet1
    Set rng = Sheets("Sheet1").Range("B2:B11")
    ' Loop through each cell in the range
```

```
    For Each cell In rng
        ' Multiply the cell value by RAND() and store the result in
the adjacent cell
        cell.Offset(0, 1).Value = cell.Value * Rnd()
    Next cell
End Sub
```

In order to create this macro, you need to click on the **Developer** tab or press *Alt + F11* to open the Visual Basic editor.

Insert a new module by going to **Insert | Module**. Once you have done this, you can type the preceding code into the window and close the editor window.

To get some clarity, let's go over what each line of the macro does:

- `Sub MultiplyByRandom()`: This line defines the start of a VBA subroutine named `MultiplyByRandom`.

- `Dim rng As Range` and `Dim cell As Range`: These lines declare two `Range` variables named `rng` and `cell`. These variables will be used to store ranges and individual cells, respectively.

- `Set rng = Sheets("Sheet1").Range("B2:B11`: This line sets the `rng` variable to refer to the range of cells from B2 to B11 on `Sheet1`. It specifies the location where the numbers are stored.

- `For Each cell In rng`: This line starts a loop that will iterate through each cell in the `rng` range. It assigns the current cell to the `cell` variable for each iteration of the loop.

- `cell.Offset(0, 1).Value = cell.Value * Rnd()`: This line multiplies the value of the current cell by a randomly generated number using the `Rnd()` function. It then stores the result in the adjacent cell, which is obtained using the `Offset` method to shift the reference one column to the right (0 rows, 1 column).

- `Next cell`: This line signifies the end of the loop. It moves the loop to the next cell in the range and repeats the process until all cells have been processed.

- `End Sub`: This line marks the end of the `MultiplyByRandom` VBA subroutine.

In order to run this macro, we can write the R code that will execute it. We are going to do this with the `RDCOMClient` library and use the `$Run()` method from the Excel `Workbook` object we create.

Let's go ahead and write that script now.

The following is a breakdown of each line in the R code, explained in simple terms.

This line loads the RDCOMClient library, which provides functionality for interacting with Microsoft Office applications, such as Excel:

```
# Load the library
library(RDCOMClient)
```

The following lines define variables for the file path and name of an Excel workbook. They will only work for the author and should be updated to reflect where you are working from. It is possible to be working in a project and use something like paste0(getwd(), "/"). The f_path, f_chapter, and f_name variables specify the directory path, subdirectory name, and filename, respectively. The paste0() function is used to concatenate these variables to create the complete file path:

```
# Set file path
f_path <- "C:/Users/steve/Documents/GitHub/Extending-Excel-with-
Python-and-R/"
f_chapter <- "chapter3/"
f_name <- "mult_by_rand_ch3.xlsm"
f <- paste0(f_path, f_chapter, f_name)
```

The next lines create an instance of the Excel application using the COMCreate() function. The xl_app variable represents the Excel application. Then, the specified workbook (f) is opened using the Open() method of the Workbooks() property of the Excel application. Finally, xl_app[['Visible']] <- TRUE sets the visibility of the Excel application to be visible:

```
# Make Excel App
xl_app <- COMCreate("Excel.Application")
xl_wkbk <- xl_app$Workbooks()$Open(f)
xl_app[['Visible']] <- TRUE
```

This line assigns the name of the macro to be executed in Excel to the macro_name variable. The macro name is set as MultiplyByRandom:

```
macro_name <- "MultiplyByRandom"
```

This line executes the MultiplyByRandom macro in the Excel application. The Run() method of the Excel application is used to run the specified macro:

```
# Run the macro
xl_app$Run(macro_name)
```

These lines save the workbook and close it using the close() method of the xl_wkbk workbook object. The TRUE argument indicates that the changes should be saved before closing. Finally, the Quit() method of the xl_app Excel application is used to close the Excel application:

```
# Save and Quit
xl_wkbk$close(TRUE); xl_app$Quit()
```

In summary, the code opens an Excel workbook using `RDCOMClient`, runs a macro named `MultiplyByRandom` in the workbook, saves the changes, and closes the workbook and the Excel application.

Let's have a look at how this works in Python!

Integrating VBA with Python using pywin32

In this section, we will dive into executing VBA code from Python, exploring the seamless integration between the two languages and the immense possibilities it unlocks for automating Excel tasks, extending functionality, and leveraging Excel's power within Python workflows.

This section will cover the motivation to work with VBA from Python, how to set up the environment on Windows, and how to write and execute VBA code. Let's dig in.

Why execute VBA code from Python?

Before delving into the details, let's explore why executing VBA code from Python can be highly beneficial.

Excel, with its extensive set of features and capabilities, serves as a vital tool for data analysis, reporting, and automation. However, Excel's built-in functionality may sometimes fall short when dealing with complex data manipulations or advanced calculations. This is where the integration of Python and VBA comes into play.

Python provides a rich ecosystem for data manipulation, analysis, and machine learning. Its libraries, such as `pandas`, `NumPy`, and `SciPy`, offer powerful tools for data processing, statistical analysis, and modeling. By leveraging Python's flexibility and extensive libraries, you can enhance Excel's capabilities and tackle complex data analysis tasks with ease.

By integrating Python with VBA, you can harness the strengths of both languages. Python provides a robust and versatile environment for data analysis, while VBA excels at automating Excel-specific tasks and accessing advanced Excel functionalities. This synergy allows you to extend Excel's capabilities using Python's extensive libraries, handle large datasets efficiently, and perform complex calculations and data transformations seamlessly.

The benefits of executing VBA code from Python extend beyond data analysis. You can leverage Python's broader ecosystem for tasks such as web scraping, text processing, machine learning, and integrating with external APIs. By combining Python's versatility with VBA's Excel-specific capabilities, you can create dynamic and efficient workflows that go beyond the limitations of Excel alone.

Furthermore, integrating Python and VBA opens up opportunities for collaboration and sharing of code. Python's popularity among data scientists, analysts, and developers ensures a vast community and a wealth of shared knowledge. By integrating Python with Excel through VBA, you can bridge the gap between these two worlds, allowing data analysts, developers, and Excel power users to collaborate and benefit from each other's expertise.

In summary, executing VBA code from Python empowers you to do the following:

- Leverage Python's extensive libraries and tools for data analysis and manipulation
- Automate repetitive tasks and build custom Excel applications using VBA
- Perform complex calculations, data transformations, and statistical analysis with Python's powerful ecosystem
- Extend Excel's functionality using Python's versatility and access external data sources and APIs
- Collaborate and share code between Python data analysts, developers, and Excel power users

The integration of Python and VBA enables you to unlock the full potential of Excel, leverage the strengths of both languages, and take your data analysis, reporting, and automation skills to new heights.

Let's proceed to set up the environment for executing VBA code from Python.

Setting up the environment

To successfully execute VBA code from Python, we need to set up the environment by installing the required dependencies and configuring the necessary connections. This section will walk you through the steps to ensure a smooth setup process in three easy steps.

Installing the pywin32 library

The `pywin32` library serves as a bridge between Python and the Windows API and COM objects. It enables Python to interact with Excel's object model and execute VBA code.

To install `pywin32`, you can use a package manager such as `pip` by running the following command in your command prompt or terminal:

```
python -m pip install pywin32==306
```

Here is how it runs:

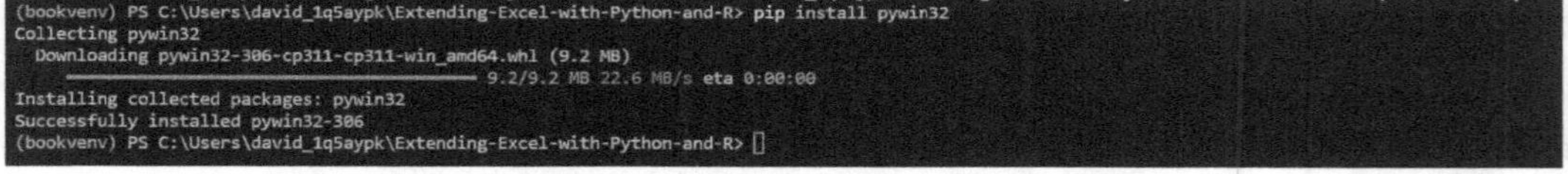

Figure 3.1 – Installing pywin32 on Windows with pip

This will install the `pywin32` package and its dependencies, allowing Python to communicate with Excel.

Establishing a connection with Excel

Once `pywin32` is installed, we can establish a connection with Excel from Python. This connection allows us to access Excel's workbooks, worksheets, ranges, and other Excel-specific functionalities programmatically.

To establish a connection, we can make use of the `win32com.client` module provided by `pywin32`. Here's an example of how to create a connection with Excel:

```
import win32com.client as win32

excel_app = win32.Dispatch("Excel.Application")
```

If the environment is set up correctly, this code returns nothing. However, if the code returns `com_error`, please go to the *Error handling with the environmental setup* section.

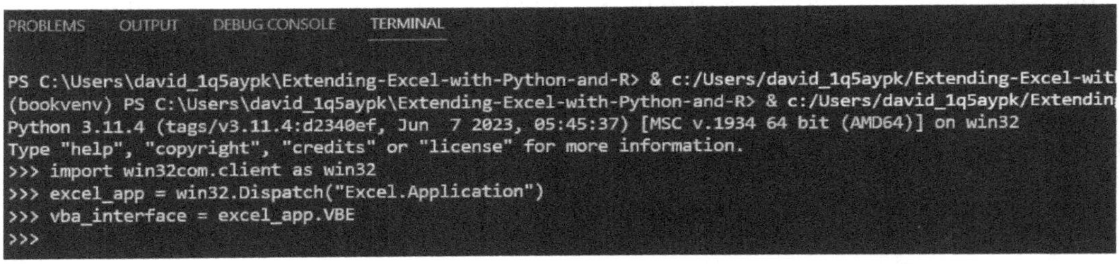

```
PROBLEMS    OUTPUT    DEBUG CONSOLE    TERMINAL

PS C:\Users\david_1q5aypk\Extending-Excel-with-Python-and-R> & c:/Users/david_1q5aypk/Extending-Excel-wit
(bookvenv) PS C:\Users\david_1q5aypk\Extending-Excel-with-Python-and-R> & c:/Users/david_1q5aypk/Extendin
Python 3.11.4 (tags/v3.11.4:d2340ef, Jun  7 2023, 05:45:37) [MSC v.1934 64 bit (AMD64)] on win32
Type "help", "copyright", "credits" or "license" for more information.
>>> import win32com.client as win32
>>> excel_app = win32.Dispatch("Excel.Application")
>>> vba_interface = excel_app.VBE
>>>
```

Figure 3.2 – Testing the connection to Excel

In the preceding code snippet, we imported the `win32com.client` module and created a new instance of the Excel application using the `win32.Dispatch` method. This creates a connection between Python and Excel, allowing us to interact with Excel's objects and execute VBA code.

Creating an interface to interact with VBA code

With the connection established, we can create an interface that enables us to execute VBA code from Python. This interface serves as a bridge between Python and VBA, allowing us to send commands, call VBA functions, and access VBA macros. To create an interface, we can use the `excel_app` object obtained from the previous step:

```
vba_interface = excel_app.VBE
```

You may receive an error along the lines of *Programmatic access to Visual Basic Project is not trusted*. In that case, you can look up a solution at `https://stackoverflow.com/questions/17033526/programmatic-access-to-visual-basic-project-is-not-trusted-from-iis`.

In the preceding code, we access the **VBA editor** (**VBE**) through the `excel_app` object. This grants us access to VBA's functionalities, including executing VBA code, manipulating modules, and interacting with Excel's objects from Python.

By following these steps, we can set up the environment to execute VBA code from Python seamlessly. The installation of the `pywin32` library and the establishment of a connection with Excel create the foundation for executing VBA code and leveraging Excel's capabilities programmatically. In the next sections, we'll dive deeper into executing VBA code, interacting with Excel's objects, and exploring various use cases for integrating Python and VBA.

Error handling with the environment setup

It is possible that the last line of code will give you the **Project is not trusted** error. As the error suggests, this is because VBA is not trusted in your Excel security settings. To programmatically access VBA, you will need to change the security settings.

> **Note**
> This has security consequences beyond the scope of this book, so only change the settings if you are OK with the risks.

To change the security settings, you will need to create a new key in the registry and add a new property to it by running PowerShell as administrator. Run the following code:

```
New-Item -path HKLM:\Software\Microsoft\Office\16.0\Excel\ -Name
"Security"
Set-ItemProperty -path HKLM:\Software\Microsoft\Office\16.0\Excel\
Security -Name "AccessVBOM" -Value 1
' ' '
```

After that, rerun the Python code to test that the environment is correctly set up.

Now that we have the environment set up, let's move on to executing VBA code from Python and exploring the possibilities it offers.

Writing and executing VBA code

Once the environment is set up, we can dive into the process of writing and executing VBA code from Python. This section will introduce you to different approaches and techniques to interact with Excel, run VBA macros, and retrieve results back into Python.

Let's explore some of the key aspects of writing and executing VBA code.

Using the win32com.client module

The `win32com.client` module, provided by the `pywin32` library, offers a convenient way to create a COM interface and interact with Excel from Python. With this module, you can access Excel's objects, open workbooks, manipulate worksheets, and execute VBA macros.

Here's an example that demonstrates how to open an Excel workbook and execute a VBA macro using `win32com.client`. Before running this code, you can ensure `iris_data.xlsm` has the macro by going to **Developer** | **Macros** (or **Visual Basic**) to see that the macro exists:

```python
import win32com.client as win32
import os

excel_app = win32.Dispatch("Excel.Application")

path =  os.getcwd().replace('\'','\\') + '\\'

workbook = excel_app.Workbooks.Open(path+"iris_data.xlsm")
excel_app.Run("examplePythonVBA")
workbook.Close(SaveChanges=True)
excel_app.Quit()
```

On a related note, here we use the `os` library to handle the working directory and the Windows-specific directory separator to make sure a correct absolute path is used. This was already commented on in previous chapters—either the file has to be in the same folder where Python is running (the working directory) or you need to provide an absolute path.

The code returns nothing as the effect we get is on the Excel side of things:

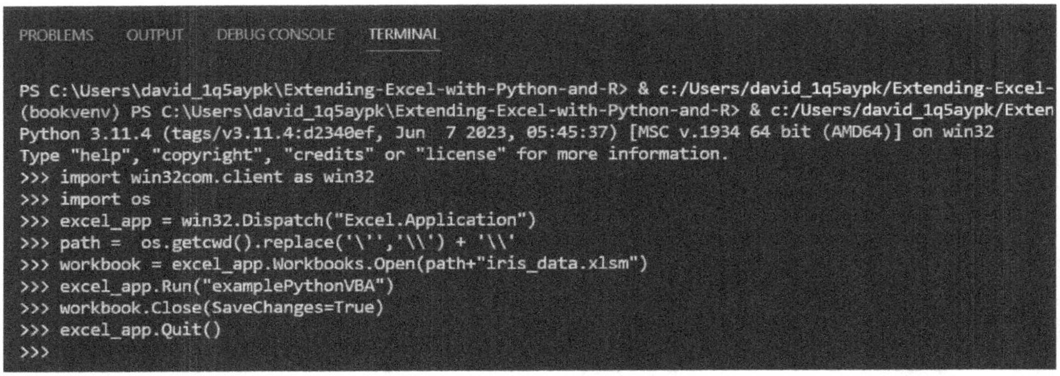

```
PROBLEMS    OUTPUT    DEBUG CONSOLE    TERMINAL

PS C:\Users\david_1q5aypk\Extending-Excel-with-Python-and-R> & c:/Users/david_1q5aypk/Extending-Excel-
(bookvenv) PS C:\Users\david_1q5aypk\Extending-Excel-with-Python-and-R> & c:/Users/david_1q5aypk/Exten
Python 3.11.4 (tags/v3.11.4:d2340ef, Jun  7 2023, 05:45:37) [MSC v.1934 64 bit (AMD64)] on win32
Type "help", "copyright", "credits" or "license" for more information.
>>> import win32com.client as win32
>>> import os
>>> excel_app = win32.Dispatch("Excel.Application")
>>> path =  os.getcwd().replace('\'','\\') + '\\'
>>> workbook = excel_app.Workbooks.Open(path+"iris_data.xlsm")
>>> excel_app.Run("examplePythonVBA")
>>> workbook.Close(SaveChanges=True)
>>> excel_app.Quit()
>>>
```

Figure 3.3 – Running the VBA macro from Python

In the preceding code, we create an instance of the Excel application using `win32.Dispatch` and open a workbook with the `Workbooks.Open` method. We then execute a VBA macro named `examplePythonVBA` using `excel_app.Run`. Finally, we close the workbook, without saving the changes, and quit the Excel application.

The macro simply creates a new sheet with a short message in a cell.

You can open the `.xlsm` workbook after running this code to see that the macro actually worked.

Interacting with Excel objects

With `win32com.client`, you have access to various Excel objects, such as worksheets, ranges, and charts, allowing you to manipulate them programmatically. For example, you can write data to a specific range, format cells, create charts, or perform calculations. Here's an example that demonstrates how to write data to an Excel worksheet using Python:

```python
import win32com.client as win32
import os

excel_app = win32.Dispatch("Excel.Application")
path =  os.getcwd().replace('\'','\\') + '\\'

workbook = excel_app.Workbooks.Open(path+"iris_data.xlsm")
worksheet = workbook.Worksheets("Sheet1")

data = [[1, 2, 3], [4, 5, 6], [7, 8, 9]]
for row_index, row_data in enumerate(data, start=1):
for col_index, value in enumerate(row_data, start=1):
worksheet.Cells(row_index, col_index).Value = value

workbook.Close(SaveChanges=True)
excel_app.Quit()
```

The code returns no output if successful:

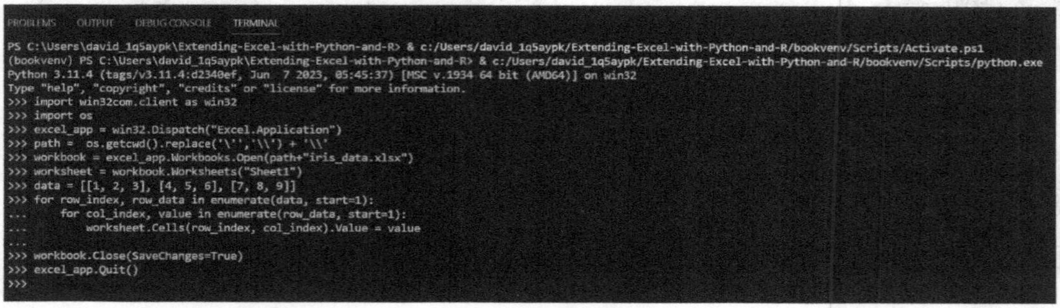

Figure 3.4 – Output for the interacting cells

In the preceding code, we open an Excel workbook, access a specific worksheet named **Sheet1**, and write data to the cells using the cells' **property**. We iterate over the data and set the values in the corresponding cells.

Retrieving results back into Python

After executing VBA code in Excel, you may want to retrieve the results back into Python for further analysis or processing. One way to accomplish this is by using Excel's object model to access specific values or ranges and retrieve them into Python variables.

Here's an example that demonstrates how to retrieve data from an Excel worksheet into a Python list:

```python
import win32com.client as win32
import os

excel_app = win32.Dispatch("Excel.Application")
path = os.getcwd().replace('\'','\\') + '\\'

workbook = excel_app.Workbooks.Open(path+"iris_data.xlsm")
worksheet = workbook.Worksheets("Sheet1")

# Access multiple cells using Range notation
range_of_cells = worksheet.Range('A1:C3')

# Read the values from the range of cells
values = range_of_cells.Value

workbook.Close(SaveChanges=False)
excel_app.Quit()

print(values)
```

The result of the code is a tuple of tuples:

```
((1.0, 2.0, 3.0), (4.0, 5.0, 6.0), (7.0, 8.0, 9.0))
```

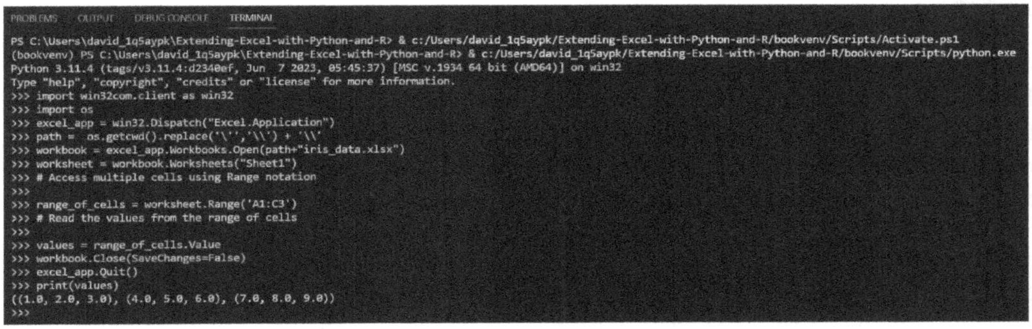

Figure 3.5 – Retrieving data from Excel

In the preceding code, we define an Excel range of cells and retrieve their values using the `Value` property. We store the values in a Python list to further process or analyze them.

By leveraging the `win32com.client` module and the Excel object model, you can write and execute VBA code from Python effectively.

The provided code examples illustrate how to interact with Excel, run VBA macros, and retrieve data back into Python for further manipulation. Experiment with these techniques, adapt them to your specific needs, and explore the possibilities of integrating Python and VBA for Excel automation and data processing.

Let's see next how this setup helps with automating tasks.

Automating Excel tasks

One of the major benefits of executing VBA code from Python is the automation of Excel tasks.

This section will discuss practical examples of automating common Excel operations using VBA from Python. By seamlessly integrating Python and VBA, you can streamline your data analysis workflows and significantly enhance your productivity.

Let's explore some of the tasks you can automate using this powerful combination.

Data manipulation

With Python and VBA integration, you can automate data manipulation tasks in Excel. This includes tasks such as sorting data, filtering records, merging datasets, and performing complex transformations. For example, you can use Python to retrieve data from external sources, process it using Python libraries such as `pandas` or `NumPy`, and then update the Excel worksheet with the transformed data using VBA. This integration allows you to automate repetitive data manipulation tasks and ensure data consistency across sources.

Formatting

Automating formatting tasks in Excel can save a significant amount of time and effort. With Python and VBA, you can define formatting rules and apply them to specific cells, ranges, or entire worksheets. This includes formatting options such as font styles, cell borders, background colors, and number formatting. By combining Python's flexibility and VBA's formatting capabilities, you can create dynamic and visually appealing Excel reports or dashboards with ease.

Chart creation

Excel's charting capabilities can be effectively utilized by automating the creation of charts from Python. You can extract data from various sources, perform necessary calculations or aggregations in Python, and then generate charts dynamically using VBA. This automation allows you to create interactive and data-driven visualizations directly from your Python analysis, saving you time and providing you with more control over the charting process.

As this topic is quite large and important, we will go into detail on it in a dedicated chapter later.

Complex calculations

Excel is well-known for its powerful built-in functions and formulas. By combining Python and VBA, you can extend Excel's calculation capabilities even further. You can leverage Python's libraries for advanced mathematical or statistical computations and integrate the results seamlessly into Excel using VBA. This integration enables you to perform complex calculations, simulations, or predictive modeling within the familiar Excel environment.

By automating Excel tasks through Python and VBA integration, you can save time, eliminate manual errors, and enhance the efficiency of your data analysis workflows. The provided code samples and explanations offer a starting point for exploring the vast possibilities of automation. Experiment with different scenarios, adapt the code to your specific requirements, and unlock the full potential of Python and VBA for Excel automation.

We know now how we can automate Excel tasks from Python. We should also think about why (or why not) to do so.

Pros and cons of executing VBA from Python

In this section, we will delve into the pros and cons of executing VBA code from Python. By understanding the advantages and limitations of this approach, you can make informed decisions when selecting the appropriate tool for your specific requirements.

Let's explore the benefits and considerations of executing VBA code from Python.

Here are the benefits of executing VBA code from Python:

- **Flexibility and power**: By combining Python and VBA, you gain access to the flexibility and power of both languages. Python offers a rich ecosystem of libraries and tools for data analysis, scientific computing, and automation. VBA, on the other hand, provides extensive functionalities within Excel, allowing you to leverage its built-in features, formulas, and macros. This combination empowers you to accomplish complex tasks and automate Excel operations efficiently.

- **Integration with external data sources**: Python excels in connecting to external data sources such as databases, APIs, or web scraping. By executing VBA code from Python, you can seamlessly integrate these external data sources with Excel. Python can retrieve data, perform calculations or transformations, and then update the Excel workbook using VBA. This integration enables you to leverage the power of Python for data manipulation and analysis while harnessing Excel's visualization and reporting capabilities.

- **Automation and efficiency**: Executing VBA code from Python allows you to automate repetitive Excel tasks, leading to increased productivity and efficiency. You can streamline your workflows by automating data import/export, data cleaning, formatting, and report generation. This automation eliminates manual errors, reduces manual effort, and frees up your time for more critical analysis and decision-making tasks.

The following are the areas of improvement in executing VBA code from Python:

- **Compatibility and platform dependency**: Executing VBA code from Python is primarily supported on Windows-based systems. If you are working on a different operating system, such as macOS or Linux, you may encounter compatibility issues. Additionally, compatibility with different versions of Excel or Office may vary, requiring careful consideration when sharing or distributing your Python and VBA integrated solutions.

- **Learning curve and skill requirements**: Successfully executing VBA code from Python requires familiarity with both languages. You need to understand the syntax and capabilities of VBA for Excel automation and Python for interacting with Excel and executing VBA code. This may require some learning and practice, especially if you are new to either language.

- **Maintenance and updates**: As with any software integration, maintenance and updates can be a consideration. If there are changes or updates to the Excel or Python ecosystem, you may need to adapt your code accordingly. Additionally, ensuring compatibility and functionality across different versions of Excel and Python may require periodic updates and testing.

Despite these considerations, executing VBA code from Python offers a powerful approach to automate Excel tasks, leverages external data sources, and creates efficient data analysis workflows. By combining the strengths of Python and VBA, you can unlock the full potential of Excel within your Python projects and enhance your productivity and data manipulation capabilities.

Summary

In this chapter, we have learned how to integrate R and Python and VBA using `RDCOMClient` and `pywin32`, respectively. We have gained knowledge on executing VBA code from Python, setting up the environment, and automating Excel tasks, and understand the pros and cons of this integration.

This knowledge will empower you to enhance your Excel automation skills.

In the next chapter, we will delve into advanced topics, building upon your existing knowledge.

4

Automating Further – Task Scheduling and Email

Sometimes, we can spend countless hours tediously creating, formatting, and emailing Excel spreadsheets. Well, fret no more! With the power of programming, specifically R or Python, you can effortlessly automate these mundane tasks and reclaim your precious time.

Imagine this: you have a list of sales data that needs to be organized into a professional-looking spreadsheet and sent to multiple recipients via email. Instead of slogging through manual data entry and formatting, you can leverage the prowess of R or Python to simplify your workflow.

In R, you can use the amazing `taskscheduleR` package to schedule tasks and run your script automatically at specified times. With this, you can set up a recurring job to generate your Excel spreadsheets and send them out without lifting a finger. For emailing, you can employ the `RDCOMClient`, `Windows365R`, or `blastula` packages, which allow you to interact with Outlook and Gmail directly. This means you can compose and send emails with the attached spreadsheets effortlessly, customizing the content and recipients as needed.

But wait, Python enthusiasts! Fear not, for you, too, can achieve the same level of automation magic. In Python, you can utilize the `pywin32` library to send out beautifully formatted emails via Gmail. It seamlessly integrates with your code, enabling you to attach your Excel spreadsheets and customize the email's content and recipients with ease.

By harnessing the power of R or Python, along with `taskscheduleR`, `RDCOMClient`, `Windows365R`, or `blastula`, you can become the hero of your office, delivering accurate, visually appealing spreadsheets promptly, all while sipping your coffee. Say goodbye to mind-numbing repetition and hello to efficient automation. Let your creativity flourish as you unlock the power of R or Python to conquer the world of Excel spreadsheets and email distribution with confidence and ease!

In this chapter, we're going to cover the following main topics:

- Installing and understanding the `taskscheduleR` library
- Using `RDCOMClient`, `Windows365R`, and `blastula` for email in Outlook or Gmail
- Scheduling Python scripts
- Email notifications and automation with Python

Technical requirements

The code for this chapter can be found here: `https://github.com/PacktPublishing/Extending-Excel-with-Python-and-R/tree/main/Chapter%204`.

You will need to install the following new R and Python packages:

- `Blastula`
- `Windows365R`
- `schedule==1.2.0`
- `apscheduler==3.10.1`

Installing and understanding the tasksheduleR library

The `taskscheduleR` R package allows you to schedule R scripts or processes with the Windows task scheduler. This means that you can automate R processes on specific time points from within R itself. The package is basically a wrapper around the `Schtasks.exe` functionality. `Schtasks.exe` is a command line tool that allows you to create, delete, query, change, run, and finish scheduled tasks on a local or remote computer. To use `taskscheduleR`, you first need to install the package from CRAN. Once the package is installed, you can use the following functions to schedule R scripts:

- `taskscheduler_create()`: This function creates a new scheduled task.
- `taskscheduler_remove()`: This function removes an existing scheduled task. If you are using version 1.8, then the function is `taskscheduler_delete()`.
- `taskscheduler_get()`: This function gets the information about an existing scheduled task.

The `taskscheduler_create()` function takes a number of arguments, including the name of the scheduled task, the R script to run, and the schedule to run the script. For example, the following code would create a scheduled task that runs the R script `my_scheduled_excel_script.R` every day at 10:00 am:

```
taskscheduler_create(
  name = "My Scheduled Excel Task",
  rscript = "my_scheduled_excel_script.R",
```

```
   schedule = "DAILY",
   start_time = "10:00:00"
)`
```

You can also use the GUI to create tasks for the job scheduler by installing `miniUI` and `shiny`. This will install the add-in capability of the package, allowing you to easily create jobs without writing a single line of code. Here is the code you can use if you want to install the preceding packages listed:

```
# The initial package itself
install.packages("taskscheduleR")

# To use the GUI
install.packages('miniUI')
install.packages('shiny')
```

Now, we see how to create scripts for this.

Creating sample scripts

The first thing we need to do is create a script that can be run via the Windows task scheduler. Let's keep the script simple and just print `Hello` and the current date and time using the R function `Sys.time()`. After this is done, we can then create a couple of jobs that will run the script.

Here is the `hello_world.R` script:

```
library("tcltk")
tkmessageBox(
   title='Message',
   message = paste0("Hello, it is: ", Sys.time()),
   type = "ok"
   )
```

The first line of code, `library("tcltk")`, loads the `tcltk` package, which provides functions for creating and interacting with **graphical user interfaces (GUIs)** in R.

The second line of code, `tkmessageBox()`, creates a message box. The message box is a pop-up window that displays a message and allows the user to take some action, such as clicking a button.

The arguments to the `tkmessageBox()` function are as follows:

- `title`: The title of the message box.
- `message`: The message that will be displayed in the message box.
- `type`: The type of message box. The possible values are `ok`, `okcancel`, `yesno`, `yesnocancel`, `retrycancel`, and `abortretryignore`.

In this case, the type of message box is `ok`, which means that the user can only click an `ok` button to close the message box.

The third line of code, `paste0("Hello, it is: ", Sys.time())`, creates a string that will be displayed in the message box. The string includes the current time, which is obtained from the `Sys.time()` function.

When this code is run, a message box will pop up that displays the current time and an `ok` button. The user can click the **OK** button to close the message box.

Here is a screenshot of what the message box will look like:

Figure 4.1 – Hello world message box

Now, let's make a couple of scripts that will pop this message up on a screen on schedule. Here is one that will run this hourly:

```
taskscheduler_create(
  taskname = "Hello World Hourly",
  rscript = "hello_world.R",
  schedule = "HOURLY"
)
```

The first line of code, `taskscheduler_create()`, calls the `taskscheduler_create()` function from the `taskscheduleR` package. The `taskscheduleR` package provides functions for creating and managing Windows task scheduler jobs.

The `taskscheduler_create()` function takes the following three arguments:

- `taskname`: The name of the task scheduler job
- `rscript`: The path to the R script that will be run by the task scheduler job
- `schedule`: The schedule for the task scheduler job

In this case, the task name is `Hello World Hourly`, the R script is `hello_world.R`, and the schedule is `"HOURLY"`.

The second line of code, `taskname = "Hello World Hourly"`, sets the task name to `Hello World Hourly`. The task name is a unique identifier for the task scheduler job.

The third line of code, `rscript = "hello_world.R"`, sets the path to the R script that will be run by the task scheduler job. The R script must be saved in a location that is accessible by the task scheduler.

The fourth line of code, `schedule = "HOURLY"`, sets the schedule for the task scheduler job. The schedule is a string that specifies when the task scheduler job will run. The schedule `"HOURLY"` means that the task scheduler job will run every hour. When this code is run, a new task scheduler job will be created that runs the `hello_world.R` R script every hour.

Now, we will move on to using `RDCOMClient` for Outlook if you are not using Microsoft 365. This will allow us to script sending emails inside of other processes.

RDCOMClient for Outlook

As we have seen, `RDCOMClient` is a powerful R package that allows you to interact with Microsoft Outlook using the COM interface. With `RDCOMClient`, you can automate tasks in Outlook, such as sending emails, accessing folders, managing appointments, and more. Sending emails via Outlook using `RDCOMClient` is straightforward and can be achieved by following a few steps. Here is the script for it:

```
install.packages("RDCOMClient")
library(RDCOMClient)
OutApp <- COMCreate("Outlook.Application")
OutMail <- OutApp$CreateItem(0)
outMail[["To"]] <- "recipient@example.com"
outMail[["Subject"]] <- "Hello from RDCOMClient"
outMail[["Body"]] <- "This is the body of the email."
outMail$Attachments$Add("C:/path/to/attachment.txt")
outMail$Send()
outMail <- NULL
OutApp <- NULL
```

Let us now understand each line of the preceding code:

1. First, you need to install and load the `RDCOMClient` package in your R environment.
2. Once installed, load the package using the `library()` function.
3. Next, create a new Outlook application object using the `COMCreate()` function.
4. This creates a connection to the Outlook application. Now, you can create a new email object using the `OutApp$CreateItem()` method and specify the email type as `olMailItem`.

5. Next, you can set various properties of the email, such as the recipient, subject, body, attachments, and more. Here's an example of how you can set these properties:

```
outMail[["To"]] <- "recipient@example.com"
outMail[["Subject"]] <- "Hello from RDCOMClient"
outMail[["Body"]] <- "This is the body of the email."
outMail$Attachments$Add("C:/path/to/attachment.txt")
```

6. After setting the desired properties, you can send the email using the `Send()` method, and that's it!

    The email will be sent from your Outlook account to the specified recipient(s) with the configured properties. Remember to release the COM object and terminate the connection once you are done.

    This ensures that the resources are properly released.

By using `RDCOMClient`, you can automate email-sending tasks in Outlook directly from R, enabling you to streamline your workflow and save time. It provides a convenient way to integrate R with Outlook and leverage its features programmatically.

Now, we will delve into the `Microsoft365R` and `blastula` packages, which work in tandem. This will be instead of using the `RDCOMClient` library, with the reason being that `Microsoft365R` works for those that are using Microsoft Azure instead of a generic SMTP connection via Outlook.

Using the Microsoft365R and blastula packages

We are now going to go over two packages that can be used in conjunction with each other to create emails via Outlook from Microsoft. These packages are Microsoft365R and blastula. Let's look at them in the following sections.

Microsoft365R

Microsoft365R is an R library that provides an interface to Microsoft 365 (formerly known as Office 365) cloud services. It is built on top of the AzureGraph package, which provides a high-level abstraction for interacting with the Microsoft Graph API. Microsoft365R currently supports the following Microsoft 365 services:

- Teams
- Outlook
- SharePoint Online
- OneDrive

The library provides several top-level client functions for accessing each of these services. For example, the `get_personal_onedrive()` function can be used to access your personal OneDrive account, and the `get_business_outlook()` function can be used to access your work or school Outlook account.

Microsoft365R also provides several helper functions for working with the Microsoft Graph API. For example, the `list_drive_contents()` function can be used to list the contents of a OneDrive drive, and the `send_email()` function can be used to send an email from Outlook.

The library is well-documented and provides several examples to help you get started. It is also actively maintained and updated with new features and bug fixes on a regular basis.

Here are some of the benefits of using Microsoft365R:

- It provides a simple and easy-to-use interface for accessing Microsoft 365 cloud services
- It is built on top of the `AzureGraph` package, which provides a high-level abstraction for interacting with the Microsoft Graph API

If you are looking for an R library that provides an easy way to access Microsoft 365 cloud services, then Microsoft365R is a great option. It is well-documented in the package vignettes, actively maintained, and supports a wide range of Microsoft 365 services. We will only be focusing on its use for Outlook.

The blastula package

The `blastula` R package is a tool that makes it easy to produce and send HTML email from R. You can use Markdown text, block-based components, and even HTML fragments to create email messages with three content areas: a body, header, and a footer. The package also provides functions to set up **simple mail transfer protocol** (**SMTP**) access credentials and send email through an SMTP server or RStudio Connect. You can install the blastula package from CRAN with `install.packages("blastula")`.

Some of the advantages of using blastula over other email packages are as follows:

- It allows you to use Markdown text, block-based components, and even HTML in order to create professional and potentially computed document emails. You can achieve this in the body, the header, and the footer of the email.
- The package also provides functions to set up SMTP access credentials and send email through a traditional SMTP server, or, if you are a RStudio Connect user, you can send emails via RStudio Connect.
- The resulting email will look great on any display.
- The syntax is intuitive, allowing you to code quickly and effectively while making your primary focus the message of the email itself.

Here is an example of using `blastula` to create and send a simple HTML email message:

1. First, we need to load the `blastula` package with `library(blastula)` and `library(glue)`.

2. Next, we can use the `compose_email()` function to create the email message. We can supply Markdown text to the body argument to be rendered in HTML; for example, see the following:

```
email <- compose_email(
  body = md(glue(
"Hello, this is {sale_file} contains the latest quarters
data. Here is a picture of the graph that will be on our
dashboard:![sales dashboard] https://dashboard.company.
com/)")
)
```

3. Then, we can preview the email message in the viewer by calling the email object:

```
email
```

4. Finally, we can send the email message through an SMTP server using the `smtp_send()` function. We need to provide the recipient's email address, the sender's email address, the subject line, and the credentials for the SMTP server:

```
email %>%
  smtp_send(
    to = "jane_doe@example.com",
    from = "joe_public@example.net",
    subject = "Testing the `smtp_send()` function",
    credentials = creds_file("email_creds")
  )
```

The `creds_file()` function is a helper function that creates a credentials file for SMTP access.

We can use the `create_smtp_creds_file()` function to generate this file interactively:

```
create_smtp_creds_file(
  file = "email_creds",
  user = "joe_public@example.net",
  provider = "gmail"
)
```

This will prompt us to enter our password and a two-factor authentication code (if enabled) for Gmail. The credentials file will be saved in a secure location and can be reused for future email messages.

Now that we have gone over both packages separately, let's see how we can use them together in a fashion that could be a bit more robust and streamlined.

Here is a full script, and then we will discuss how it works:

```
install.packages("blastula")
install.packages("Microsoft365R")
library(blastula)
library(Microsoft365R)

# Get work/school email
outlb <- get_business_outlook()

# compose an email with blastula
bl_body <- "## Hello!

You can write email in **Markdown** with the blastula package."

bl_em <- compose_email(
    body=md(bl_body),
    footer=md("sent via Microsoft365R and R")
)
em <- outlb$create_email(bl_em, subject="Hello from R", to="email@
example.com")

# add an attachment and send it
em$add_attachment("mydocument.docx")
em$send()
```

Now, let's go over each part of the script to understand what is happening.

1. First, we must install both the `blastula` and `Microsoft365R` packages.
2. Then, we call those libraries into the current session using the `library()` function.
3. We then create a variable called `outlb` that holds the variable for the `get_business_outlook()` function.
4. We then create the body of the email. We can write the email using Markdown syntax.
5. After we make the body of the email, we then create a variable to hold the email itself that is created using the function `compose_email()`.
6. From here, we then add the attachment and send the email.

The email is sent using the configured work/school email account retrieved earlier. So, in conclusion, these lines of code install the necessary packages, load the required libraries, retrieve the work/school email account, compose an email using the `blastula` package, add an attachment to the email, and finally, send the email using the `Microsoft365R` package.

You have learned about scheduling and email integration in R. Now, let's have a look at how the same can be achieved in Python!

Scheduling Python scripts

Automation is not limited to executing scripts manually; it also involves scheduling them to run at specific intervals or events. Scheduling Python scripts allows you to automate repetitive tasks, perform periodic data updates, generate reports, and carry out system maintenance without manual intervention.

In this section, we will explore various techniques and tools to schedule Python scripts and achieve efficient and timely execution.

By the end of this section, you will have a comprehensive understanding of various scheduling techniques and tools available for Python scripts. You will be equipped with the knowledge and skills to schedule your Python scripts effectively, automate routine tasks, and maximize your productivity. Whether you are running scripts on Windows or Unix-like systems, this chapter will empower you to implement reliable and efficient Python script scheduling solutions.

Introduction to Python script scheduling

We will start by discussing the importance of scheduling Python scripts and its benefits in streamlining workflows. You will learn why scheduling is crucial for automating tasks and how it can save time and effort. We will also highlight real-world scenarios where Python script scheduling is commonly applied.

Scheduling Python scripts plays a vital role in automating tasks and improving workflow efficiency. By scheduling scripts to run at specific intervals or events, you can eliminate the need for manual execution and ensure timely and accurate data processing, report generation, and system maintenance.

In this section, we will explore the importance of Python script scheduling and highlight its benefits in the various domains listed as follows:

- **Automating repetitive tasks**: Many tasks in data processing, analysis, and reporting involve repetitive actions. Scheduling Python scripts allows you to automate these tasks, reducing the time and effort required for manual execution. Whether it's fetching data from external sources, performing calculations, generating reports, or updating databases, scheduling scripts ensures consistent and reliable automation.

- **Periodic data updates**: In many applications, data need to be regularly updated from external sources or refreshed from internal systems. Python script scheduling enables you to define a schedule for fetching, transforming, and updating data automatically. By specifying the desired frequency, you can ensure that your data remain up to date without manual intervention.

- **Generating reports**: Reports are often generated periodically, such as daily, weekly, or monthly. With Python script scheduling, you can automate the generation of reports by scheduling the script to run at specific intervals. This ensures that the reports are produced consistently and delivered on time, saving valuable time and effort.

- **System maintenance**: Python script scheduling is not limited to data-related tasks; it can also be used for system maintenance activities. From performing backups and database maintenance to running system checks and executing routine cleanup tasks, scheduling Python scripts enables you to keep your systems running smoothly without manual intervention.

- **Real-world scenarios**: Python script scheduling finds application in various industries and domains. For example, in ecommerce, scripts can be scheduled to update product inventory, synchronize prices, and generate sales reports. In finance, scheduled scripts can fetch stock market data, calculate portfolio performance, and generate financial statements. In IT operations, scripts can be scheduled for system monitoring, log analysis, and automated incident response. These are just a few examples of how Python script scheduling can be leveraged to enhance productivity and efficiency across different domains.

By understanding the importance of Python script scheduling and its benefits, you can identify opportunities to automate tasks, streamline workflows, and improve overall productivity.

In the following sections, we will explore different methods and tools for scheduling Python scripts, providing you with the knowledge and techniques to implement effective and reliable automation solutions.

Built-in scheduling options

Python provides built-in scheduling options on both Windows and Unix-like systems without the need for external libraries. These options provide a convenient and lightweight way to schedule and execute your Python scripts at predefined intervals. In this section, we will explore the built-in scheduling options and discuss their features, usage, and limitations.

We will explore **Windows Task Scheduler** and **crontab** on Unix-like systems. You will learn how to set up scheduled tasks using these native scheduling tools, specify the frequency of execution, and configure various options to meet your specific requirements.

Here is a list of the built-in options and their key features:

cron (Unix-like systems)

The following are the key features of cron:

- cron is a time-based job scheduler available on Unix-like operating systems, including Linux and macOS

- It allows you to schedule recurring tasks by specifying the time, date, and frequency using a cron expression

- cron provides flexibility in defining schedules, such as running scripts at specific times, on specific days of the week, or at regular intervals

- It is widely supported and has been the de facto standard for scheduling tasks on Unix-like systems for many years
- While cron is not a Python-specific tool, you can use it to schedule the execution of Python scripts by specifying the appropriate command line invocation

Windows Task Scheduler (Windows systems)

The following points list the features of Windows systems:

- Windows Task Scheduler is the built-in task scheduling tool provided by the Windows operating system
- It allows you to schedule tasks to run at specific times or events on Windows machines
- You can create scheduled tasks through the graphical user interface or using the command line tool `schtasks`
- Windows Task Scheduler provides a range of options for defining triggers, such as specific times, daily, weekly, or monthly schedules, or even based on system events
- It offers a user-friendly interface for managing scheduled tasks, including setting up dependencies, priority settings, and error handling

Python's time.sleep() function

This is a list of the key features of the `time.sleep()` function:

- While not specifically designed for scheduling tasks, Python's built-in `time` module provides a simple way to introduce delays between script executions
- The `time.sleep()` function pauses the script for a specified number of seconds, allowing you to control the timing between script runs
- While this option lacks the sophistication and advanced features of dedicated scheduling tools, it can be useful for simple cases where a fixed delay is sufficient
- However, keep in mind that using `time.sleep()` as a scheduling mechanism may not be suitable for precise or complex scheduling requirements

It's important to note that these built-in scheduling options have their strengths and limitations. They are suitable for many use cases but may not provide the advanced features and flexibility required for complex scheduling scenarios. In such cases, external libraries and tools can offer more robust solutions.

In the next section, we will explore some popular third-party libraries for scheduling Python scripts, providing additional features and customization options.

Third-party scheduling libraries

While Python's built-in scheduling options can handle many common scheduling tasks, there are several third-party libraries available that provide more advanced features and customization options. These libraries offer greater flexibility and control over scheduling Python scripts, allowing you to handle complex scheduling scenarios with ease.

In this section, we will explore some popular third-party scheduling libraries and discuss their features and benefits. We will cover topics such as defining schedules using cron-like syntax, handling time zones, and managing concurrent execution.

schedule

Here are the features and benefits of the `schedule` library:

- The `schedule` library is a lightweight Python library that simplifies the process of scheduling tasks
- It offers an intuitive and easy-to-use API for defining schedules using a fluent interface
- The library supports various scheduling options, such as specific times, intervals, and cron-like expressions
- `schedule` allows you to execute functions, methods, or even shell commands at the defined schedule
- It is designed to be simple and lightweight, making it suitable for smaller projects or cases where a minimalistic scheduling solution is desired

Here is an easy-to-demonstrate usage of `schedule` in Python:

```
import schedule
import time

def job():
    print("This job is executed every day at 8:00 AM.")

# Schedule the job to run every day at 8:00 AM
schedule.every().day.at("08:00").do(job)

# Keep the program running
while True:
    schedule.run_pending()
    time.sleep(1)
```

In this example, we import the `schedule` library and define a function called `job()`, which prints a message. We then use the `schedule.every().day.at(08:00).do(job)` syntax to schedule the `job` function to run every day at 8:00 am. Finally, we use a `while` loop to continuously check for pending scheduled jobs and execute them. Note that this solution means the console is `blocked`, meaning the Python process running this infinite loop will not be available for other tasks. To stop the scheduler, simply interrupt the kernel/console or kill the underlying Python process.

You can customize the scheduling behavior by using different methods provided by the `schedule` library, such as `.every().day.at()`, `.every().monday`, `.every().hour`, and more. Additionally, you can schedule jobs to run at specific intervals or combine multiple scheduling patterns as per your requirements.

Let's have a look at `APScheduler` next.

Advanced Python Scheduler (APScheduler)

Here are the features and benefits of `APScheduler`:

- **Advanced Python Scheduler** (**APScheduler**) is another popular choice for scheduling tasks in Python
- It provides a rich set of features, including various trigger types, such as intervals, cron expressions, and date-based triggers
- APScheduler supports multiple job stores, including in-memory, SQL databases, and Redis
- It offers advanced scheduling options, such as job coalescing, distributed scheduling, and time zone support
- APScheduler has a well-documented API and is widely used in various applications, ranging from simple scripts to complex web applications

Here's a sample code snippet demonstrating how to schedule tasks using the `APScheduler` library:

```
from apscheduler.schedulers.blocking import BlockingScheduler

# Create a scheduler instance
scheduler = BlockingScheduler()

# Define a task function
def send_email():
    # Code to send an email
    print("Email sent!")

# Schedule the task to run every hour
scheduler.add_job(send_email, 'interval', hours=1)

# Start the scheduler
scheduler.start()
```

From the preceding example, we understand the following:

1. We first import the `BlockingScheduler` class from the `apscheduler.schedulers.blocking` module. Then, we create an instance of the scheduler using `BlockingScheduler()`.

2. Next, we define a function called `send_email()`, which represents the task of sending an email. Inside this function, you can write the code to send an email or perform any other desired action.

3. To schedule the task, we use the `add_job()` method of the scheduler. In this case, we specify the `send_email` function as the task to be executed. We also provide the scheduling parameters using the `interval` option, which indicates that the task should be executed at regular intervals. In this example, we set it to run every hour (`hours=1`).

4. Finally, we start the scheduler by calling the `start()` method. This will initiate the scheduler and begin executing the tasks according to the defined schedule.

The `APScheduler` library provides various scheduling options, such as fixed intervals, cron expressions, date/time triggers, and more. You can customize the scheduling behavior according to your specific requirements by exploring the documentation and using the appropriate scheduling options provided by APScheduler.

Next up, let's have a look at the Celery package for completeness' sake.

Celery

The following are the features and benefits of Celery:

*   Celery is a distributed task queue library that can be used for both task execution and scheduling

*   It provides a robust and scalable solution for scheduling Python tasks across multiple workers or machines

*   Celery supports various scheduling options, including intervals, crontab-like expressions, and more

*   It offers advanced features such as task prioritization, result tracking, retries, and task chaining

*   Celery integrates well with message brokers such as **RabbitMQ**, **Redis**, or **Apache Kafka**, providing reliable and scalable task-scheduling capabilities

By using the Celery scheduler, you can automate the execution of tasks based on specific schedules, allowing you to perform recurring or time-based operations in your application. Configuring and deploying Celery apps is beyond the scope of this book, though, so it only stands here for completeness' sake. You can consult the official documentation if you wish to delve deeper: `https://docs.celeryq.dev/en/stable/userguide/periodic-tasks.html`.

These third-party scheduling libraries provide powerful and flexible solutions for scheduling Python scripts. Depending on your specific requirements and the complexity of your scheduling tasks, you can choose the library that best fits your needs. Each library has its own strengths and capabilities, so it's important to evaluate them based on your project's requirements.

In the next section, we will explore practical examples of using these libraries to schedule Python scripts for various use cases.

Best practices and considerations for robust automation

When working with scheduling Python scripts, it's essential to follow best practices and consider various factors to ensure efficient and reliable automation. This section provides insights into the best practices and considerations for scheduling Python scripts effectively.

These best practices will help you create robust and maintainable scheduled tasks. Let's discuss these best practices in the following sections.

Error handling and logging

Here are the best practices for error handling and logging:

- Implement robust error-handling mechanisms to handle any unexpected exceptions and errors that may occur during script execution
- Use logging frameworks to capture detailed information about script execution, including errors, warnings, and information messages
- Proper error handling and logging allow you to diagnose issues, track script performance, and ensure that scheduled tasks are executed as expected

Resource management

Here are the best practices for resource management:

- Consider the resources required by your scheduled Python scripts, such as CPU, memory, and disk space
- Optimize resource usage by identifying and minimizing any resource-intensive operations or bottlenecks
- Ensure that your scripts release resources properly to avoid resource leaks or conflicts

Security considerations

Here are the best practices for security considerations:

- Evaluate the security implications of scheduling Python scripts, especially if they involve sensitive data or interact with external systems

- Implement necessary security measures, such as encrypting credentials, securing API endpoints, and adhering to authentication and authorization protocols
- Regularly review and update security measures to mitigate potential risks and vulnerabilities

Testing and validation

Here are the best practices for testing and validation:

- Thoroughly test and validate your scheduled Python scripts to ensure their correctness and reliability
- Perform unit testing, integration testing, and end-to-end testing to verify that your scripts function as expected and handle various scenarios
- Consider creating a staging environment where you can test scheduled tasks before deploying them to a production environment

Monitoring and alerting

Here are the best practices for monitoring and alerting:

- Establish monitoring and alerting mechanisms to track the execution status of scheduled tasks
- Monitor the performance and health of your scheduling system, including script execution times, resource usage, and any potential errors or failures
- Configure alerts to notify you when tasks fail, enabling prompt intervention and troubleshooting

Documentation and maintenance

Here are the best practices for documentation and maintenance:

- Document the scheduling process, including the configuration, dependencies, and any specific instructions for managing scheduled tasks
- Maintain an up-to-date schedule of your scheduled Python scripts, including the frequency and expected outcomes of each task
- Regularly review and update your scheduling setup, scripts, and dependencies to adapt to changing requirements and technologies

By following these best practices and considering the relevant factors, you can ensure the reliability, efficiency, and security of your scheduled Python scripts. Incorporating these considerations into your scheduling workflow will contribute to the smooth execution of tasks and help you maintain a well-structured and sustainable automation system.

In the next section, we will explore practical examples and use cases that illustrate the application of these best practices and considerations in real-world scenarios.

By completing this section on scheduling Python scripts, you have gained valuable knowledge and skills in automating and managing the execution of your scripts. Let's summarize what you have learned:

- You explored the various built-in scheduling options available in different operating systems, such as cron jobs on Unix-like systems and Task Scheduler on Windows, enabling you to schedule Python scripts at specific times or intervals

- You discovered third-party scheduling libraries, such as `APScheduler` and `Schedule`, which provide more advanced scheduling capabilities, such as cron-like expressions and interval-based scheduling

- You understood the best practices for scheduling Python scripts, including error handling, resource management, security considerations, testing, validation, monitoring, and alerting, as well as documentation and maintenance

- Through practical examples and use cases, you gained hands-on experience in implementing and managing scheduled Python scripts, ensuring the efficient and reliable automation of your tasks

By mastering the concepts and techniques covered in this section, you are now equipped to schedule Python scripts effectively, automate repetitive tasks, and streamline your workflow. The ability to schedule scripts opens a world of possibilities for automating various processes, increasing productivity, and freeing up valuable time for more critical tasks.

In the next section, we will delve into the exciting realm of email notifications and explore how you can enhance your automation workflows by integrating email functionality into your Python scripts.

Email notifications and automation with Python

Much like scheduling Python scripts, email notifications and automation can make your daily work much more efficient. This section will cover the basics, such as the motivation behind using emails from Python, moving on to setting up the environment and sending basic emails, and then covering a real-life use case: sending email notifications for script status.

Introduction to email notifications in Python

Email notifications play a crucial role in automation by providing timely updates, alerts, and reports. In this section, we will explore the significance of integrating email functionality into your Python scripts. We'll discuss various use cases where email notifications can be beneficial, and we'll delve into the advantages they offer for streamlining workflows and enhancing communication.

Let's start with the most basic considerations: why would you do this?

Use cases and benefits of integrating email functionality into your scripts

Email notifications are versatile and can be applied to a wide range of scenarios. Some common use cases include the following:

- **Task completion notifications**: These send notifications to indicate the successful completion of a task or process, helping to keep stakeholders informed and reassuring them that everything is running smoothly.

- **Error and exception reporting**: This involves alerting relevant team members or administrators when errors or exceptions occur during script execution, allowing for prompt troubleshooting and issue resolution.

- **Progress updates**: This provides periodic progress updates to stakeholders or clients, ensuring transparency and maintaining open lines of communication.

- **Data analysis reports**: These automate the generation and delivery of data analysis reports via email, saving time and effort by eliminating the need for manual report creation and distribution.

- **System monitoring**: This involves setting up email notifications to monitor system status, such as server uptime, disk space usage, or application performance. Immediate alerts can help address potential issues before they impact operations.

By incorporating email notifications into your Python scripts, you can benefit from the following:

- **Realtime updates**: Stay informed about the progress, status, and results of automated tasks

- **Enhanced collaboration**: Facilitate communication and collaboration among team members by providing timely notifications

- **Error detection and resolution**: Receive alerts about errors or exceptions in your scripts, enabling you to identify and resolve issues quickly

- **Customization and personalization**: Tailor email notifications to suit your specific requirements, including content, formatting, and recipients

- **Streamlined workflows**: Automate the delivery of reports, updates, and alerts, saving time and effort in manual distribution

Throughout this section, we will explore the various aspects of email notifications in Python, empowering you to leverage this powerful communication tool within your automation workflows.

Let's dive in and explore how to set up and use email functionality effectively.

Setting up email services

Before diving into sending email notifications from Python, it's essential to set up the necessary email services to establish a connection between your script and the email server.

By the end of this section, you will have a clear understanding of how to set up email services for your Python scripts. You'll be equipped with the necessary knowledge to choose the right email service provider, obtain the required SMTP server credentials, configure secure connections, and test the connection. With your email services in place, you'll be ready to move on to the next steps of sending email notifications seamlessly from your Python scripts.

Let's get started and set up your email services effectively.

In this section, we will cover the steps involved in configuring email services, including the following aspects.

Choosing an email service provider

There are several email service providers available, each offering different features and options. In this section, we will be using Gmail as an example but the code can easily be adapted to other providers, such as Microsoft Exchange, as well.

Obtaining SMTP server credentials

To send emails programmatically, it's important to obtain the SMTP server credentials provided by your email service provider. These credentials are essential for establishing a connection with the email server and sending emails securely.

In this section, we'll guide you through the process of acquiring the necessary information to configure your email settings effectively.

- **SMTP server address**: The SMTP server address is the hostname or IP address of the server responsible for sending outgoing emails. Your email service provider will provide you with this information, which typically follows a format such as `smtp.example.com` or `mail.example.com`. Make sure you verify the correct SMTP server address for your specific email service.

- **Port number**: The port number specifies the communication endpoint for the SMTP server. Common port numbers for SMTP communication include 25, 465 (for SSL/TLS encrypted connections), and 587 (for STARTTLS encrypted connections). Your email service provider will specify the appropriate port number to use for sending emails.

- **Authentication details**: To authenticate yourself with the SMTP server, you will need to provide a username and password. These credentials are used to establish a secure connection and ensure that only authorized users can send emails. Your email service provider will provide you with the necessary authentication details. In some cases, an API key or access token may be required for authentication instead of a traditional username and password.

It's important to note that the process of obtaining SMTP server credentials may vary depending on your email service provider. Some providers offer specific instructions or account settings where you can find the required information. If you're unsure about where to find your SMTP server credentials, it's recommended that you consult the documentation or support resources provided by your email service provider.

By obtaining the SMTP server credentials, you'll be equipped with the necessary information to establish a connection with the email server and send emails programmatically. This allows you to leverage the power of Python to automate email notifications, updates, and other communication tasks within your applications or scripts.

Testing the connection

To ensure a successful setup, it's important to test the connection between your Python script and the email server.

In the next section, we'll demonstrate how to perform a connection test by sending a test email using the provided SMTP server credentials. This will help verify that the connection is established correctly and that your script can communicate with the email server.

Sending basic emails

Now that we have set up our email services, we can proceed to the next step: sending basic emails from Python.

By the end of this section, you will have a solid understanding of how to send basic emails from Python. You'll know how to import the required libraries, create email messages, establish a connection with the email server, and send the email using the SMTP protocol. With this knowledge, you'll be able to send simple text-based emails from your Python scripts and lay the foundation for more advanced email notifications.

In this section, we will explore the fundamental concepts and techniques for sending emails programmatically.

Importing the required libraries

To send emails from Python, we need to import the necessary libraries that provide email-related functionality. Ahead, we'll discuss popular libraries, such as `smtplib` and `email.mime`, which offer convenient features for creating and sending emails. We'll guide you through the installation process and demonstrate how to import these libraries into your Python script.

Creating the email message

Before sending an email, we need to construct the email message, which includes the sender, recipient, subject, and body of the email. We'll show you how to create an email message using the `email.mime` library, allowing you to customize various aspects of the email, such as adding attachments or setting HTML content. We'll provide code examples and explanations to help you understand the structure and components of an email message.

Establishing the connection

To send an email, we need to establish a connection with the email server using the SMTP protocol. We'll demonstrate how to establish a connection using the SMTP server credentials obtained earlier. We'll guide you through the process of creating an SMTP object, setting up the connection, and handling any potential errors or exceptions that may arise during the establishment of the connection.

Sending the email

Once the connection is established, we can proceed to send the email. We'll demonstrate how to use the `smtplib` library to send an email message. We'll cover the necessary steps, including authenticating with the email server, specifying the sender and recipient addresses, and invoking the `sendmail()` method. We'll also discuss error handling and provide best practices for ensuring the successful delivery of the email.

The preceding sections are the steps that are implemented in the following code sample:

```python
import smtplib
from email.mime.text import MIMEText
from email.mime.multipart import MIMEMultipart

# Define email server and credentials
smtp_server = 'your_smtp_server'
smtp_port = 587
smtp_username = 'your_username'
smtp_password = 'your_password'

# Create a MIME message
message = MIMEMultipart()
message['From'] = 'sender@example.com'
message['To'] = 'recipient@example.com'
message['Subject'] = 'Test Email'

# Add the email body
body = MIMEText('This is the email body.')
message.attach(body)

# Establish a connection with the email server
with smtplib.SMTP(smtp_server, smtp_port) as server:
    # Start the TLS encryption
    server.starttls()

    # Log in to the email server
```

```
server.login(smtp_username, smtp_password)

# Send the email
server.send_message(message)
```

From this code example, we can observe the following:

1. We first import the `smtplib` library to establish an SMTP connection and the `MIMEText` and `MIMEMultipart` classes from the `email.mime` module for creating the email message.

2. Next, we define the SMTP server details, including the server address, port, and the credentials (username and password) required for authentication.

3. We then create a `MIMEMultipart` object called message, which represents the email message. We set the sender and recipient addresses, as well as the subject of the email.

4. Then, we send the email using the `send_message()` method of the SMTP server object, passing the message as an argument.

5. Remember to replace the placeholder values (`your_smtp_server` and `your_username`). To add the email body, we create a `MIMEText` object called body and attach it to the message.

6. Afterward, we establish a connection with the email server using the `smtplib.SMTP` class, passing the server address and port as arguments. We start the TLS encryption using the `starttls()` method.

7. Next, we log in to the email server using the `login()` method and provide the username and password.

Finally, use `your_password`, `sender@example.com`, and `recipient@example.com` with your actual SMTP server details and email addresses.

By following this code example, you'll be able to send basic emails using the `smtplib` and `email.mime` libraries in Python.

Sending email notifications for script status

In this section, you'll learn how to define triggers, implement email notification logic, customize email content, and handle email delivery and errors effectively. With these skills, you'll be able to enhance the monitoring and reporting capabilities of your scripts and stay informed about the progress and outcomes of your automated processes.

By the end of this section, you will have a clear understanding of how to incorporate email notifications into your Python scripts to receive updates on script execution and status.

One of the key use cases for email notifications in Python is to receive updates on the status of your scripts or processes. In this section, we will delve into the process of sending email notifications to keep track of the execution and status of your scripts. By implementing this functionality, you can stay informed about the progress and outcomes of your automated processes and take the necessary actions when needed.

To begin, let's explore the steps involved in sending email notifications for script status.

Defining triggers

Before we can send email notifications, we need to define triggers that determine when the notifications should be sent. Triggers can be based on specific conditions or events that occur during script execution. For example, you may want to send an email notification when a script completes successfully, encounters an error, or reaches a specific milestone. By defining triggers, you have full control over when and under what circumstances email notifications are sent.

Implementing email notification logic

Once the triggers are defined, we can proceed to implement the logic for sending email notifications. This involves incorporating the necessary code within your script to check the triggers and initiate the email-sending process. You will need to import the required libraries, establish a connection with the email server, and customize the email content. The logic should be designed to efficiently handle the sending of email notifications based on the specified triggers.

Customizing email content

To provide relevant and informative content in your email notifications, you can customize various aspects of the email, such as the subject, body, and any additional details. The content can include information about the script's execution status, error messages, relevant data or statistics, and any other details that are important for understanding the script's progress. By customizing the email content, you can ensure that recipients have the necessary information to take appropriate actions or make informed decisions.

Handling email delivery and errors

Sending emails involves interacting with email servers, and various factors can affect the successful delivery of emails. It's important to handle potential issues such as network connectivity problems, email server errors, or recipient email address errors. By implementing error-handling mechanisms, you can gracefully handle email delivery issues and ensure that notifications are sent reliably. Additionally, logging and error reporting can be useful for troubleshooting and diagnosing any email-related problems that may occur.

In summary, by implementing email notifications for script status, you can stay informed about the progress and outcomes of your automated processes. You have the flexibility to define triggers, customize email content, and handle potential email delivery issues effectively. This functionality enhances the monitoring and reporting capabilities of your scripts and enables you to take timely actions based on the script's status. With these techniques in place, you can confidently automate your processes while staying updated on their execution.

Summary

In the sections on scheduling and email notifications in Python, you have gained a comprehensive understanding of the key concepts. You have learned about different scheduling options for Python scripts, including built-in options and third-party libraries such as `schedule` and `APScheduler`. The chapter also emphasizes the importance of following best practices for email notifications, such as error handling, resource management, security considerations, testing, monitoring, documentation, and maintenance.

You can now recognize the value of email notifications in providing timely updates on the status and results of processes in automated systems. We have explored Python's powerful libraries and modules, such as `smtplib` and `email.mime`, which enable the creation and customization of email messages. Additionally, you have acquired the knowledge required to set up email services by configuring SMTP servers, authentication credentials, and other relevant settings. We have also learned about packages in R, such as `tasksheduleR`, `blastula`, and `Microsoft365R`, that will perform these functions as well. They have a solid and simple syntax, which makes them very powerful tools.

With a solid understanding of the basics, you have learned how to construct simple email messages with the necessary headers and content to implement basic email functionality. You have also discovered the versatility of email notifications in providing updates on script execution, including success, failure, or specific events. Now that you are armed with these insights, readers are well-equipped to integrate email notifications effectively into their Python projects.

By completing this chapter, you should have gained a comprehensive understanding of scheduling Python scripts and email notifications in Python. You have learned when and how to use various scheduling tools, set up email services, and send basic emails. In the next chapter, we will learn how to format Excel with Python and R.

Part 2:
Making It Pretty – Formatting, Graphs, and More

In this part, we delve into enhancing the visual appeal and functionality of your Excel sheets. You will learn how to format your data elegantly using libraries such as `styledTables`, `tablaxlsx`, `excelR`, `basictabler`, and `tidyxl` in R and `pandas` and `openpyxl` in Python. You will discover techniques to seamlessly insert `ggplot2` and `matplotlib` graphs into your Excel sheets, bringing your data to life. Additionally, you will master the art of creating pivot tables using `tidyquant` in R and `win32com` and `pypiwin32` in Python, along with advanced summary table creation using `{gt}`.

This part has the following chapters:

- *Chapter 5, Formatting Your Excel Sheet*
- *Chapter 6, Inserting ggplot2/matplotlib Graphs*
- *Chapter 7, Pivot Tables and Summary Tables*

5

Formatting Your Excel Sheet

In this chapter, we are going to go over two different libraries in R and various libraries in Python that can be used to format tables and data in an Excel worksheet.

There are several packages in R that we will be discussing, including the following:

- `styledTables`
- `basictabler`

We are going to create some fictitious data along with using one of R's built-in datasets, Iris, and then we are going to apply styling to it from the aforementioned packages. Each package will have its methods to apply this styling, so it's good to go over them and see which type of workflow you prefer.

In the Python section of this chapter, we will explore the advanced options available in `pandas` and `openpyxl` to create beautiful tables and pivot tables from Python in Excel. In particular, we will use `pandas`, `openpyxl`, and `pywin32`.

In this chapter, we will understand the following topics:

- Installing and using `styledTables` in R
- Advanced options for formatting with Python

By the end of this chapter, you will have a deep understanding of cell formatting, conditional formatting, and pivot tables. So, without further delay, let's get into them.

Technical requirements

The code for this chapter can be found on GitHub at the following link: `https://github.com/ PacktPublishing/Extending-Excel-with-Python-and-R/tree/main/Chapter5`.

As mentioned previously, we are going to be working with a few different packages in the R section. The `styledTables` package can only be installed from GitHub via the `devtools` package.

For the Python section, you will need one new package (specifically for the formatting tasks with pandas): `jinja2==3.1.2`.

Installing and using styledTables in R

As we have done before, we will need to install the necessary packages before we can use them. In this section, we are going to install the `styledTables` package. Because `styledTables` is not on CRAN, we cannot install it using the typical method of using the `install.packages()` function, so we will need to install this package from GitHub. This will require us to also install the `devtools` package, which has the functionality to do this very sort of thing.

Here is the full code you'll need to install the package:

```
install.packages("devtools")
# Install development version from GitHub
devtools::install_github(
'R-package/styledTables',
build_vignettes = TRUE
)
```

After running the preceding code, we can call the library into the current session in the typical fashion by issuing `library(styledtables)` in the console. Now that we have loaded the library in, we can go ahead and create our first script, which will style a table based on a simple criterion. Let's get started:

```
library(TidyDensity)
library(styledTables)
library(xlsx)

st <- tidy_normal() |>
  styled_table(keep_header = TRUE) |>
  set_border_position("all", row_id = 1) |>
  set_bold(row_id = 1) |>
  set_fill_color("#00FF00", col_id = 3,
                 condition = X >= 0.5)

# open new xlsx workbook and create a worksheet
```

```
wb <- createWorkbook()
sheet <- createSheet(wb, "tidy_normal")

# insert the styled table in the worksheet
write_excel(sheet, st)

# save the workbook
saveWorkbook(wb, "chapter5/styledTables_test.xlsx")
```

This R code uses several libraries (`TidyDensity`, `styledTables`, and `xlsx`) to create a styled table from a dataset, save it to an Excel file, and apply some formatting to it. Let's break down the code step by step:

1. First, we load the required libraries – `TidyDensity` for creating a table of randomly generated data from a Gaussian distribution, `styledTables` for styling tables, and `xlsx` for working with Excel files.

2. Then, we create and style the table. This code creates a styled table, `st`, from the output of the `tidy_normal()` function. The `tidy_normal()` function generates some data from a Gaussian distribution and presents it in a tibble format. The table is then styled using the `styled_table()` function with `keep_header = TRUE`, which means the header row will be retained and styled separately from the data rows. The next three lines of code apply specific styles to the first row (header row) of the table. It sets a border around all cells in the first row, makes the text bold in the first row, and sets a fill color (`#00FF00`, which is green) to cells in the third column if the corresponding value (denoted by X) in that column is greater than or equal to 0.5.

3. Then, we create a new Excel workbook and worksheet using the `xlsx` package by creating a new workbook with the `createWorkbook()` function. Once this workbook has been created, we use the `createSheet()` function to create the sheet in the workbook with a sheet name of `tidy_normal`.

4. Next, we insert the styled table into the worksheet by using the `write_excel()` function from the `styledTables` library. This takes the styled table, `st`, and places it into the `tidy_normal` worksheet.

5. Finally, we save the workbook to an Excel file with the `saveWorkbook()` XLSX function, where we tell it to save the wb workbook into an Excel file named `styledTables_test.xlsx` in a subdirectory called `chapter5`.

In summary, this R code generates a styled table from some data (obtained from `tidy_normal()`), applies specific formatting to the header row and cells in the third column, saves the styled table in an Excel file, and places it in a worksheet named `tidy_normal`. The resulting Excel file will contain the styled table with the specified formatting.

Installing and using basictabler in R

The `basictabler` R package provides an easy way to create rich tables from `DataFrame` or matrices. The tables can be rendered as HTML, HTML widgets, or Excel spreadsheets.

To create a `basictabler` object, you need to create a `DataFrame` or matrix. Once you have your data, you can create a `basictabler` object by calling the `qhtbl()` function. The `qhtbl()` function takes two arguments: the `DataFrame` or matrix, and a list of formatting options. We are going to spend time on the `qhtbl()` function and the `BasicTable()` function. The `qhtbl()` function is a quick way to generate a table, while the `BasicTable()` function is a way to build it piece by piece. First, we are going to create a very basic example using the `qhtbl()` function, as follows:

```
# Load in the library
library(basictabler)

# Create a data frame
data <- data.frame(
  name = c("John Doe", "Jane Doe"),
  age = c(30, 25),
  salary = c(100000, 50000))

# Create a Plain table
table_plain <- qhtbl(data, theme = "largeplain")
table_plain
```

Here is the output of the code:

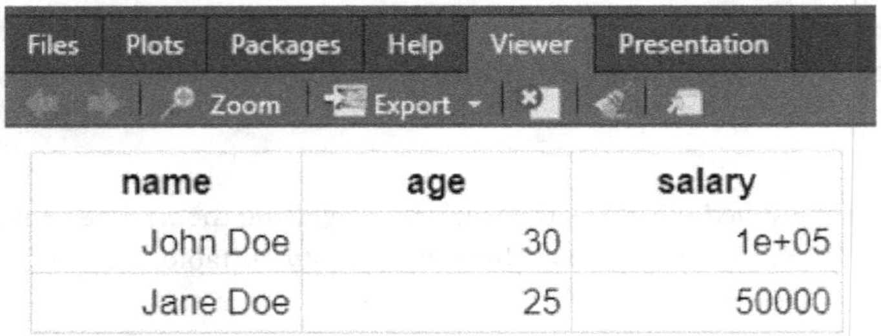

name	age	salary
John Doe	30	1e+05
Jane Doe	25	50000

Figure 5.1 – Using basictabler to create a plain table

Now that we can see what it looks like, let's go over what just happened. First, we created a dataset named `data`. This was a small simple dataset purely to help illustrate the use of the `basictabler` package. Once the data has been created, we simply call the `ghtbl()` function on the data, give it a theme of `largeplain`, and then assign it to the `table_plain` variable. This only makes the table – it does not send it to Excel. We will go over that later.

Now, let's look at another example that is a little bit more involved:

```
# Create a basictabler object
table <- qhtbl(data,
  theme = "largeplain",
  tableStyle = list("border-color" = "maroon"),
  headingStyle = list(
    "color" = "cornsilk", "background-color" = "maroon",
    "font-style" = "italic", "border-color" = "maroon"
  ),
  cellStyle = list(
    "color" = "maroon", "background-color" = "cornsilk",
    "border-color" = "maroon"
  )
)
# Render the table to HTML
table
```

This piece of code will produce a table that consists of the same data. However, the difference here is that this one will have some styling. Let's go over the styling options we used; then, we will see the finished product.

The first difference is that we used the `tableStyle` option. This option in the function takes in as its argument a list object of CSS style declarations that will be applied to the table. For this option, we provided a value of `"border-color" = "maroon"`.

The next option that we used is `headingStyle`, which also takes a list object of CSS style declarations that get applied to the headings of the table. In the preceding code, we used four different options inside the list. First, we chose to use the `color` option with a value of `cornsilk` and then we chose `background-color` with a value of `maroon`. The next option we chose was `font-style` for `italics` and then finally `border-color` with `maroon`. Let's see what this looks like:

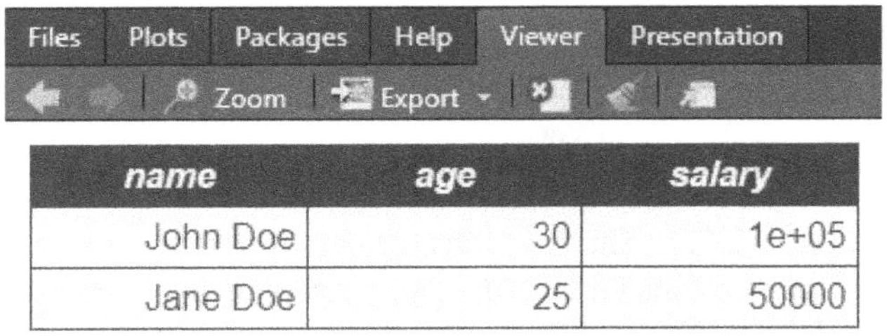

Figure 5.2 – A second basictabler example using some different styling

Now, let's walk through a longer example that will use some different features of the `basictabler` package to map styles according to some sort of logic that we dictate. Refer to the following code:

```
# A longer example
library(TidyDensity)
tn <- tidy_normal(.n = 10)
```

`library(TidyDensity)` imports the `TidyDensity` package into the R environment. This package provides tools for visualizing and summarizing distributions. We use it specifically to generate a tibble of a normal distribution with 10 points. We do not need to call in `basictabler` because it is already loaded at this point.

Next, we assign `tn <- tidy_normal(.n = 10)`. This line creates a dataset called `tn` by generating 10 random points from a standard normal distribution. The function also creates the density of the data (`dx`, `dy`), along with `pnorm` and `qnorm`, as columns of the table:

```
tbl <- BasicTable$new()
# formatting values (explained in the introduction vignette)
columnFormats <- list(
  NULL, NULL, "%.4f", "%.4f", "%.4f", "%.4f", "%.4f"
)
```

`tbl <- BasicTable$new()` creates a new instance of a `BasicTable` object called `tbl`. The `BasicTable` class is an R6 class object from the `basictabler` package. This function has many different public methods associated with it. These methods help create the table itself, as well as its styling:

```
tbl$addData(tn,
  firstColumnAsRowHeaders = TRUE,
  explicitColumnHeaders = c(
"Simulation", "x", "y", "dx", "dy", "p", "q"
  ),
  columnFormats = columnFormats
)
```

From the preceding code snippet, we understand the following:

- `tbl$addData(tn, ...)`: This line adds the data from the `tn` dataset to the `tbl` table object. It also sets some options for how the data should be displayed, such as using the first column as row headers and explicitly setting the column headers.

- `columnFormats <- list(...)`: Here, a list named `columnFormats` is created, which contains formats for each column of the table. The formats that are specified are for the second to the seventh column (index 1 to 6) and are represented using `strings`. `tbl$renderTable()`. Here, we used `%.4f`.

- `tbl$renderTable()`: This line renders the table based on the data and formatting provided earlier and displays it in the R environment. This gives us the necessary table pre-styling so that we can see a base table versus what we've done to it.

Next, we have the following code:

```
# Add some conditional formatting
cells <- tbl$getCells(
rowNumbers = 2:11,
columnNumbers = 3:7,
matchMode = "combinations"
)
```

Here, the `cells <- tbl$getCells(...)` line retrieves a subset of cells from the `tbl` table object. It selects cells from rows 2 to 11 and columns 3 to 7 (y, dx, dy, p, q) using the `getCells()` method:

```
tbl$mapStyling(
   cells = cells,
   styleProperty = "background-color",
   valueType = "color",
   mapType = "logic",
   mappings = list(
      "v<=-3", "red",
      "-3<v<=-2", "orange",
      "-2<v<=-1", "pink",
      "-1<v<= 0", "white",
      "0<v<=1", "white",
      "1<v<=2", "lightgreen",
      "2<v<=3", "lightblue",
      "3<v", "green"
   )
)
```

The `tbl$mapStyling(...)` line applies conditional formatting to the selected cells. The `mapStyling()` method is used to map styles (such as background color) to cell values based on certain conditions:

```
tbl$renderTable()
```

After applying conditional formatting, the `tbl$renderTable()` line renders the updated table with the formatted cells, and it will be displayed in the R environment again.

To summarize, the preceding R code imports a package, creates a dataset of random numbers, generates a table with formatted data, displays the table, applies conditional formatting to specific cells, and finally displays the table again with the formatted cells. Conditional formatting assigns different background colors to cells based on the values in the specified columns.

Now, let's look at what we created. Remember that the data may be different for you as the values are random. First, we will look at the plain table, and then the styled table:

Files	Plots	Packages	Help	Viewer	Presentation

Simulation	x	y	dx	dy	p	q
1	1	1.9349	-2.6076	0.0014	0.9735	1.9349
1	2	0.1192	-1.9991	0.0743	0.5475	0.1192
1	3	-1.6738	-1.3907	0.0858	0.0471	-1.6738
1	4	1.3319	-0.7822	0.0998	0.9085	1.3319
1	5	0.2334	-0.1737	0.3896	0.5923	0.2334
1	6	0.5718	0.4348	0.5633	0.7163	0.5718
1	7	0.4775	1.0433	0.1871	0.6835	0.4775
1	8	0.5126	1.6518	0.1610	0.6959	0.5126
1	9	-0.2764	2.2602	0.0758	0.3911	-0.2764
1	10	-0.4009	2.8687	0.0014	0.3442	-0.4009

Figure 5.3 – BasicTable R6 plain table

The following is the styled table according to the logic created in the `mapStyling()` function:

Files	Plots	Packages	Help	Viewer	Presentation

Simulation	x	y	dx	dy	p	q
1	1	1.9349	-2.6076	0.0014	0.9735	1.9349
1	2	0.1192	-1.9991	0.0743	0.5475	0.1192
1	3	-1.6738	-1.3907	0.0858	0.0471	-1.6738
1	4	1.3319	-0.7822	0.0998	0.9085	1.3319
1	5	0.2334	-0.1737	0.3896	0.5923	0.2334
1	6	0.5718	0.4348	0.5633	0.7163	0.5718
1	7	0.4775	1.0433	0.1871	0.6835	0.4775
1	8	0.5126	1.6518	0.1610	0.6959	0.5126
1	9	-0.2764	2.2602	0.0758	0.3911	-0.2764
1	10	-0.4009	2.8687	0.0014	0.3442	-0.4009

Figure 5.4 – BasicTable R6 styled table

Now that we have made the tables, let's see how we can use the `basictabler` package to save them to an Excel file. First, we are going to rely on a package that was introduced earlier: `openxlsx`.

Here's the script we are going to use; you will notice that the `chapter5` directory has been used as it was created first:

```
# Write styled table out to Excel
library(openxlsx)

# Create Workbook
wb <- createWorkbook()

# Add a sheet called Data
addWorksheet(wb, "Data")

# Use basictabler to write the tbl to excel
tbl$writeToExcelWorksheet(
  wb = wb,
  wsName = "Data",
  topRowNumber = 1,
  leftMostColumnNumber = 1,
  applyStyles = TRUE
  )

# Use openxlsx to save the file
saveWorkbook(
  wb,
  file="chapter5/basictabler_excel.xlsx",
  overwrite = TRUE
)
```

Here, we used the public method of `writeToExcelWorksheet()` from the `basictabler` package. While it does not directly write to an Excel file, it does get the object into a format that can be written to Excel using a package such as `openxlsx`.

Now that you've learned about some of the possibilities to write in R, let's have a look at similar tools in Python. Once again, we will go over how to format cells and tables for Excel. For more details, you can take a look at some extra packages, such as `gt` and `gtextras`.

Advanced options for formatting with Python

The Python section of this chapter is organized into the following three sections:

- *Cell formatting*: Cell formatting is crucial for presenting data in a visually appealing and organized manner. We will demonstrate how to apply various formatting styles to cells, such as setting font properties (for example, size, color, bold, and italic), adjusting cell background colors, and aligning text within cells. You will learn how to create professional-looking tables with well-formatted cells that enhance data readability.

- *Conditional formatting*: Conditional formatting allows you to dynamically format cells based on specific conditions. We will walk you through the process of applying conditional formatting to highlight important data points, visualize trends, and identify outliers. You will discover how to use `pandas` and `openpyxl` to implement various conditional formatting rules, such as color scales, data bars, and icon sets, making your data stand out in the Excel sheet.

- *Pivot tables*: Pivot tables are powerful tools for summarizing and analyzing data in Excel. We will show you how to create pivot tables using `pywin32`, as well as how to adjust subtotals and grand totals and customize labels and styles.

Throughout this chapter, we will provide practical examples and detailed explanations to guide you through the process of formatting your Excel sheets effectively. By mastering cell formatting, conditional formatting, and pivot tables, you will be able to present your data professionally and make it visually compelling, facilitating better insights and data analysis.

Let's get started with cell formatting!

Cell formatting

Cell formatting is a crucial aspect of presenting data effectively in Excel. With `pandas` and `openpyxl`, you have powerful tools at your disposal to customize the appearance of cells. You can apply a wide range of formatting styles to make your tables visually appealing and enhance data readability.

To get started with cell formatting, you will learn how to set various font properties, such as font size, color, boldness, and italics. These adjustments allow you to emphasize certain data points and create a consistent visual hierarchy in your tables.

Additionally, you can control the background color of cells to group related data or highlight specific values. By setting cell background colors, you can create clear demarcations between different sections of your table, making it easier for readers to interpret the data.

Aligning text within cells is another important formatting technique. With `pandas` and `openpyxl`, you can align text horizontally and vertically, ensuring that your data is presented in a tidy and organized manner.

In this section, we will walk you through practical examples of cell formatting using both `pandas` and `openpyxl`. You will learn how to apply different formatting styles, adjust font properties, change cell background colors, and align text within cells. Armed with these skills, you will be able to create professional-looking tables that effectively convey your data's message and insights.

Setting font properties

Let's start by exploring how to set font properties for cells using both `pandas` and `openpyxl`.

In pandas, for more advanced styling, including custom CSS-like styles, we can use the Styler. apply method, along with custom functions to format the cells, to apply the font properties to suit our preferences, as shown here:

```
# import pandas
import pandas as pd

data = {'Name': ['John', 'Alice', 'Michael'],
        'Age': [25, 30, 22],
        'City': ['New York', 'London', 'Paris']}

df = pd.DataFrame(data)

# Define a function to apply font properties
def apply_font_properties(value):
    return 'font-weight: bold; font-size: 14px; font-style: italic;
color: blue'

# Applying font properties
styled_df = df.style.applymap(apply_font_properties, subset='Name')

# Save the styled DataFrame to an Excel file
styled_df.to_excel('styled_table_pandas.xlsx', index=False)
```

The resulting Excel sheet is available in this chapter's GitHub repository.

In openpyxl, you can use the Font class to set font properties. For instance, to make text bold, you can set the bold attribute of the font object to True. You can also adjust other font properties, such as size and color, to achieve the desired formatting. Refer to the following example:

```
# OpenPyXL example for setting font properties
from openpyxl import Workbook
from openpyxl.styles import Font
wb = Workbook()
ws = wb.active

# Applying font properties
font = Font(size=14, bold=True, italic=True, color='0000FF')
ws['A1'].font = font
ws['A1'] = 'Name'
ws['B1'] = 'Age'
ws['C1'] = 'City'
wb.save('styled_table_openpyxl.xlsx')
```

Cell background colors

Changing the background color of cells is another formatting technique that can help you visually distinguish different parts of your table. In `pandas`, you can set the `background-color` CSS style using the `Styler` object, as shown here:

```
# Pandas example for cell background colors
import pandas as pd
data = {'Name': ['John', 'Alice', 'Michael'],
        'Age': [25, 30, 22],
        'City': ['New York', 'London', 'Paris']}
df = pd.DataFrame(data)

# Create a styler object
styled_df = df.style

# Define the style for the cells
styled_df = styled_df.applymap( \
    lambda _: 'background-color: yellow', \
    subset=pd.IndexSlice[0, ['Name', 'Age']])

# Save the styled DataFrame to an Excel file
styled_df.to_excel('colored_table_pandas.xlsx', index=False)
```

The preceding code demonstrates how to use `pandas` to create a `DataFrame` containing some sample data and then apply cell background colors to specific cells in the `DataFrame`. The `DataFrame` contains information about individuals' names, ages, and cities. By using the `pandas` `Styler` object, we can define the background color for specific cells. In this example, the first row's `Name` and `Age` columns are highlighted with a yellow background color. Finally, the styled `DataFrame` is saved to an Excel file named `colored_table_pandas.xlsx`. This technique allows for easy and flexible cell formatting when exporting data from Python to Excel.

Now, let's have a look at how we can achieve something similar with `openpyxl`!

In `openpyxl`, you can set the background color of cells using the `Fill` class, as follows:

```
# openpyxl example for cell background colors
from openpyxl import Workbook
from openpyxl.styles import PatternFill

wb = Workbook()
ws = wb.active

# Applying cell background colors
yellow_fill = PatternFill(start_color='FFFF00', end_color='FFFF00',
```

```
fill_type='solid')
ws['A1'].fill = yellow_fill
ws['A1'] = 'Name'
ws['B1'] = 'Age'
ws['C1'] = 'City'
wb.save('colored_table_openpyxl.xlsx')
```

Aligning text within cells

Properly aligning text within cells can significantly improve the table's visual presentation. In pandas, you can use the Styler object to apply text alignment styles:

```
# Pandas example for aligning text within cells
import pandas as pd
data = {'Name': ['John', 'Alice', 'Michael'],
        'Age': [25, 30, 22],
        'City': ['New York', 'London', 'Paris']}
df = pd.DataFrame(data)

# Applying text alignment
alignment_styles = {'text-align': 'center'}
styled_df = df.style.set_properties( \
    subset=['Name', 'Age', 'City'], **alignment_styles)
styled_df.to_excel('aligned_table_pandas.xlsx', index=False)
```

With this code, the text in the specified columns of the DataFrame will be aligned to the center. This code uses the set_properties method to apply the text alignment to the specified columns. The resulting DataFrame is then saved to an Excel file named aligned_table_pandas.xlsx.

In openpyxl, you can set text alignment using the Alignment class, as follows:

```
# OpenPyXL example for aligning text within cells
from openpyxl import Workbook
from openpyxl.styles import Alignment
wb = Workbook()
ws = wb.active

# Applying text alignment
alignment = Alignment(horizontal='center', vertical='center')
ws['A1'].alignment = alignment
ws['A1'] = 'Name'
ws['B1'] = 'Age'
ws['C1'] = 'City'
wb.save('aligned_table_openpyxl.xlsx')
```

With these examples, you have learned how to customize cell formatting, set font properties, change cell background colors, and align text within cells using both `pandas` and `openpyxl`. By utilizing these formatting options, you can create visually appealing and informative tables to present your data effectively in Excel.

Now, we continue our deep dive with conditional formatting.

Conditional formatting

Conditional formatting is a powerful feature in Excel that allows you to automatically apply formatting to cells based on specific conditions. It enables you to visually highlight important data, identify trends, and make your Excel sheets more interactive. In this chapter, we will explore how to implement conditional formatting using `openpyxl`. We'll cover various scenarios, such as highlighting cells based on value ranges, text, and date criteria. Additionally, we'll demonstrate how to create custom conditional formatting rules to suit your specific needs.

By the end of this chapter, you'll have the skills to add dynamic and visually appealing conditional formatting to your Excel sheets directly from Python. Let's dive in and learn how to make your data stand out with conditional formatting!

Visualizing data with conditional formatting

By applying conditional formatting to your Excel sheets, you can effectively visualize your data and gain valuable insights at a glance. For example, you can highlight the highest and lowest values in a column, color cells based on specific categories, or emphasize significant changes over time.

Conditional formatting is particularly useful when dealing with large datasets as it allows you to quickly identify key information and make data-driven decisions.

`openpyxl` provides functionalities to implement conditional formatting in Excel sheets. The library offers a range of options to apply different formatting styles based on specific conditions. The process of using `openpyxl` for conditional formatting involves the following steps:

1. Import the required modules from `openpyxl` and load your data into a workbook object.

2. Create a conditional formatting rule using `openpyxl.formatting.rule`.

3. Define the rule's conditions, such as applying styles based on cell values, text, or date criteria.

4. Apply the rule to the desired range of cells using `openpyxl.worksheet.conditional.ConditionalFormatting.add()`.

With `openpyxl`, you can easily implement conditional formatting rules and add visual cues to your Excel sheets, enhancing the presentation of your data and facilitating data analysis.

Let's have a look at some code that implements the preceding concepts:

```python
import pandas as pd
import openpyxl
from openpyxl.formatting.rule import ColorScaleRule, CellIsRule

# Create some sample data
data = {'Name': ['John', 'Alice', 'Michael', 'Emily'],
        'Age': [25, 30, 22, 28],
        'City': ['New York', 'London', 'Paris', 'Sydney'],
        'Sales': [1000, 800, 1200, 900]}
df = pd.DataFrame(data)

# Write the DataFrame to a worksheet
df.to_excel("conditional_formatting.xlsx", index=False)

# Load the workbook
wb = openpyxl.load_workbook('conditional_formatting.xlsx')
ws = wb.active

# Define conditional formatting rule for red text
red_text_rule = CellIsRule( \
    operator="lessThan", formula=["1000"], stopIfTrue=True, \
    font=openpyxl.styles.Font(color="FF0000"))
ws.conditional_formatting.add(f"D2:D{len(df)+1}", red_text_rule)

# Define the condition for the green fill color scale
min_sales = min(df['Age'])
max_sales = max(df['Age'])

green_fill_rule = ColorScaleRule( \
    start_type='num', start_value=min_sales, start_color='0000FF00', \
    end_type='num', end_value=max_sales, end_color='00FFFF00')

ws.conditional_formatting.add(f"B2:B{len(df)+1}", green_fill_rule)

# Save the Excel workbook
wb.save('conditional_formatting.xlsx')
```

In this code, we create an Excel workbook from a pandas DataFrame. Then, we define two conditional formatting rules: red text if the Sales value is less than 1000 while green_fill_rule uses the minimum and maximum age values from the Age column to set up the color scale condition. This way, the cells in the Age column will be filled with green colors based on their relative values within the minimum and maximum values. These rules are added to the worksheet's conditional_ `formatting` property. Finally, we save the Excel workbook, and conditional formatting will be applied when you open the Excel file with Microsoft Excel.

Custom conditional formatting rules provide you with precise control over how your data is displayed, making it easier to identify patterns, trends, and outliers in your Excel sheets.

Next, we'll cover a case study where conditional formatting can really shine: a dynamic heatmap!

Case study – using a dynamic heatmap with conditional formatting

To further demonstrate the power of conditional formatting, we'll walk through a case study where we create a dynamic heatmap using Python and Excel. We'll use conditional formatting to color cells in the heatmap based on the data's magnitude, enabling us to visualize the data's intensity and patterns effectively. What's created here is also called a **highlight table**, given there is an annotation (numbers) in the table and not just the heatmap colors.

Let's have a look at the implementation of such a heatmap:

```python
import pandas as pd
import openpyxl
from openpyxl.utils.dataframe import dataframe_to_rows
from openpyxl.formatting.rule import ColorScaleRule

# Sample data for the heatmap
data = {
    'Category': ['A', 'B', 'C', 'D'],
    'Jan': [10, 20, 30, 40],
    'Feb': [15, 25, 35, 45],
    'Mar': [12, 22, 32, 42],
    'Apr': [18, 28, 38, 48]
}

# Convert data to a pandas DataFrame
df = pd.DataFrame(data)

# Write the DataFrame to a worksheet
df.to_excel("heatmap_with_conditional_formatting.xlsx", index=False)

# Load the workbook
wb = openpyxl.load_workbook( \
    'heatmap_with_conditional_formatting.xlsx')
ws = wb.active

# Define the range for conditional formatting (excluding the
'Category' column)
```

```
data_range = f'B2:E{len(df) + 1}'  # Adjust the range based on the
DataFrame size

# Apply color scale conditional formatting to the range
color_scale_rule = ColorScaleRule(start_type='min', \
    start_color='FFFFFF', end_type='max', end_color='FF0000')
ws.conditional_formatting.add(data_range, color_scale_rule)

# Save the workbook
wb.save('heatmap_with_conditional_formatting.xlsx')
```

Conditional formatting is a valuable tool for enhancing the visual representation of data in Excel. Whether you're using `pandas` or `openpyxl`, you can easily implement conditional formatting rules to dynamically format cells based on specified conditions. By incorporating conditional formatting into your Excel sheets, you can create compelling visualizations and better understand your data, making data analysis and decision-making more efficient and effective.

Pivot tables

Pivot tables are powerful tools in Excel that allow you to summarize and analyze large datasets quickly. They provide a flexible way to aggregate, group, and calculate data, enabling you to gain valuable insights from your data with just a few clicks. In this section, we will explore how to create and manipulate pivot tables from Python using `pywin32`. Additionally, we will cover some techniques for adjusting subtotals and grand totals and customizing labels and styles.

Creating pivot tables with pywin32

`pywin32` allows you to interact with Microsoft Excel via the COM interface. With this library, you can control Excel's features, including creating pivot tables.

To create a pivot table with `win32com.client` in Python, you can use the code snippets provided in this section.

First, set everything up by importing the required module, starting an Excel instance as we did in *Chapter 3*, and getting a sheet we can work with:

```
# Import the required modules from the `win32com.client` package:
import win32com.client as win32
import os.path

# Create a new instance of Excel and make it visible:
excel = win32.Dispatch('Excel.Application')
excel.Visible = True

# Create a new workbook or open an existing one:
```

```
workbook = excel.Workbooks.Add()  # Create a new workbook
# Or to open an existing workbook:
# workbook = excel.Workbooks.Open('path/to/your/workbook.xlsx')

# Get the reference to the sheet where you want to create the Pivot
Table:
sheet = workbook.ActiveSheet  # Get the active sheet
# Or specify the sheet by its name:
# sheet = workbook.Sheets('Sheet1')
```

Next, generate some sample data and write it to the sheet (this is optional; that is, only do this if you have data to analyze):

```
# Sample data
data = [
    ['Product', 'Category', 'Sales'],
    ['Product A', 'Category 1', 100],
    ['Product B', 'Category 2', 200],
    ['Product C', 'Category 1', 150],
    ['Product D', 'Category 2', 50],
    # Add more data rows here...
]

# Write the data to the sheet
for row_index, row in enumerate(data, start=1):
    for col_index, value in enumerate(row, start=1):
        sheet.Cells(row_index, col_index).Value = value
```

> **Fun fact**
>
> You can watch the workbook populate with values when this nested `for` loop runs!

Now, we can start on the actual pivot table! We'll begin by creating a new sheet where the pivot will go:

```
# Add a new worksheet to the workbook to hold the Pivot Table:
pivot_table_sheet = workbook.Worksheets.Add()
pivot_table_sheet.Name = 'Pivot Table'
```

Next, we can create the pivot table itself by using the `Create()` method of the `PivotCaches` property of the workbook and then calling `CreatePivotTable()`:

```
# Create a Pivot Cache using the data range (UsedRange highlights the
whole used range in the sheet):
pivot_cache = workbook.PivotCaches().Create(SourceType=1, \
    SourceData=sheet.UsedRange)
```

```
# Create the Pivot Table on the new sheet using the Pivot Cache:
pivot_table = pivot_cache.CreatePivotTable( \
    TableDestination=pivot_table_sheet.Cells(3, 1), \
    TableName='MyPivotTable')
```

With the pivot table defined, we can add the fields we want to use as row, column, and data fields:

```
# Add fields to the Pivot Table, specifying their orientation (rows,
columns, data, etc.):
pivot_table.PivotFields('Product').Orientation = 1 # row field
pivot_table.PivotFields('Category').Orientation = 2 # column field
pivot_table.PivotFields('Sales').Orientation = 4 # data field
```

We're almost there! We now have a working pivot table, but we may want to switch grand totals and subtotals on or off:

```
# Control row and column grandtotals
pivot_table.ColumnGrand = False
pivot_table.RowGrand = False


# Decide which fields have Subtotals
pivot_table.PivotFields('Sales').Subtotals = [False]*12
pivot_table.PivotFields('Product').Subtotals = [False]*12
pivot_table.PivotFields('Category').Subtotals = [True]*12
```

Finally, we can customize the labels and styles:

```
# Customize labels and styles
pivot_table.ShowTableStyleRowStripes = True
pivot_table.PivotFields('Product').Caption = 'Product Name'
pivot_table.PivotFields('Sales').NumberFormat = '#,##0'
pivot_table.PivotFields('Sales').Caption = 'Total Sales'
# Note: labels change the Pivot Table wizard available when clicking
into the Pivot Table, not the table itself.


# Save the workbook and close Excel:
  # Note: you will want to change the path to a path that exists on
your computer.
file_path = os.path.join('C:' + os.sep, 'Users', 'david_1q5aypk',
'Extending-Excel-with-Python-and-R')
workbook.SaveAs(os.path.join(file_path, 'pivot_table.xlsx'))


workbook.Close()
excel.Quit()
```

With that, you've learned how to create a pivot table in Excel using `win32com.client`, enabling you to analyze and summarize your data effectively. The library allows you to have full control over Excel, including creating and customizing pivot tables based on your specific data analysis needs.

Summary

In this chapter, we delved into the art of formatting Excel sheets to present data in a visually appealing and organized manner. Divided into three sections, we covered essential techniques to transform raw data into professional-looking tables that enhance data readability.

The first section focused on cell formatting, where we demonstrated how to apply various styles to cells, such as adjusting font properties, cell backgrounds, and text alignment. By mastering cell formatting, you can create well-organized and visually appealing tables.

Next, we explored conditional formatting, a powerful feature that allows you to dynamically format cells based on specific conditions. We provided practical examples of using `styledTables` and `basictabler` for R and then `pandas` and `openpyxl` for Python to implement various conditional formatting rules, such as color scales, data bars, and icon sets, making your data stand out and revealing critical insights.

Lastly, we unlocked the potential of pivot tables, which are indispensable tools for summarizing and analyzing data. Using `pywin32`, we created pivot tables and learned how to adjust subtotals and grand totals, as well as customize labels and styles.

Throughout this chapter, you've gained valuable skills in Excel manipulation using `styledTables`, `basictabler`, `pandas`, `openpyxl`, and `pywin32`, thus enabling you to present your data professionally, make it visually compelling, and uncover meaningful insights for more informed decision-making. With these techniques at your disposal, you are well-equipped to excel in data analysis and visualization, taking your Excel proficiency to new heights.

Stay tuned for the next chapter, *Inserting ggplot2/matplotlib Graphs*! There, you will learn how to add beautiful data visualizations to your Excel sheets using R and Python.

6
Inserting ggplot2/matplotlib Graphs

As a programmer, data visualizations are an indispensable tool for analyzing and presenting complex information in a more accessible and intuitive manner. They play a vital role in various domains, from data analysis and business intelligence to scientific research and even everyday decision-making. One of the reasons that visuals are beneficial to decision-making is that they help an analyst understand data to help communicate items that can help in the decision-making process. Here are some other reasons:

- **Enhanced understanding**: Visualizations provide a clear and concise representation of data, making it easier for both technical and non-technical stakeholders to grasp complex relationships, trends, and patterns. They help identify outliers, correlations, and insights that might otherwise be overlooked in raw data.

- **Effective communication**: Visualizations are a powerful communication tool that transcends language barriers and simplifies complex concepts. Presenting data in charts, graphs, and interactive dashboards allows for a more compelling and persuasive narrative during meetings, presentations, and reports. When data is presented visually, it becomes easier to digest and understand. For example, a Sankey chart helps to make a visualization of how data flows from a starting point to an endpoint easily digestible.

- **Geospatial analysis**: Geographic data visualizations enable deeper exploration.

Examples of popular data visualizations include line charts for time series analysis, bar and pie charts for categorical data comparison, scatter plots for correlation analysis, bubble charts for multivariate comparisons, and choropleth maps for geospatial data representation.

In conclusion, data visualizations are indispensable for programmers, as they facilitate data understanding, communication, decision-making, and exploration, making them an essential tool in today's data-driven world.

In the following sections, we are going to explore the use of `ggplot2` and `cowplot` to build some visualizations, such as histograms, ordered bar charts, and dumbbell charts.

In this chapter, we are going to learn the following topics:

- Visualizing data with `ggplot2`
- Enhancing your Excel reports with `plotnine2`, `matplotlib`, and `plotly` graphs
- Enhancing Excel reports with visualizations
- An introduction to data visualization libraries
- Creating graphs with `plotnine` (Python's `ggplot2`)
- Other visualization libraries
- Embedding visualizations in Excel

Technical requirements

For this chapter, you will need to make sure that you have a few different R packages installed. These include the following:

- `ggplot2 3.4.4`
- `cowplot 1.1.3`

The code for this chapter can be found on GitHub at the following link: `https://github.com/PacktPublishing/Extending-Excel-with-Python-and-R/tree/main/chapter6`.

Some basics

Before we dive into the core of this chapter, here are some things that it will help us understand:

- **Effective communication**: Visualizations are a powerful communication tool that transcends language barriers and simplifies complex concepts. Presenting data in charts, graphs, and interactive dashboards allows for a more compelling and persuasive narrative during meetings, presentations, and reports.

- **Data-driven decision making**: Visualizations empower decision-makers to base their judgments on data evidence. When data is presented visually, it becomes easier to identify potential opportunities, risks, and areas for improvement, leading to more informed and effective decisions.

- **Identifying trends and anomalies**: Visualization tools enable programmers to spot trends, changes, and anomalies in data quickly. This is particularly valuable in fields such as finance, where spotting irregularities promptly can prevent significant financial losses.

- **Exploratory Data Analysis (EDA)**: Data visualizations are essential during the exploratory phase of data analysis. By creating scatter plots, histograms, box plots, and heatmaps, programmers can explore data's distribution and relationships before diving into more in-depth analysis.

- **Real-time monitoring**: In applications that deal with constantly changing data, real-time visualizations offer a dynamic way to monitor key metrics and respond swiftly to emerging situations.

- **Geospatial analysis**: Geographic data visualizations, such as maps and heatmaps, are invaluable for analyzing location-based information, such as customer distribution, disease outbreaks, or environmental changes.

- **Forecasting and predictive analysis**: Visualizations help in presenting predictive models' results and trends, making it easier for stakeholders to understand potential future scenarios and make proactive decisions.

- **Interactive reporting**: Interactive visualizations allow end users to customize and interact with data, creating a more personalized experience and enabling deeper exploration.

Let us now go into the details of these basics.

Visualizing data with ggplot2

ggplot2 is a powerful and widely used data visualization package in the R programming language. Developed by Hadley Wickham, it is part of the tidyverse ecosystem. With ggplot2, users can create high-quality and customizable graphics through a declarative approach, where plots are constructed by specifying data, mapping aesthetics to variables, and adding layers of geometric shapes, statistics, and themes. Its grammar of graphics paradigm allows you to easily create complex visualizations, making it a popular choice for exploratory data analysis and presentation of insights.

In this section, we will make a few graphs using the ggplot2 library and the iris dataset that comes with R. The first thing we need to do is install it and load it into the current environment:

```
install.packages("ggplot2")
library(ggplot2)
```

Now that we have the library installed and loaded, we can first see how the graph will look in base R, using the hist() function and then looping through the Species column of data for Sepal. Width.

Let's see the rest of the script with an explanation to accompany it:

```
hist(iris$Sepal.Width)

par(mfrow = c(2,2))
for (species in unique(iris$Species)) {
  hist(iris$Sepal.Width[iris$Species == species], main = species,
       xlab = species)
}
hist(iris$Sepal.Width, main = "All Species")
par(mfrow = c(1,1))
```

The first line of code, `hist(iris$Sepal.Width)`, makes a histogram of the sepal width for all species of iris. The iris dataset is built into R, so we don't need to load it with the `data()` function. The `Sepal.Width` column of the iris dataset contains the sepal width measurements for each flower. The `hist()` function plots a histogram of the data in a specified column.

The second line of code, `par(mfrow = c(2,2))`, tells R to split the plotting area into four quadrants. This will allow us to plot four histograms side by side.

The third line of code, `for (species in unique(iris$Species))` {, starts a `for` loop. The `for` loop will iterate over the unique values of the `Species` column in the iris dataset. The `unique()` function returns a vector of all the unique values in a column.

The body of the `for` loop, `hist(iris$Sepal.Width[iris$Species == species]`, `main = species, xlab = species)`, makes a histogram of the sepal width for the current species. The `iris$Sepal.Width[iris$Species == species]` expression selects the sepal width measurements for the current species. The `main` argument specifies the title of the histogram, and the `xlab` argument specifies the label for the x axis.

The fourth line of code, `hist(iris$Sepal.Width, main = "All Species")`, makes a histogram of the sepal width for all species. This histogram is plotted in the last quadrant of the plotting area.

The fifth line of code, `par(mfrow = c(1,1))`, tells R to reset the plotting area to a single quadrant. Now that we have gone over the code, let's see what the output looks like:

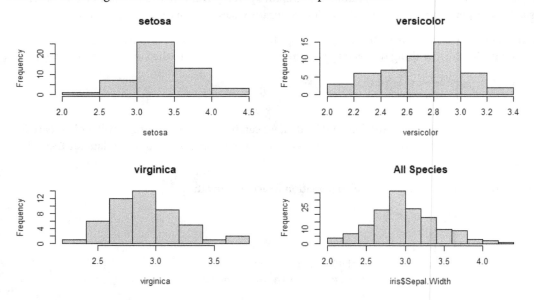

Figure 6.1 – Base R histograms

Now that we have the base R version done, let's see what this will look like in ggplot2:

```
# Make a histogram of the sepal width for all species
iris |>
ggplot(aes(x = Sepal.Width)) +
  geom_histogram(alpha = 0.328) +
  theme_minimal()

# Make a histogram of the sepal width for each species
iris |>
ggplot(aes(x = Sepal.Width, fill = Species)) +
  geom_histogram(alpha = 0.328) +
  theme_minimal()
```

The first line of code, `iris |> ggplot(aes(x = Sepal.Width)) + geom_histogram(alpha = 0.328) + theme_minimal()`, makes a histogram of the sepal width for all species of iris. The iris dataset is built into R, so we don't need to load it with the `data()` function. The `ggplot()` function is a powerful plotting function in R that allows us to create customized visualizations. The `aes()` function specifies the aesthetic mappings for the plot. In this case, we are mapping the sepal width to the *x*-axis. The `geom_histogram()` function plots a histogram of the data in the specified column. The alpha argument specifies the transparency of the bars in the histogram. The `theme_minimal()` function applies a minimal theme to the plot.

The second line of code, `iris |> ggplot(aes(x = Sepal.Width, fill = Species)) + geom_histogram(alpha = 0.328) + theme_minimal()`, makes a histogram of the sepal width for each species. The `fill` argument in the `aes()` function specifies the fill color of the bars in the histogram. In this case, we are using the `Species` column to color the bars in the histogram. This will allow us to see the distribution of sepal width for each species. Now that we have gone over the code, let's see the output.

This will be in two plots, as ggplot2 objects are not plotted in a similar fashion to base R using the `par()` function.

Here is the first plot:

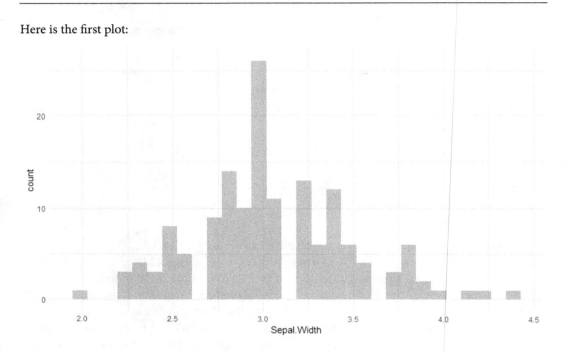

Figure 6.2 – A ggplot2 histogram of Sepal.Width for all species

This is the second plot:

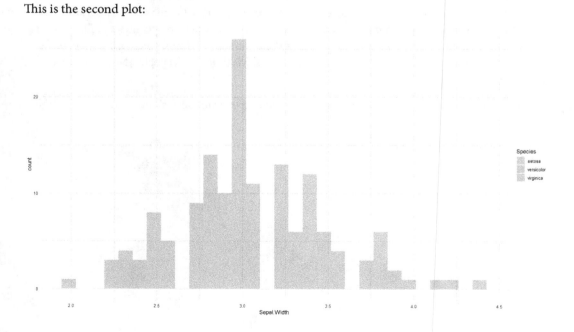

Figure 6.3 – A ggplot2 histogram of Sepal.Width filled by species

Now, there is one way in which we can see the histograms side by side in ggplot2, and that is by using the facet_wrap() function:

```
iris |>
  ggplot(aes(x = Sepal.Width, fill = Species)) +
  geom_histogram(alpha = 0.328) +
  facet_wrap(~ Species, scales = "free") +
  theme_minimal()
```

The aes() function specifies the aesthetic mappings for the plot. In this case, we are mapping the sepal width to the *x*-axis and the species to the fill color of the bars. The geom_histogram() function plots a histogram of the data in the specified columns. The alpha argument specifies the transparency of the bars in the histogram. The facet_wrap() function creates a separate plot for each value of the Species column. The scales = "free" argument tells the facet_wrap() function to allow the x axis and y axis scales to vary for each plot. The theme_minimal() function applies a minimal theme to the plot. The output of the code is a series of three histograms, one for each species of iris. The histograms show the distribution of sepal width for each species. The different colors of the bars make it easy to see the distribution of sepal width for each species. Here is the result:

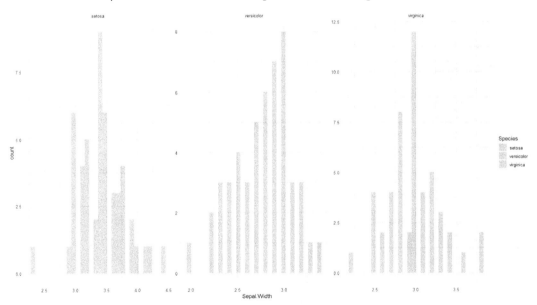

Figure 6.4 – The ggplot2 histogram of Sepal.Width using facet_wrap

In this section, we learned how to plot some simple histograms using both base R and ggplot2. We learned how to facet the histogram by species in both situations as well.

We have finished working in ggplot, and now it is time to see how we can extend plots with the use of a cowplot, which can help us build more complex and publication-ready graphics.

Visualizing data with the cowplot package

The R `cowplot` package provides numerous functions for plotting data that is of high quality. The `cowplot` package is an R library that provides various features to help with creating publication-quality figures. It can be used for the following:

- **Arranging plots into a grid**: The `plot_grid()` function can be used to arrange multiple plots into a grid, with labels and annotations

- **Aligning plots**: The `align_plots()` function can be used to align the axes and other elements of multiple plots so that they look consistent

- **Mixing different plotting frameworks**: The `plot_grid()` function can be used to mix plots from different plotting frameworks, such as `ggplot2` and base graphics

- **Adding annotations to plots**: The `ggdraw()` and `draw_*()` functions can be used to add annotations to plots, such as text, images, and shapes

- **Creating publication-quality themes**: The `cowplot` package includes several themes that are designed for publication-quality figures

Now that we understand what `cowplot` is, let's dive into the first example:

```
# Install Libraries
install.packages("ggplot2")
install.packages("cowplot")

# Load required libraries
library(ggplot2)
library(cowplot)

# Load the Iris dataset
data(iris)
```

In the preceding code, we install both the `ggplot2` and `cowplot` libraries; this will work even if they are already installed, but we will install the latest version.

Now, let's use a `for` loop to create a plot for each species of the iris dataset:

```
# Create separate histograms for each species
histograms <- list()
for (species in unique(iris$Species)) {
  data_subset <- iris[iris$Species == species, ]

  histogram <- ggplot(data_subset, aes(x = Sepal.Width)) +
      geom_histogram(binwidth = 0.1, fill = "lightblue", color =
"black") +
```

```
    labs(title = paste("Sepal Width Histogram for", species)) +
    labs(x = "", y = "") +
    theme_minimal()

  histograms[[species]] <- histogram
}
```

Let's break the code down step by step in simple terms.

The `histograms <- list()` line creates an empty list called `histograms`, where we'll store the histograms for each species.

In the next line, for `(species in unique(iris$Species)) { ... }`, the loop goes through each unique species in the Iris dataset and performs the following steps for each species. Next is `data_subset <- iris[iris$Species == species, ]`; this line creates a subset of the Iris dataset, including only the rows where the species matches the current species in the loop. It helps us focus on data for one species at a time.

The `histogram <- ggplot(data_subset, aes(x = Sepal.Width)) + ...` line is where the magic happens. We're using the `ggplot2` library to create a histogram. It's like drawing a graph that shows how many flowers have a specific sepal width. The `aes(x = Sepal.Width)` option tells R that we're interested in plotting the `Sepal.Width` on the *x*-axis.

The fifth line, `geom_histogram(binwidth = 0.1, fill = "lightblue", color = "black")`, adds the bars to the histogram. It specifies how the bars should look, such as their width and color. It's like building the columns of the histogram.

The `labs(title = paste("Sepal Width Histogram for", species))` line adds a title to the histogram, telling us what it's about. The title changes based on the current species in the loop. It's like writing a name tag for each histogram. The next line, `labs(x = "", y = "")`, removes the *x*- and *y*-axis labels, making the histogram look cleaner. We then add a theme to the plot using `theme_minimal()`, which makes the background of the histogram simple and clean. Finally, the `histograms[[species]] <- histogram` line takes the histogram for the current species, and we store it in the `histograms` list. We use the species name to access this histogram later. The following code is slightly different but produces the same exact plots:

```
histograms <- lapply(unique(iris$Species), function(species) {
  data_subset <- iris[iris$Species == species, ]

  histogram <- ggplot(data_subset, aes(x = Sepal.Width)) +
    geom_histogram(binwidth = 0.1, fill = "lightblue", color =
"black") +
    labs(title = paste("Sepal Width Histogram for", species)) +
    labs(x = "", y = "") +
    theme_minimal()
```

```
    return(histogram)
})
```

So, in summary, this code creates histograms for the sepal width of different species in the iris dataset. It does this by looping through each species, creating a subset of data for that species, and then creating a histogram with appropriate formatting and labels. All the histograms are stored in a list called `histograms`, so we can use them later. In this list, each species is a histogram object, and the object is named after the species it visualizes. Now, we are going to create and explain the histogram created on the full dataset and then combine them all, using the `plot_grid()` function from cowplot. Here is the code:

```
# Create histogram for all species combined
all_species_hist <- ggplot(iris, aes(x = Sepal.Width)) +
    geom_histogram(binwidth = 0.1, fill = "lightblue", color = "black")
+
    labs(title = "Sepal Width Histogram for All Species") +
    theme_minimal()

# Arrange histograms using cowplot
plot_grid(
    histograms[["setosa"]],
    histograms[["versicolor"]],
    histograms[["virginica"]],
    all_species_hist,
    ncol = 2,
    align = "hv"
    )
```

The first line of code that creates the `all_species_hist` variable creates a histogram of the `Sepal.Width` column for all species combined. The histogram has a binwidth of `0.1`, and the fill color is light blue. The color of the borders is black. The title of the histogram is `Sepal Width Histogram for All Species`. The theme of the histogram is `theme_minimal()`.

The next line of code, `plot_grid(histograms[["setosa"]], histograms[["versicolor"]], histograms[["virginica"]], all_species_hist, ncol = 2, align = "hv")`, uses the cowplot package to arrange the histograms for each species into a grid. The histograms are arranged in two columns, and they are aligned horizontally and vertically.

The `plot_grid()` function takes a list of plots as its arguments. The plots are arranged in a grid according to the number of columns and rows specified by the `ncol` and `nrow` arguments. The `align` argument specifies how the plots are aligned with each other. In this case, the plots are aligned horizontally and vertically with the `align = "hv"` argument.

The output of the `plot_grid()` function is a grid of plots that can be saved to a file or displayed in the R console. Now, let's see the final output:

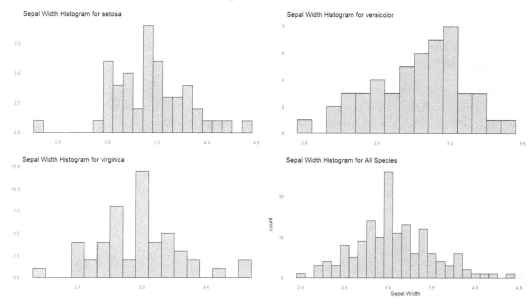

Figure 6.5 – Using cowplot to plot four histograms together

Now that we have seen how to effectively use `cowplot` to combine plots and control other parts of the graphic, we can move on to the next type of plot, bar charts and dumbbell plots.

Bar charts and dumbbell plots

A bar chart and dumbbell plot are all types of visualizations used to represent data. Here is a description of each and their pros and cons. First up is the bar chart. A bar chart, also known as a bar graph, uses rectangular bars to compare different categories of data. The length or height of each bar represents the value of a particular category. The bars can be plotted vertically or horizontally, with the most common type being vertical. Some of the pros of a bar chart are as follows:

- **Easy to read and interpret**: Bar charts are straightforward and intuitive, making them easy to understand even for people without a background in statistics or data visualization

- **Effective for comparisons**: Bar charts allow for quick and easy comparisons between different categories, making them useful for identifying patterns or trends

- **Suitable for categorical data**: Bar charts are ideal for representing categorical or discrete variables

Here are some of the cons:

- **Limited for continuous data**: Bar charts are not as effective for representing continuous variables or data with many distinct values

- **Potential readability issues**: When the number of bars is large or the values are close in magnitude, it can be challenging to read the exact values on the chart

A dumbbell plot, also known as a connected dot plot or a range bar chart, compares the values of two categories or groups. It consists of two dots or markers connected by a line, with each dot representing a value and the line indicating the range between them. Here are its pros:

- **Highlights differences and comparisons**: Dumbbell plots are effective for emphasizing the differences or comparisons between two categories or groups

- **Shows ranges and variances**: The line connecting the dots in a dumbbell plot represents the range or variance between the values, providing additional information

- **Suitable for categorical or continuous data**: Dumbbell plots can be used for both ordinal and continuous variables

Here are the cons:

- **Limited for multiple comparisons**: Dumbbell plots are best suited for comparing two categories or groups. If there are more than two groups, the plot can become cluttered and confusing.

- **Less common and familiar**: Dumbbell plots are not as widely used or recognized as bar charts or time series charts, which may make them less familiar to some viewers.

In summary, bar charts are useful for comparing values between groups, and dumbbell plots are suitable for comparing two categories or groups. Each visualization has its strengths and limitations, and the choice depends on the nature of the data and the specific insights you want to convey.

Now that we have some information about the different types of plots, along with their pros and cons, it's time to delve into creating them and seeing the output.

Bar charts with ggplot2

Bar charts can be plotted vertically or horizontally, with the most common type being vertical. The vertical axis on the left or right side of the bar chart is called the y axis, while the horizontal axis at the bottom of the chart is called the x axis. The height or length of each bar represents the value of a particular category of data. Bar charts can be used to compare different sets of data among different groups easily, and they can illustrate important changes in data throughout a period. They can be of great use when explaining the meaning of complex data, as they allow for quick and easy comparisons between different categories. Bar charts are particularly useful for showing segments of information and are commonly used to present data or concepts involving data visually. Some key properties of bar charts include the following:

- The bars are rectangular and of equal width, with varying heights
- The gap between one bar and another should be uniform throughout
- They can be either horizontal or vertical

Overall, bar charts are a useful tool to convey relational information quickly in a visual manner and can be used to compare different sets of data among different groups easily. Now that we have a basic understanding of a bar chart and how it is useful, let's go through an example using the ggplot2 library.

First, let's load in the required libraries, of which healthyR and healthyR.data may need to be installed on your machine, as they may not have been already:

```
library(healthyR.data)
library(healthyR)
library(ggplot2)
library(dplyr)
library(forcats)
library(purrr)
```

Here, we're loading several packages that provide functions and tools for data manipulation (dplyr, forcats, and purrr) and visualization (ggplot2). These packages extend R's capabilities for handling data and creating plots. We load in the healthyR.data library for the dataset to work with and the healthyR library for the use of the category_counts_tbl() function.

The next block of code is used to create the dataset that we are going to plot:

```
df <- healthyR_data |>
  filter(payer_grouping != '?') |>
  category_counts_tbl(
    .count_col = payer_grouping
    , .arrange = TRUE
    , ip_op_flag
  ) |>
  group_by(ip_op_flag) |>
  mutate(order_var = paste0(
    sprintf("%02i", as.integer(rank(n))),
    " - ",
    payer_grouping
    )) |>
  ungroup()
```

In this step, a pipeline (| >) is used to perform a series of operations on the data:

- `healthyR_data` is a dataset provided by the `healthyR.data` package.
- The `filter()` function removes rows where the `payer_grouping` column is not equal to '?'.
- The `category_counts_tbl()` function is applied, which counts the occurrences of each unique value in the `payer_grouping` column within each combination of `ip_op_flag` values. The `.count_col` argument specifies the column to count, `.arrange` sorts the counts in descending order, and `ip_op_flag` groups the data by this column.
- The data is grouped by the `ip_op_flag` column using `group_by()`.
- The `mutate()` function adds a new column named `order_var`, which contains formatted rank values based on the count column, n. This is done using the `sprintf()` function to format the rank as a two-digit integer. We then ungroup the data, as the groups are no longer necessary.

Now, let's make the plot:

```
ggplot(df, aes(x = order_var, y = n)) +
  geom_col(alpha = 0.328) +
  labs(x = "", y = "") +
  theme(legend.position = "none") +
  facet_wrap(~ ip_op_flag, scale = "free") +
  scale_x_discrete(
    labels =  with(df, as.character(payer_grouping) |>
                          set_names(order_var))) +
  xlab(NULL) +
  theme(axis.text.x = element_text(
    angle = 90, hjust=1, vjust=.5)) +
  coord_flip() +
  theme_minimal()
```

This section creates a bar plot using `ggplot2`:

- `ggplot()` initializes the plot, and `aes()` specifies aesthetics (such as what goes on the x axis and y axis).
- `geom_col()` adds bars to the plot, where the height of each bar represents the value of *n*. The alpha parameter controls the transparency of the bars.
- `labs()` sets the axis labels to be empty.
- `theme()` allows theme adjustments to be made, such as removing the legend and using a minimal theme.

- `facet_wrap()` is used to create separate panels for each unique value of `ip_op_flag`.

- `scale_x_discrete()` is used to customize the *x*-axis labels using the `payer_grouping` values, indexed by `order_var`.

- `xlab(NULL)` removes the *x*-axis label.

- `theme(axis.text.x = element_text(angle = 90, hjust = 1, vjust = .5))` adjusts the appearance of the *x*-axis text, making it vertical.

- `coord_flip()` flips the *x* and *y* axes.

- `theme_minimal()` applies a minimalistic theme to the plot.

In summary, this code takes a dataset, filters and processes it, and then creates a bar plot with multiple facets, each displaying bars based on counts of a categorical variable. The plot's appearance is customized using various `ggplot2` functions and settings. Now, after all of that, let's see the final output:

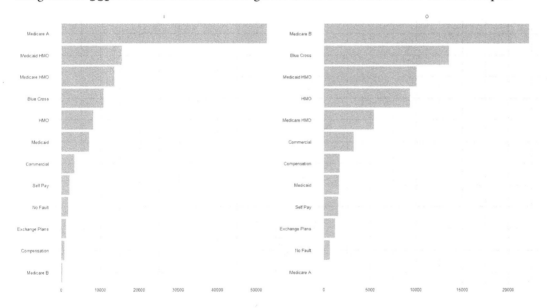

Figure 6.6 – Using ggplot2 to create bar plots

In this section, we have learned how to make a fairly sophisticated horizonal bar chart. We created an ordered one that allowed us to see information in two different groups ordered by the same factor column. It shows us volumes by insurance payer group for inpatient and outpatient facets. Now, we will move onto the dumbbell plot.

Dumbbell plots with ggplot2

A dumbbell plot, also known as a *dot plot with lines*, is a visualization that displays the change between two points for different categories. It often uses dots (representing the categories) connected by lines to show the change. In R, you can create a dumbbell plot using libraries such as ggplot2. Here's how you can do it.

First, make sure you have the ggplot2 and dplyr packages installed and loaded. You can install them if needed using install.packages("ggplot2") and install.packages("dplyr").

Let's make a data frame; we will make this with two columns for the initial and final values, and a categorical variable to group them. Your data might look something like this:

```
# Sample data
data <- data.frame(
  Category = c("A", "B", "C", "D"),
  Initial = c(10, 15, 8, 12),
  Final = c(18, 22, 14, 16)
)
```

Now, let's create a midpoint of our data before we make the actual plot:

```
data <- data |>
  mutate(Midpoint = (Initial + Final)/2)
```

Now, we can go ahead and create the plot:

```
# Create the dumbbell plot using ggplot2
dumbbell_plot <- ggplot(data, aes(x = Category, xend = Category,
   y = Initial, yend = Final)) +
  geom_segment(color = "gray50") +  # Lines connecting dots
  geom_point(color = "blue", size = 3) +  # Initial values
  geom_point(aes(y = Final),
             color = "orange", size = 3) +  # Final values
  geom_text(aes(label = Midpoint),
            vjust = -0.5, size = 3) +  # Midpoint labels
  labs(title = "Dumbbell Plot",
       x = "Category",
       y = "Values") +
  theme_minimal()

# Print the plot
dumbbell_plot
```

This example assumes you have a `Category` column in your data frame that defines the groups/categories. The plot will display initial values (blue dots), final values (red dots), lines connecting them, and midpoint labels above the lines. You can customize the aesthetics, colors, labels, and other elements according to your preferences. Now, let's see what we have created.

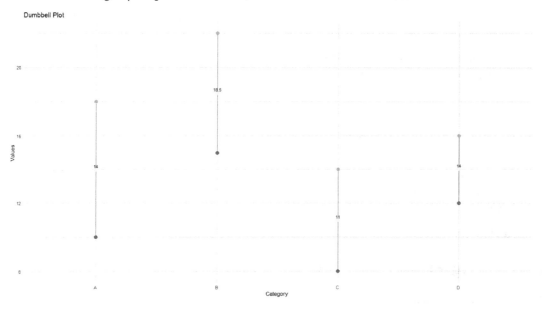

Figure 6.7 – A dumbbell plot with ggplot2

Remember that this is just a basic example. Depending on your data and requirements, you might need to adjust the code to fit your needs. It is now time for some time series graphs.

Enhancing your Excel reports with plotnine2, matplotlib, and plotly graphs

The Python section of this chapter explores the integration of popular data visualization libraries, such as `plotnine`, `matplotlib`, and `plotly`, with Microsoft Excel using Python.

You'll learn how to leverage the strengths of each library to visualize data effectively and enhance your Excel reports.

This part of the chapter is organized into the following sections:

- *Enhancing Excel reports with visualizations*: We'll provide guidance on effectively using visualizations to communicate insights and patterns.

- *Introduction to visualization libraries*: We'll provide an overview of the key visualization libraries – `plotnine`, `matplotlib`, and `plotly`. Understanding these and the use cases is essential for selecting the right library for your needs.

- *Creating graphs with* `plotnine`: This section will delve into using the `plotnine` library to craft sophisticated graphs. You'll learn how to generate various plot types, customize visual elements, and incorporate additional layers for enhanced clarity.

- *Generating graphs with* `matplotlib`: `matplotlib` is a versatile library for creating static visualizations. We'll walk you through the process of generating different types of graphs using `matplotlib` and then transferring them into Excel for inclusion in your reports.

- *Embedding visualizations into Excel*: This section covers the practical aspects of inserting graphs and charts generated with Python libraries into Excel sheets.

By the end of this chapter, you'll have the skills to seamlessly bridge the gap between data visualization in Python and Excel reporting. Whether you're creating static graphs or interactive visualizations, you'll be equipped to present data in a visually compelling and insightful way within Excel, facilitating more engaging and impactful reports.

Let's get plotting! (You can now imagine breaking out in an evil laugh!)

Enhancing Excel reports with visualizations

In this section of the chapter, we dive into the practical aspect of using visualizations to enhance your Excel reports. Beyond the technical aspects of generating and embedding visualizations from Python, we will explore the broader significance of these visual aids in the context of data-driven decision-making. Visualizations in Excel aren't just about aesthetics; they're powerful tools for effectively communicating insights, patterns, and trends hidden within your data. Whether you're preparing reports for stakeholders, colleagues, or clients, mastering the art of incorporating visualizations will elevate your data-driven narratives and facilitate more informed decision-making.

The upcoming sections provide guidance on how to strategically use visualizations within your Excel reports to maximize their impact. You'll learn not only how to create compelling graphs and charts but also how to interpret and present them effectively to convey your data's story.

Integrating visualizations into Excel reports goes beyond mere aesthetics – it's about transforming data into insights that drive informed decisions. We will delve into various strategies to enhance the impact of your reports by effectively utilizing visualizations.

The power of visualizations lies not just in their aesthetics but also in their ability to tell compelling stories with data. By mastering the art of choosing the right visualization type, utilizing annotations, simplifying complex data, and adhering to design principles, you'll be well equipped to elevate your Excel reports to new levels of impact and clarity.

An introduction to data visualization libraries

Data visualization is a fundamental aspect of data analysis, and Python offers a rich ecosystem of libraries to create engaging and informative visualizations. In this section, we will introduce you to three prominent data visualization libraries – `plotnine`, `matplotlib`, and `plotly`. Understanding the strengths and applications of each library is crucial for effectively conveying your data's story in Excel reports.

Plotnine – elegant grammar of graphics

The `ggplot2` library is a popular data visualization library in the R programming language, known for its expressive and declarative syntax. The Python adaptation is called `plotnine`.

It is based on the **grammar of graphics** concept, which allows you to build visualizations by composing individual graphical elements. `plotnine` excels in creating intricate, publication-quality plots. It offers fine-grained control over aesthetics, enabling you to customize every aspect of your visualization.

Plotly – interactive visualizations

`plotly` is a versatile Python library that specializes in creating interactive, web-based visualizations. It allows you to build interactive dashboards, scatter plots, line charts, and more. Users can hover over data points, zoom in, or filter data for a dynamic user experience.

`plotly` integrates seamlessly with Jupyter notebooks, making it a favorite choice for data scientists and analysts. It is ideal for generating interactive visualizations for web applications, reports, and data exploration.

Matplotlib – classic and customizable plots

`matplotlib` is a foundational library for creating static, high-quality visualizations in Python. It provides a wide range of plotting functions, making it suitable for various chart types, such as line plots, bar charts, and scatter plots.

`matplotlib` is highly customizable, allowing you to control every detail of your plots, from colors and labels to fonts and gridlines. It is the go-to choice for generating custom, static plots for research papers, presentations, and Excel reports.

Understanding the capabilities and best use cases of these libraries will empower you to select the right tool for your data visualization needs. Whether you want to create elegant, static plots with `plotnine`, interactive dashboards with `plotly`, or highly customized visualizations with `matplotlib`, you'll have the knowledge to choose the library that aligns with your goals.

In the following sections, we'll delve deeper into each library, providing practical examples and insights to help you master the art of data visualization in Python for Excel reports.

Let's dive into `plotnine` first.

Creating graphs with plotnine (Python's ggplot2)

In this section, we will explore the powerful capabilities of the `plotnine` library in Python, which draws inspiration from R's `ggplot2`, covered by the R section of this chapter. You will see that (other than accounting for differences in syntax between R and Python) the code and features are extremely similar – `plotnine` and *ggplot2* are truly sister packages.

By the end of this section, you'll be well versed in generating a wide range of visualizations, customizing every detail, and incorporating additional layers for enhanced clarity.

Understanding the grammar of graphics

Before we dive into creating impressive graphs with `plotnine`, it's essential to understand the grammar of graphics. This structured approach to data visualization forms the core of `plotnine` and enables you to build complex plots by combining data, aesthetics, and geometric objects.

Let's break down some key concepts:

- **Data mapping**: `plotnine` links data to visual elements in your plot. You'll specify which variables represent the x and y axes, color, shape, size, and so on.

- **Aesthetics**: Aesthetics control how data attributes are represented visually. You can use aesthetics to encode information such as color, shape, and size.

- **Layers**: `plotnine` encourages a layered approach. Each layer adds a new element to your plot, such as points, lines, or labels. This allows for intricate, information-rich visualizations.

Generating various plot types

One of the `plotnine` library's strengths is its versatility. You can create numerous plot types, catering to different data visualization needs.

In this section, we'll illustrate the construction of various plot types using `plotnine`:

- **Scatter plots**: Simple yet effective, scatter plots help visualize relationships between two numerical variables:

```
from plotnine import ggplot, aes, geom_point, geom_bar, geom_
histogram, geom_boxplot, geom_tile, geom_violin, theme_minimal,
labs
import pandas

# Sample data
data = pandas.DataFrame({'x': [1, 2, 3, 4, 5],
```

```
                                'y': [2, 4, 1, 3, 5]})

# Create a scatter plot
gg = ggplot(aes(x='x', y='y'), data) + geom_point()
print(gg)
```

Here is the plot the preceding code generates:

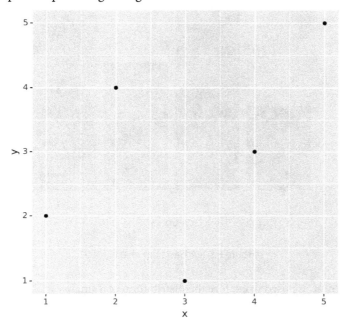

Figure 6.8 – A basic scatter plot

- **Bar charts**: Ideal for displaying categorical data, bar charts are excellent for comparisons:

```
# Sample data
data = pandas.DataFrame({'category': ['A', 'B', 'C', 'D'],
                         'value': [10, 25, 15, 30]})

# Create a bar chart
gg = ggplot(aes(x='category', y='value'),
    data) + geom_bar(stat='identity')
print(gg)
```

Here is the plot for it:

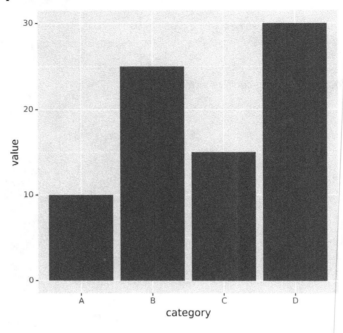

Figure 6.9 – A basic bar chart

- **Histograms**: These are used to explore the distribution of a single variable:

```
# Sample data
data = pandas.DataFrame({'values': [1, 2, 2, 3, 3, 3, 4, 4, 5]})

# Create a histogram
gg = ggplot(aes(x='values'), data) + geom_histogram(binwidth=1,
    fill='blue', color='black', alpha = 0.5)
print(gg)
```

Here is the plot for it:

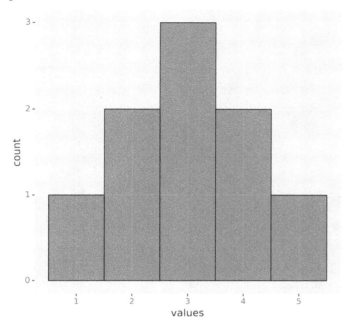

Figure 6.10 – A basic histogram

Note how we can use a syntax completely analogue to the R ggplot2 syntax up to and including the alpha parameter to control the transparency. It goes to show that R and Python are essentially similar tools with similar syntax in some packages!

- **Box plots**: Box plots provide a summary of the distribution of a dataset, including the median, quartiles, and potential outliers:

```
# Sample data
data = pandas.DataFrame({'category': ['A', 'A', 'B', 'B', 'C',
'C'],
                         'value': [10, 15, 20, 25, 30, 35]})

# Create a box plot
gg = ggplot(aes(x='category', y='value'), data) + geom_boxplot()
print(gg)
```

Here is the plot for it:

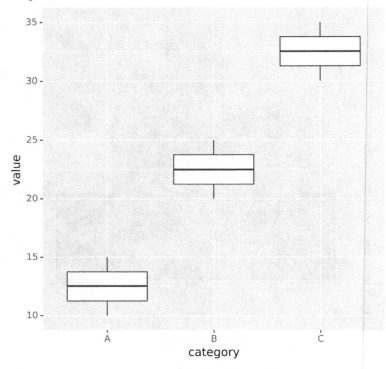

Figure 6.11 – A basic box plot

- **Heatmaps**: Perfect for revealing patterns in large datasets, heatmaps use color intensity to represent data values. We will use `geom_tile()` to achieve this:

```
data = {
        'x': ['A', 'A', 'A', 'A', 'B', 'B', 'B', 'B', 'C', 'C',
'C', 'C', 'D', 'D', 'D', 'D'],
        'y': ['W', 'X', 'Y', 'Z', 'W', 'X', 'Y', 'Z', 'W', 'X',
'Y', 'Z', 'W', 'X', 'Y', 'Z'],
        'value': [10, 15, 5, 20, 25, 30, 35, 40, 45, 50, 55, 60,
65, 70, 75, 80]
}

# Convert data to a DataFrame
data = pandas.DataFrame(data)

# Create a heatmap
gg = (ggplot(data, aes(x='x', y='y', fill='value'))
            + geom_tile()
            + theme_minimal()
```

```
                    + labs(title='Heatmap Example', x='X-Axis', y='Y-
Axis', fill='Values'))
print(gg)
```

Here is the plot for it:

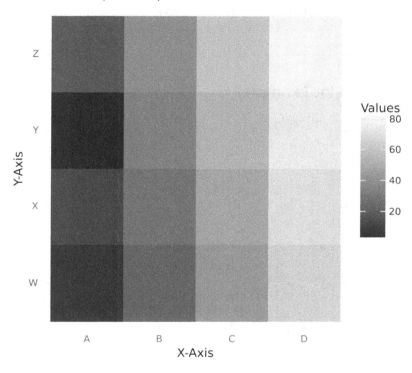

Figure 6.12 – A basic heatmap

- **Violin plots**: Combining box plots and kernel density estimation, violin plots showcase data distributions with rich detail:

```
# Sample data
data = {
        'Category': ['A', 'A', 'B', 'B', 'B', 'C', 'C', 'D',
'D', 'D'],
        'Value': [10, 15, 25, 30, 35, 45, 50, 65, 70, 75]
}

# Convert data to a DataFrame
```

```
df = pandas.DataFrame(data)

# Create a violin plot
gg = (ggplot(df, aes(x='Category', y='Value', fill='Category'))
            + geom_violin()
            + theme_minimal()
            + labs(title='Violin Plot Example', x='Category',
y='Value', fill='Category'))
print(gg)
```

Here is the plot for it:

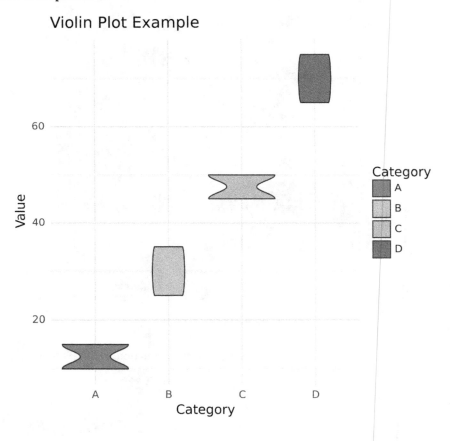

Figure 6.13 – A basic violin plot

Now that the basics are covered, let's have a look at what makes plotnine so special – all the customization possibilities!

Customizing the visual elements of a plotnine plot

The `plotnine` library's strength extends to customization. You can tailor every aspect of your visualizations to meet specific requirements. Here's a detailed explanation of how you can customize various aspects of your visualizations:

- **Labels and titles**: In `plotnine`, you can customize labels for the *x* and *y*-axes using the `xlab()` and `ylab()` functions, respectively. To add a title and subtitle to your plot, use the `ggtitle()` and `labs()` functions:

  ```
  # Customize labels and titles
  gg = gg + xlab("Custom X Label") + ylab("Custom Y Label")
  gg = gg + ggtitle("Custom Plot Title") + labs(subtitle="Custom
  Subtitle")
  ```

- **Axes and legends**: You have the flexibility to adjust axis scales, add breaks, and fine-tune legends. Use functions such as `scale_x_continuous()` and `scale_y_continuous()` to customize scales and legends:

  ```
  # Customize axes and legends
  gg = gg + scale_x_continuous(breaks=[1, 2, 3, 4, 5],
      labels=["One", "Two", "Three", "Four", "Five"])

  gg = gg + scale_y_continuous(limits=(0, 10))
  gg = gg + scale_color_manual(values={'A': 'red', 'B': 'blue'})
  ```

- **Themes**: Applying themes ensures consistent styling across your plots. You can use themes such as `theme_minimal()` or `theme_light()` to maintain a clean look throughout your reports or presentations.

  ```
  # Apply themes
  # gg = gg + theme_minimal()
  gg = gg + theme_light()
  ```

- **Text formatting**: You can control text size, style, and alignment using the `theme()` function. Adjust parameters such as `text`, `text_size`, `text_family`, and `text_align` to achieve the desired text formatting:

  ```
  # Control text formatting
  gg = gg + theme(text=element_text(size=12, family="Arial",
      face="bold", color="black"),
      axis_text_x=element_text(angle=45, hjust=1)
  ```

The preceding customizations result in the following graph:

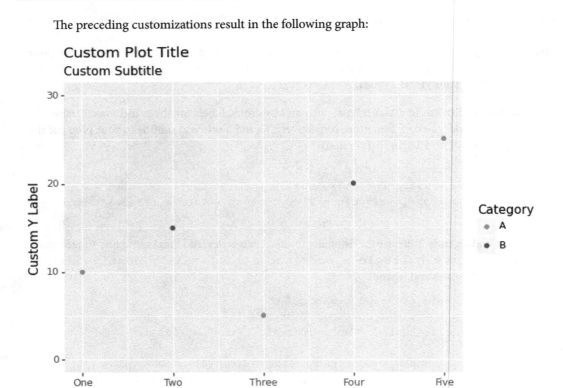

Figure 6.14 – Custom visual elements

By customizing these elements, you can create visually appealing and highly tailored visualizations to effectively communicate your data insights.

Beyond customization, `plotnine` has another trick up its sleeves – layers! In the next section, we will have a look at what layers are and how to use them to deliver the best visualization possible.

Incorporating additional layers

Layering is a powerful concept in `plotnine`. It allows you to superimpose multiple layers on a single plot, each conveying different aspects of your data. In this section, we'll explore some common layers:

- **Trendlines**: Add trendlines to reveal underlying patterns in your data

- **Error bars**: Visualize variability and uncertainty by incorporating error bars

- **Annotations**: Highlight specific data points or regions with text labels or geometric shapes

To add error bars, you can use the following code:

```python
from plotnine import (
    ggplot, aes, geom_line, geom_point, geom_errorbar,
    position_dodge, geom_text, labs, geom_smooth
    )
import pandas
import numpy
# Sample data
data = pandas.DataFrame({
        'x': [1, 2, 3, 4, 5],
        'y': [10, 15, 8, 12, 18],
        'group': ['A', 'A', 'B', 'B', 'C'],
        'error': [1, 2, 1.5, 1, 2.5],
        'label_x': [2, 4, 3, 1, 5],
        'label_y': [16, 11, 6, 13, 17],
        'annotation_text': ['Peak', 'Valley', 'Low', 'High', 'Bottom']
})

# Create a ggplot object
gg = ggplot(data, aes(x='x', y='y', group='group')) + \
        geom_line() + \
        geom_point() + \
        geom_errorbar(aes(ymin='y - error', ymax='y + error'),
        width=0.1, size=0.5,
        position=position_dodge(width=0.2)) + \
        geom_text(aes(x='label_x', y='label_y',
        label='annotation_text'), size=10)

# Draw the plot
print(gg)
```

This results in the following plot:

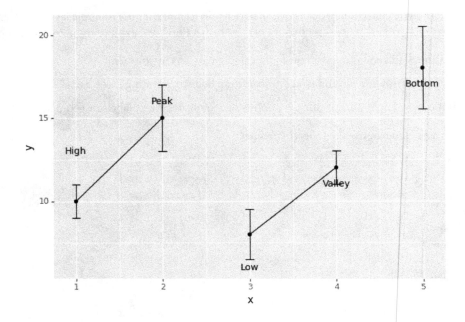

Figure 6.15 – Error bars added

For trendlines, you can use the following:

```
# Sample data
data = pandas.DataFrame({
        'X': numpy.arange(1, 21),
        'Y': numpy.random.randint(1, 101, size=20)
})

# Create a base plot
gg = (ggplot(data, aes(x='X', y='Y')) +
            geom_point() +
            labs(title='Scatter Plot with Trendline')
        )

# Add a trendline
gg = gg + geom_smooth(method='lm', se=False, linetype='dashed',
    color='red', size=1)

print(gg)
```

This results in a trendline added to the plot:

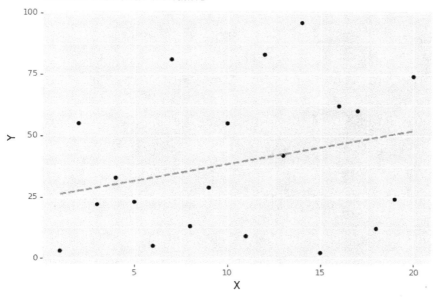

Figure 6.16 – A scatter plot with a trendline

Finally, for annotations, we have the following:

```
# Sample data
data = pandas.DataFrame({
        'X': numpy.arange(1, 11),
        'Y': numpy.random.randint(1, 101, size=10)
})

# Create a base plot
gg = (ggplot(data, aes(x='X', y='Y')) +
        geom_point() +
        labs(title='Scatter Plot with Annotations')
    )

# Add an annotation and adjust the position of the labels along the
y-axis using nudge_y by 5 units
gg = gg + geom_text(aes(label='Y'), nudge_y=5, color='blue')

print(gg)
```

This results in the following plot:

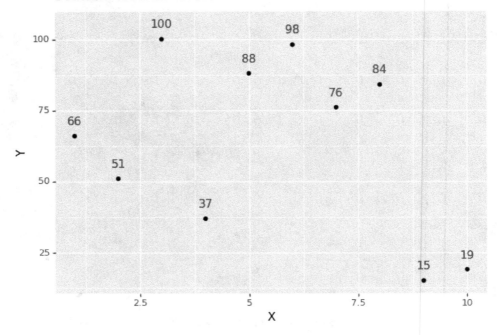

Figure 6.17 – An annotated scatter plot

Whether you're communicating insights, comparing datasets, or exploring trends, plotnine will empower you to create engaging and data-driven narratives for your Excel reports.

Next, let's have a look at similar plots using matplotlib!

Generating graphs with matplotlib

In this section, we will dive into the versatile world of matplotlib, one of the most widely used data visualization libraries in Python. With matplotlib, you have the power to create an array of static visualizations, fine-tune their appearance, and tailor them to your specific needs. Whether you're looking to craft scatter plots, bar charts, histograms, or other graphical representations of your data, matplotlib provides the tools to turn your data into compelling visual insights.

Creating diverse plot types with matplotlib

matplotlib is celebrated for its versatility, offering a wide array of plot types to meet diverse data visualization requirements. In this section, we'll delve into the construction of various plot types using matplotlib, allowing you to craft scatter plots, bar charts, histograms, box plots, heatmaps, and violin plots. Whether you're seeking to explore relationships between variables, display categorical data, or analyze data distributions, matplotlib equips you with the tools to create the visualizations you need:

- **Scatter plots**: Here is the code for them:

```
import numpy
import pandas
import matplotlib.pyplot as plt

### scatter plot
data = {
        'Height': [155, 162, 168, 173, 179],
        'Weight': [50, 56, 61, 65, 72]
}

df = pandas.DataFrame(data)

# Create a scatter plot
df.plot.scatter(x='Height', y='Weight',
    title='Scatter Plot of Height vs. Weight')

# Save the plot to a file (e.g., .png) in your working directory
plt.savefig('matplotlib_scatter_plot.png')

# Show the plot
plt.show()()
```

This code will create a scatter plot of height versus weight and save it as a .png image. You can further customize the plot as needed. The result is shown as follows:

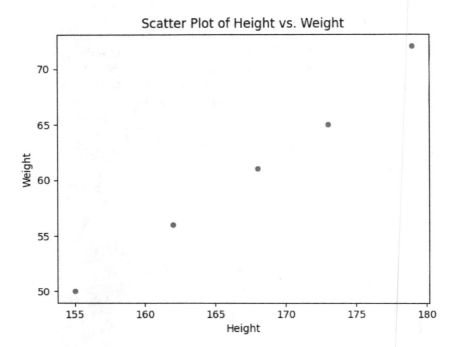

Figure 6.18 – A basic scatter plot with matplotlib

- **Bar charts**: Here is the code for them:

```
data = {'Category': ['A', 'B', 'C', 'D', 'E'],
          'Values': [15, 28, 24, 20, 32]}

df = pandas.DataFrame(data)

# Create a basic bar chart
plt.figure(figsize=(8, 6))
plt.bar(df['Category'], df['Values'], color='skyblue')
plt.xlabel('Categories')
plt.ylabel('Values')
plt.title('Basic Bar Chart')

# Save the plot to a file (e.g., .png)
plt.savefig('matplotlib_bar_chart.png')

plt.show()
```

This code creates a simple bar chart with categories on the *x*-axis and corresponding values on the *y*-axis, resulting in the following:

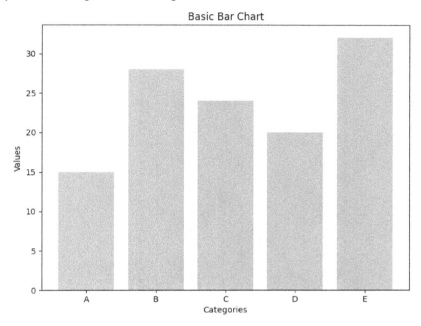

Figure 6.19 – A basic bar chart with matplotlib

- **Histograms**: Here is the code for them:

```
# Generate some random data for the histogram
data = numpy.random.normal(0, 1, 1000)


# Create a basic histogram
plt.figure(figsize=(8, 6))
plt.hist(data, bins=20, color='lightblue', edgecolor='black')
plt.xlabel('Values')
plt.ylabel('Frequency')
plt.title('Basic Histogram')

# Save the plot to a file (e.g., .png)
plt.savefig('matplotlib_histogram.png')

plt.show()
```

This code generates a histogram from random data, showcasing the frequency distribution of values. You can adjust the number of bins, colors, labels, and other properties to customize the histogram as needed. The histogram generated is shown as follows:

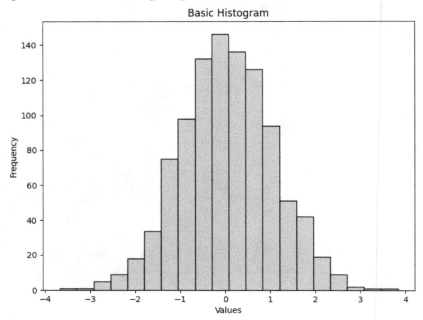

Figure 6.20 – A basic histogram with matplotlib

- **Box plots:** Here is the code for them:

```
# Generate some random data for the box plot
data = [numpy.random.normal(0, 1, 100) for _ in range(3)]   #
Three sets of random data

# Create a basic box plot
plt.figure(figsize=(8, 6))
plt.boxplot(data, vert=False,
    labels=['Set 1', 'Set 2', 'Set 3'])
plt.xlabel('Values')
plt.ylabel('Data Sets')
plt.title('Basic Box Plot')

# Save the plot to a file (e.g., .png)
plt.savefig('matplotlib_boxplot.png')

plt.show()
```

This code generates a basic box plot from random data, comparing three different datasets. You can adjust various parameters to customize the appearance of the box plot as needed. The preceding code results in this visualization:

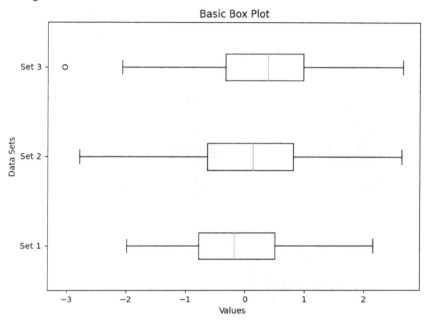

Figure 6.21 – A basic box plot with matplotlib

- **Heatmaps**: Here is the code for them:

```
# Generate some random data for the heatmap
numpy.random.seed(42)
data = numpy.random.rand(5, 5)  # Create a 5x5 matrix of random
values

# Create a heatmap
plt.figure(figsize=(8, 6))
heatmap = plt.imshow(data, cmap='viridis',
    interpolation='nearest')
plt.colorbar(heatmap)
plt.title('Heatmap Example')

# Save the plot to a file (e.g., .png)
plt.savefig('matplotlib_heatmap.png')

plt.show()
```

In this code, we generate a random 5x5 matrix of values and create a heatmap from it. We will use the `viridis` colormap, but you can choose from various colormaps to adjust the color scheme. This example demonstrates how to create a basic heatmap; you can further customize it according to your data and preferences. The resulting heatmap is shown as follows:

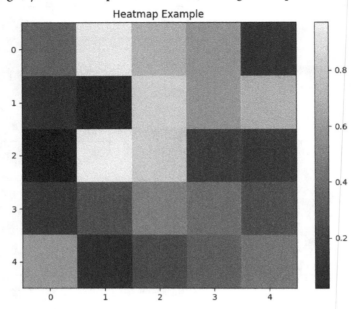

Figure 6.22 – A basic heatmap with matplotlib

- **Violin plots**: Here is the code for them:

```
# Generate some random data for the violin plot
numpy.random.seed(42)
data = [numpy.random.normal(0, std, 100) for std in range(1, 4)]

# Create a violin plot
plt.figure(figsize=(8, 6))
plt.violinplot(data, showmedians=True)
plt.title('Violin Plot Example')
plt.xticks([1, 2, 3], ['Group 1', 'Group 2', 'Group 3'])
plt.xlabel('Groups')
plt.ylabel('Values')

# Save the plot to a file (e.g., .png)
plt.savefig('matplotlib_violinplot.png')

plt.show()
```

In this code, we generate three sets of random data and create a violin plot to visualize their distributions. The `showmedians=True` argument displays the median values inside each violin. You can adjust the data, labels, and other plot properties to fit your specific dataset and requirements. Let's have a look at the plot generated:

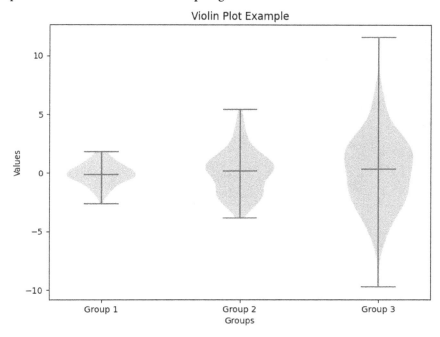

Figure 6.23 – A basic violin plot with matplotlib

Next, let's see how to customize the visual elements in a plot of matplotlib.

Customizing visual elements of a matplotlib plot

The plots created by `matplotlib` can, of course, be customized in many ways, just like the plots generated with `plotly`. In this section, we will explore the most important aspects and provide some examples along the way.

Labels and titles

`matplotlib` allows you to customize axis labels, plot titles, and subtitles easily. You can set labels for the *x*- and *y*-axes, title your plot for context, and even add subtitles to provide additional information or context. Here's an example of how to customize labels and titles in `matplotlib`:

```
# Sample data
x = [1, 2, 3, 4, 5]
y = [10, 20, 25, 30, 35]
```

```
# Create a scatter plot
plt.scatter(x, y)

# Customize labels and titles
plt.xlabel('X-axis Label')
plt.ylabel('Y-axis Label')
plt.title('Custom Title')
plt.suptitle('Subtitle for Additional Context')

# Display the plot
plt.show()
```

Here is the graph for it:

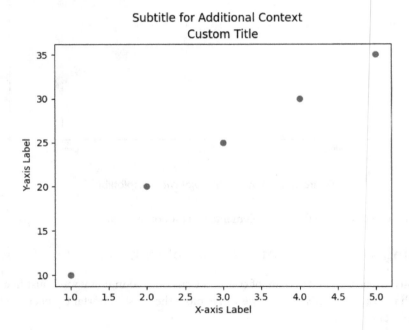

Figure 6.24 – Customizing labels with matplotlib

Axes and legends

matplotlib allows you to adjust axis scales, add axis breaks, and fine-tune legends. You can change the range, scale, and tick positions on both the *x*- and *y*-axes. Additionally, you can customize legends to better represent data series or categories.

Here's an example of customizing axes and legends:

```python
import matplotlib.pyplot as plt

# Sample data
x = [1, 2, 3, 4, 5]
y = [10, 20, 25, 30, 35]

# Create a line plot
plt.plot(x, y, label='Data Series A')

# Customize axes and legend
plt.xlim(0, 6)
plt.ylim(0, 40)
plt.xticks([1, 2, 3, 4, 5])
plt.yticks([0, 10, 20, 30, 40])
plt.legend()

# Display the plot
plt.show()
```

Here is the plot for it:

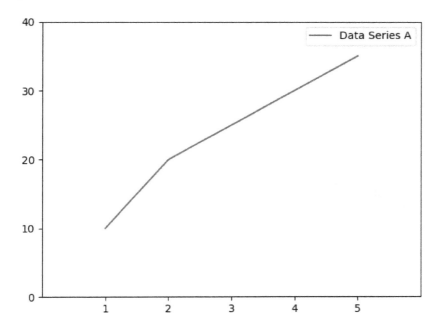

Figure 6.25 – Customizing axes and the legend with matplotlib

Themes

`matplotlib` offers a variety of themes to maintain consistency in your visualizations. You can choose from different predefined styles to match your report or presentation's aesthetics. Here's how you can apply a different theme. As an example, we will apply the `ggplot` theme you became familiar with earlier in the chapter:

```
import matplotlib.pyplot as plt

# Apply a different theme
plt.style.use('ggplot')

# Sample data and plot
x = [1, 2, 3, 4, 5]
y = [10, 20, 25, 30, 35]
plt.plot(x, y)

# Display the plot
plt.show()
```

Here is the plot:

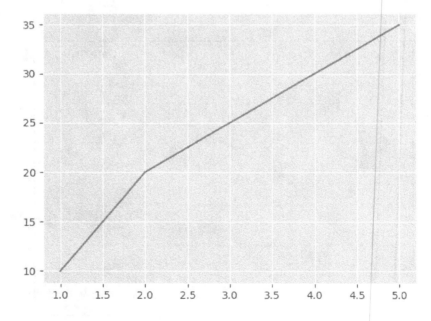

Figure 6.26 – Using themes with matplotlib

Text formatting

`matplotlib` allows you to control text size, style, and alignment for a polished look. You can adjust the font size, use bold or italic styles, and specify alignment for text elements such as titles, labels, and annotations. Here's an example of text formatting:

```
import matplotlib.pyplot as plt

# Sample data and plot
x = [1, 2, 3, 4, 5]
y = [10, 20, 25, 30, 35]
plt.plot(x, y)

# Customize text formatting
plt.title('Custom Title', fontsize=16, fontweight='bold',
    color='blue')
plt.xlabel('X-axis Label', fontsize=12, fontstyle='italic',
    color='green')
plt.ylabel('Y-axis Label', fontsize=12, fontweight='bold',
    color='red')

# Display the plot
plt.show()
```

Here is the plot for it:

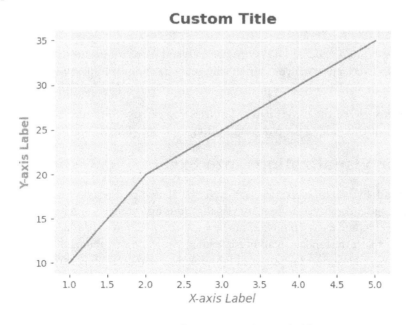

Figure 6.27 – Text formatting with matplotlib

These examples showcase how you can achieve various customization aspects in your `matplotlib` visualizations.

This concludes our overview of the most popular and powerful visualization libraries in Python. The next section covers short descriptions of the other choices available.

Other visualization libraries

For completeness's sake, here is a brief description of other popular libraries as well.

plotly

`plotly` is a popular Python library known for creating interactive and visually appealing data visualizations. It excels in generating dynamic charts, dashboards, and interactive plots. Unfortunately, the full power of the `plotly` library's interactivity does not work seamlessly with the most recent versions of Excel, due to security considerations introduced by Microsoft. This limitation can hinder its integration into Excel for users who rely on the latest Excel features and functionalities. Since the focus of this book is enhancing your Excel-based workflows, we will not cover `plotly` in detail.

seaborn

`seaborn` is another Python library designed for statistical data visualization. While it offers a wide range of customization options and the ability to create complex plots, it often requires more code to achieve the same results compared to libraries such as `matplotlib` and `plotnine`. Given the focus on simplicity and ease of use in the chapter, we chose to emphasize libraries that provide a more straightforward and concise approach to data visualization.

In this section, we primarily focused on `matplotlib` and `plotnine` due to their simplicity and compatibility with Excel, ensuring you can quickly generate and integrate visualizations into Excel reports without unnecessary complexity.

Now that we have covered the most popular libraries you can use to create visualizations, we can continue with the distribution of the plots: embedding them into Excel!

Embedding visualizations into Excel

When working with Python libraries such as `matplotlib` and `plotnine` to create visualizations, you might want to seamlessly integrate these visualizations into your Excel reports or spreadsheets. Embedding these plots and charts into Excel can be a valuable addition to your data analysis toolkit. In this section, we'll explore the fundamentals of embedding `matplotlib` and `plotnine` visualizations into Excel, helping you leverage the power of Python's data visualization libraries alongside Excel's reporting capabilities.

A basic embedding process

The process of embedding `matplotlib` and `plotnine` visualizations into Excel typically involves exporting your plots or charts as image files (such as PNG or JPEG) and then importing these images into your Excel sheet. While this approach doesn't offer the same level of interactivity as some other methods, it's a straightforward way to enhance your Excel reports with data visualizations generated in Python.

Here are the basic steps:

1. **Generate your visualization**: Create your `matplotlib` or `plcotnine` visualization in your Python script or Jupyter notebook. Customize it to meet your data analysis and reporting requirements.

2. **Export as an image**: Use `matplotlib` or `plotnine` to save your visualization as an image file. Common image formats such as PNG or JPEG work well for this purpose. Ensure that you save the image in a location accessible from your Excel sheet.

3. **Insert the image in Excel**: This can be done in two ways:

   - **Option 1**: Here, we manually insert the image. Open your Excel sheet and navigate to the location where you want to insert the visualization. Use Excel's **Insert** or **Picture** option to import the image file you generated in *step 2*. You can then resize and position the image as needed within your Excel sheet.

   - **Option 2**: Insert the image programmatically from Python using `pywin32`:

```
import win32com.client as win32

# Initialize Excel
excel = win32.gencache.EnsureDispatch('Excel.Application')
excel.Visible = True

# Create a new workbook
workbook = excel.Workbooks.Add()

# Define the (absolute) image path
image_path = 'path\\to\\your\\image.png'

# Insert the image into a specific sheet and cell
sheet = workbook.ActiveSheet
cell = sheet.Range("A1")  # You can specify the cell where you
want to insert the image

# Add the image to the worksheet (note that Width and Height
might need to be adjusted)
sheet.Shapes.AddPicture(image_path, LinkToFile=False,
```

```
          SaveWithDocument=True, Left=cell.Left,
          Top=cell.Top, Width=300, Height=200)

# Save the workbook
workbook.SaveAs('your_excel_with_image.xlsx')

# Close Excel
excel.Application.Quit()
```

4. **Scheduling a script for updates (optional)**: If your data changes regularly, you may want to consider scheduling script-generating the image in Excel and inserting it, using the method from the preceding *option 2*. This way, your visualization regularly updates automatically. You can do this with what you learned in *Chapter 4*.

While this method provides a static representation of your visualizations, it's a practical way to enhance your Excel reports with Python-generated charts and plots.

Summary

Embedding visualizations in Excel reports offers a practical way to enhance data presentation, customization, and automation. Whether you're working with sales data, financial reports, or any other dataset, this approach empowers you to create insightful reports that convey your data-driven insights effectively.

In this chapter, you learned about data visualization techniques in general, the ways to extend your Excel workflows and reports with those techniques, and how to implement them in R and Python.

We have covered the most popular and powerful R packages and Python libraries in detail. You learned about the typical plots used to carry out your analysis and how to communicate your findings, along with use cases and examples where those data visualizations can be used.

The next time you prepare an Excel report, you will be in a position to dazzle your audience with the most beautiful and insightful visualizations they have ever seen!

In the next chapter, we will look at another way to communicate your findings to audiences for whom the details of raw data are too much: automating pivot tables.

7

Pivot Tables and Summary Tables

In the realm of data analysis and spreadsheet manipulation, a pivot table is a powerful tool that enables users to transform and summarize large datasets into more manageable and insightful formats. By providing an organized and dynamic way to analyze data, pivot tables have become an indispensable asset for professionals across various domains.

So, what is a pivot table? A pivot table is a data processing technique employed in spreadsheet software, such as Microsoft Excel or Google Sheets, to analyze and extract meaningful insights from complex datasets. It allows users to restructure and condense large amounts of information into a concise, comprehensible format, facilitating better decision-making and data exploration.

In the world of data analysis, pivot tables stand as versatile tools that empower users to transform raw data into actionable insights. By organizing, summarizing, and presenting data in a user-friendly format, pivot tables streamline decision-making processes and promote a deeper understanding of complex datasets. Their adaptability, interactivity, and simplicity make them an invaluable asset across diverse industries and analytical tasks.

In this chapter, we will cover the following topics:

- Making a table with the Base R `xtabs` function
- Making a table with the `gt` package
- Creating pivot tables with `tidyquant`
- Creating and managing pivot tables in Python with `win32com` and `pypiwin32`
- Creating pivot tables with Python basics

Technical requirements

For this chapter, you will be able to find the code used at the following link: `https://github.com/PacktPublishing/Extending-Excel-with-Python-and-R/tree/main/Chapter7`.

Some of the packages that will be covered for the R language are as follows:

- `tidyquant >= 1.0.6`
- `gt >- 0.10.0`

Making a table with the Base R xtabs function

Before we move onto the core of the topic, let us understand a few of the important components.

Here is a list of some key components of a pivot table:

- **Rows and columns**: Pivot tables typically involve two primary components – rows and columns. The data rows contain individual records or observations, while the columns contain the attributes or variables that define those records.

- **Values**: Pivot tables allow users to aggregate and summarize data by calculating values based on specific metrics, such as sum, average, count, or percentage.

- **Filters and slicers**: Filters and slicers enable users to focus on specific subsets of data within the pivot table, enhancing the granularity of analysis. These tools are especially useful when dealing with large datasets.

- **Row and column labels**: Pivot tables allow users to drag and drop attributes into row and column labels, defining the layout and structure of the table dynamically.

The core functionality of a pivot table revolves around rearranging and summarizing data based on user-defined criteria. By "pivoting" the data, the table generates a multidimensional summary, providing insights that might not be readily apparent in the original dataset. The following details how a pivot table works:

- **Selection**: Users select the dataset they want to analyze and identify the columns containing the relevant attributes and metrics.

- **Arrangement**: Users place these attributes and metrics into specific areas of the pivot table layout, such as rows, columns, values, and filters.

- **Calculation**: Pivot tables automatically calculate the specified metrics for various combinations of the chosen attributes. For instance, it can show the total sales amount for each product category in different regions.

- **Interactivity**: Pivot tables are interactive; users can easily modify the layout by dragging and dropping attributes, allowing real-time exploration of the data.

Pivot tables offer several advantages that make them indispensable tools for data analysis:

- **Data summarization**: Pivot tables allow quick and effective summarization of data, helping users understand patterns, trends, and anomalies within large datasets

- **Quick insights**: Users can swiftly generate insights without the need for complex coding or intricate formulas

- **Flexible analysis**: Pivot tables enable users to experiment with different perspectives by rearranging attributes, thereby aiding in the identification of correlations and trends

- **Report generation**: Pivot tables are pivotal (pun intended) in creating comprehensive and informative reports, dashboards, and visualizations

- **Data cleaning**: Before analyzing data, pivot tables can be employed to identify missing values, outliers, or inconsistencies

The xtabs() function in R is used to create a contingency table from factor columns in a data frame. You would use this function with the familiar formula input: x ~ y. A contingency table is a table that displays the frequency distribution of two or more categorical variables. In this case, we will use the UCBAdmissions dataset to demonstrate how to use the xtabs() function.

The syntax for the xtabs() function is as follows:

```
xtabs(formula, data, subset, sparse, na.action, addNA, exclude, drop.
unused.levels)
```

The meaning of each is as follows:

- formula: A formula object with the cross-classifying variables (separated by ~)
- data: A data frame containing the variables in the formula
- subset: An optional expression specifying a subset of observations to be used
- sparse: A logical value indicating whether to return a sparse matrix
- na.action: A function to handle missing values
- addNA: A logical value indicating whether to add a row and column for missing values
- exclude: A vector of values to exclude from the table
- drop.unused.levels: A logical value indicating whether to drop unused factor levels

To use the `xtabs()` function with the `UCBAdmissions` dataset, we first need to convert it to a data frame using the `as.data.frame()` function. The `UCBAdmissions` dataset contains the number of male and female applicants and the number of male and female applicants who were admitted or rejected. We can use the `xtabs()` function to create a contingency table that displays the frequency distribution of gender and admission status. Here is the code for it:

```
# Convert the dataset to a data frame
df <- as.data.frame(UCBAdmissions)

# Create a contingency table using xtabs()
xtabs(Freq ~ Gender + Admit, df)
        Admit
Gender   Admitted Rejected
  Male       1198     1493
  Female      557     1278
```

The output of the `xtabs()` function will be a table that displays the frequency distribution of gender and admission status. The rows represent the gender, and the columns represent the admission status. The values in the table represent the frequency of each combination of gender and admission status.

In summary, the syntax for the `xtabs()` function includes several arguments that allow for customization of the output. To use the `xtabs()` function with the `UCBAdmissions` dataset, we first need to convert it to a data frame using the `as.data.frame()` function. We can then use the `xtabs()` function to create a contingency table that displays the frequency distribution of gender and admission status.

Now that we have produced a contingency table in base R, we can move on to the `gt` package, which will allow us to make something we are more familiar with: a pivot table, as we have come to know it.

Making a table with the gt package

The `gt` package in R allows users to create beautiful and customizable tables in R. One of the main pros of the `gt` package is its ease of use. The package is designed to be user-friendly, with a simple syntax that makes it easy to create tables quickly. Additionally, the package offers a wide range of customization options, allowing users to create tables that are tailored to their specific needs.

Another pro of the `gt` package is its ability to handle large datasets. The package is optimized for performance, which means that it can handle large datasets without slowing down. This is particularly useful for users who need to create tables from large datasets, as it allows them to do so quickly and efficiently.

The `gt` package also offers a wide range of styling options, allowing users to create tables that are visually appealing and easy to read. Users can customize the fonts, colors, and formatting of their tables, making it easy to create tables that match their branding or design preferences.

Finally, the gt package is open source, which means that it is constantly being updated and improved by the R community. This ensures that the package remains up to date and relevant, with new features and improvements being added regularly.

In summary, the gt package is a powerful tool for creating tables in R. Its ease of use, performance, customization options, and open source nature make it a popular choice among R users who need to create tables quickly and efficiently. Let's check out an example using the gt package with the mtcars dataset.

In this section, we are checking whether the gt package is installed. If it's not installed, we use the install.packages function to install it. The gt package is a package for creating nicely formatted tables in R:

```
# The gt package
if (!require(gt)) {
   install.packages("gt", dependencies = TRUE)
}
```

Here, we are loading two additional packages: dplyr and tibble. These packages provide useful functions and data structures for data manipulation and analysis in R:

```
library(dplyr)
library(tibble)
```

In this section, we are performing several operations on the mtcars dataset:

```
tab <- mtcars |>
   rownames_to_column() |>
   arrange(factor(cyl), mpg) |>
   group_by(cyl) |>
   slice(1:3) |>
   gt()
```

The operations are as follows:

- rownames_to_column(): We are converting the row names of the dataset into a regular column so that we can work with it. This is a function from the tibble package.
- arrange(factor(cyl), mpg): We are sorting the dataset first by the cyl column in ascending order and then by the mpg column in ascending order. This, along with group_by and slice, is a function from dplyr.
- group_by(cyl): We are grouping the dataset by the cyl column.
- slice(1:3): We are selecting the first three rows within each group.
- gt(): We are creating a table using the gt package to display the resulting data.

In this next section, we are adding a `Performance` spanner (a label for a group of columns) to the table. We specify the columns we want to include under this spanner: `mpg`, `disp`, `hp`, `drat`, `wt`, and `qsec`. These columns are related to the performance of the cars:

```
tab <- tab |>
  tab_spanner(
    label = "Performance",
    columns = c(mpg, disp, hp, drat, wt, qsec)
  )
```

Similarly, in this section, we are adding a `Specs` spanner to the table, and we specify the columns to be included under this spanner: `vs`, `am`, `gear`, and `carb`. These columns contain specification information about the cars:

```
tab <- tab |>
  tab_spanner(
    label = "Specs",
    columns = c(vs, am, gear, carb)
  )
```

In the final section, we are setting the table header with a title and subtitle. The title is `The Cars of mtcars` with some Markdown formatting, and the subtitle is `These are some fine automobiles`:

```
tab <- tab |>
  tab_header(
    title = md("The Cars of **mtcars**"),
    subtitle = "These are some fine automobiles"
  )
tab
```

So, in summary, this R code loads the necessary packages, manipulates the `mtcars` dataset to create a customized table with performance and specification information, and sets a header for the table. Now that we have gone through all of the code, let's see the output of it all. If you want to do this on your own, just call up the tab in the console. The table appears as follows:

The Cars of **mtcars**										
These are some fine automobiles										
	Performance						Specs			
	mpg	disp	hp	drat	wt	qsec	vs	am	gear	carb
4										
Volvo 142E	21.4	121.0	109	4.11	2.780	18.60	1	1	4	2
Toyota Corona	21.5	120.1	97	3.70	2.465	20.01	1	0	3	1
Datsun 710	22.8	108.0	93	3.85	2.320	18.61	1	1	4	1
6										
Merc 280C	17.8	167.6	123	3.92	3.440	18.90	1	0	4	4
Valiant	18.1	225.0	105	2.76	3.460	20.22	1	0	3	1
Merc 280	19.2	167.6	123	3.92	3.440	18.30	1	0	4	4

Figure 7.1 – mtcars and the gt package

Now that we have seen how to create a pivot table with the gt package by creating different spanners and headers, we can move on to the tidyquant package, which will give users an even more familiar feeling when creating pivot tables in R.

Creating pivot tables with tidyquant

The pivot_table() function from the tidyquant library is a useful tool for creating summary tables from data frames in R. It allows you to specify the rows, columns, values, and aggregation functions for your table and to employ other options such as sorting, formatting, and filtering.

To use the pivot_table() function, you need to load the tidyquant library first by using the library(tidyquant) command. Then, you can pass your data frame as the first argument to the function, followed by the other arguments that define your table. For example, if you want to create a table that shows the average sepal length and sepal width of different iris species, you can use the following code:

```
# Load the tidyquant library
library(tidyquant)
library(purrr)
# Create a pivot table
pivot_table(.data = iris,
            .rows = ~ Species,
```

```
            .values = c(~ mean(Sepal.Length),
                      ~ mean(Sepal.Width))) |>
set_names("Species","Mean_Sepal_Length","Mean_Sepal_Width")
```

The output of this code is as follows:

```
# A tibble: 3 x 3
  Species    Mean_Sepal_Length Mean_Sepal_Width
  <fct>                  <dbl>            <dbl>
1 setosa                  5.01             3.43
2 versicolor              5.94             2.77
3 virginica               6.59             2.97
```

Here's a breakdown of the code in simple terms:

- **Load libraries**: The code starts by loading two R libraries: `tidyquant` and `purrr`. These libraries provide functions and tools for data manipulation and analysis.

- **The pivot table function**: The `pivot_table` function is used to reshape the data in the iris dataset. It takes three main arguments:

  - `.data`: This is the dataset you want to work with, which in this case is the iris dataset.

  - `.rows`: This specifies how you want to group or categorize your data. In this code, it groups the data by the `Species` column, which represents different species of iris flowers.

  - `.values`: This argument specifies which columns you want to calculate and display values for. Here, it calculates the mean (average) of two columns – `Sepal.Length` and `Sepal.Width` – for each species.

- **The set names function**: The `set_names` function is used to rename the columns of the resulting table. The names are set to `Species`, `Mean_Sepal_Length`, and `Mean_Sepal_Width`.

So, in summary, this code takes the iris dataset, groups it by species, calculates the mean sepal length and mean sepal width for each species, and then renames the resulting table's columns to make it more understandable. The result is a new table that shows the mean sepal length and mean sepal width for each species of iris flower.

Now that we have gone over the material in R, let's move on to Python!

Creating and managing pivot tables in Python with win32com and pypiwin32

Pivot tables are powerful tools in data analysis, allowing you to summarize and explore large datasets quickly and efficiently. While they are a staple feature in spreadsheet software such as Microsoft Excel, you can also create and manipulate pivot tables programmatically using Python. In this section of the chapter, we will delve into the world of pivot tables and learn how to harness their potential with the `win32com` and `pywin32` libraries.

Creating pivot tables with Python: the basics

Pivot tables are an indispensable tool in the world of data analysis. They provide a dynamic way to summarize, explore, and gain insights from complex datasets. However, when dealing with extensive data, setting up and customizing pivot tables can be a time-consuming and error-prone process, often requiring manual intervention.

In this chapter, we'll explore how Python, in combination with the `win32com` and `pywin32` libraries, can streamline and automate the creation and management of pivot tables. This powerful combination empowers data analysts and professionals to efficiently process large volumes of data without the need for repetitive, manual tasks.

Imagine being able to create pivot tables, apply advanced calculations, and refresh data with just a few lines of Python code. This is precisely what we aim to achieve in this section. We'll equip you with the knowledge and tools to harness the full potential of pivot tables while eliminating the tedious aspects of manual setup.

Setting up the Python environment

Before we dive into creating pivot tables, you need to set up your Python environment with the required libraries. `win32com` and `pywin32` are essential for interacting with Microsoft Excel, so ensure they are installed on your system. We have covered the installation process in *Chapter 3* and have provided a basic example of how to connect Python with Excel. See the *Integrating VBA with Python using pywin32* section for details, in particular, the *Setting up the environment subsection*. Please refer to that chapter if you have not set `pywin32` up yet.

Creating pivot tables

The foundation of working with pivot tables is, of course, creating them. We'll start with the basics, teaching you how to build pivot tables from scratch. The following is a step-by-step guide to help you get started:

1. **Connecting to Excel**: Create an instance of Excel and open a workbook. If the workbook doesn't exist, you can create a new one as follows:

```python
import win32com.client as win32

# Create an Excel workbook and add a sheet
excel = win32.gencache.EnsureDispatch('Excel.Application')
workbook = excel.Workbooks.Add()
worksheet = workbook.Worksheets(1)
```

2. **Adding data to the worksheet**: You'll need data to create a pivot table. Usually, that data is already there, but for the purposes of this example, you can add sample data to the worksheet as follows:

```
worksheet.Cells(1, 1).Value = 'Name'
worksheet.Cells(1, 2).Value = 'Category'
worksheet.Cells(1, 3).Value = 'Sales'

worksheet.Cells(2, 1).Value = 'John'
worksheet.Cells(2, 2).Value = 'Electronics'
worksheet.Cells(2, 3).Value = 1000

worksheet.Cells(3, 1).Value = 'Alice'
worksheet.Cells(3, 2).Value = 'Clothing'
worksheet.Cells(3, 3).Value = 800

worksheet.Cells(4, 1).Value = 'John'
worksheet.Cells(4, 2).Value = 'Clothing'
worksheet.Cells(4, 3).Value = 300

# Add more data as needed
```

3. **Selecting the data range**: Define the data range that you want to use for your pivot table. You can do this by specifying the start and end cells of your data:

```
data_range = worksheet.Range('A1:C4')  # Adjust the range as
needed
```

4. **Creating the pivot table**: Now, you can create the pivot table based on the selected data range. Specify where you want the pivot table to be located and which columns should be used for rows, columns, and values in your pivot table:

```
# Add a new worksheet to the workbook to hold the Pivot Table:
pivot_table_sheet = workbook.Worksheets.Add()
pivot_table_sheet.Name = 'Pivot Table'

# Create a Pivot Cache using the data range:
pivot_cache = workbook.PivotCaches().Create(SourceType=1,
SourceData=data_range)

# Create the Pivot Table on the new sheet using the Pivot Cache:
pivot_table = pivot_cache.CreatePivotTable(
    TableDestination=pivot_table_sheet.Cells(3, 1),
```

```
        TableName='MyPivotTable')

    # Add the row, column and data fields
    pivot_table.PivotFields('Name').Orientation = 1 # row field
    pivot_table.PivotFields('Category').Orientation = 2 # column
    field
    pivot_table.PivotFields('Sales').Orientation = 4 # data field

    # Add the calculated fields
    calculated_field = pivot_table.CalculatedFields().Add(
        "Total Sales", "=SUM(Sales)")

    # Refresh the PivotTable to apply changes
    pivot_table.RefreshTable()
```

In this example, the `SourceType` parameter specifies the type of data source for `PivotTable`. In this case, `SourceType = 1` indicates that the data source is an Excel spreadsheet. The `SourceType` parameter can take on one of the following values (or a number between one and three representing them):

- `xlDatabase`: This indicates that the data source is an Excel spreadsheet or an external database. It is the most common type of data source for pivot tables.

- `xlExternal`: This indicates that the data source is an OLAP cube or an external data source that is not directly accessible from Excel.

- `xlConsolidation`: This indicates that the data source is a consolidation. A consolidation is a pivot table that aggregates data from multiple worksheets or workbooks.

5. **Save the workbook and close Excel**: Don't forget to save your Excel workbook with the newly created pivot table:

```
    workbook.SaveAs('PivotTableExample.xlsx')
    workbook.Close()
    excel.Quit()
```

When saving the Excel sheet, you can provide a full path if you don't want to save the spreadsheet to the Python working directory.

That's it! You've created a pivot table using `pywin32` in Python. You can adjust the data, pivot table location, and formatting options to suit your specific needs.

Now that you have a basic pivot table ready, let's have a look at how to change one to fit your needs the best.

Manipulating pivot tables

Once you have your pivot tables, you may want to perform various operations on them, such as filtering, sorting, and refreshing data. Here are the steps for it:

1. First, open the Excel file from the previous section and select the pivot table created:

```
import win32com.client as win32

# Connect to Excel
excel = win32.gencache.EnsureDispatch('Excel.Application')

# Open the workbook with the pivot table
workbook = excel.Workbooks.Open('PivotTableExample.xlsx')  #
Replace with your workbook path
worksheet = workbook.Worksheets(1)

# Access the Pivot Table
pivot_table = worksheet.PivotTables('MyPivotTable')  # Use the
name of your pivot table
```

2. You can filter the data within the pivot table based on values. In this example, we'll filter the Category field to show only Electronics:

```
# Filter by value (need to make the field a Page field instaed
of a column field)
category_field = pivot_table.PivotFields('Category')
category_field.Orientation = 3 # page field
category_field.CurrentPage = "Electronics"
```

3. You may have to sort rows or columns within the pivot table. In this example, we'll sort the Name field in ascending order:

```
# Sort Rows or Columns
name_field = pivot_table.PivotFields('Name')
name_field.AutoSort(1, "Name")
```

4. If your source data has changed, you can refresh the pivot table to update it:

```
# Define the new source data range
new_source_data_range = 'Sheet1!A1:C2'

# Update the SourceData property of the pivot table's Table
object
pivot_table.TableRange2(workbook.Sheets('Sheet1').Range(
    new_source_data_range))

# Refresh data
pivot_table.RefreshTable()
```

5.   After manipulating the pivot table, save your changes and close the workbook:

```
workbook.Save()
workbook.Close()
excel.Quit()
```

> **Note**
>
> Do not have the spreadsheet open (in Excel) while accessing or manipulating it from Python as it leads to `com_errors` instances that are difficult to debug.

These steps should help you get started with manipulating pivot tables using `pywin32`. You can adjust the filters, sorting criteria, and refresh frequency to meet your specific requirements and automate various tasks involving pivot tables.

Once your pivot table is set up as you want it, you may need to enhance it further by grouping some (or all) of your categories to better reflect the information you are trying to convey. In the next subsection, we go into the details of how to do just that.

Groupings in pivot tables

Grouping data in a pivot table can help you create a more organized and insightful view of your dataset. You can group data by specific criteria, such as date ranges, numeric intervals, or custom categories. In this section, we'll explore how to apply groupings to your pivot tables using Python with the `pywin32` library.

Creating date groupings

One common use case for grouping is aggregating data by date ranges. For example, you might want to group sales data into monthly or quarterly intervals. To do this, you can create date groupings within your pivot table.

We will start by generating some sample data:

```python
# Sample Data Generation
import pandas as pd
import random
from datetime import datetime, timedelta
import win32com.client as win32
import os
import numpy as np

data = {
    'Date': [datetime(2023, 1, 1) + timedelta(days=i) for i in
range(365)],
```

```
    'Sales': [random.randint(100, 1000) for _ in range(365)]
}

df = pd.DataFrame(data)

# Create an ExcelWriter object and write the DataFrame to the Excel
worksheet
df.to_excel("GroupingExample.xlsx", sheet_name='Sheet1', index=False)
```

With the data saved in an Excel sheet (in the Python working directory by default but can be specified otherwise), we can follow the usual steps of opening the Excel sheet, adding a dedicated tab for the pivot table, and creating the pivot table. The steps that have been covered before are omitted here (but are available in GitHub). The steps are as follows:

```
# Connect to Excel

# Open the Excel workbook and add a sheet

# Add a new worksheet to the workbook to hold the Pivot Table:

# Define the range of data to be used as input for the pivot table

# Create a Pivot Cache using the data range:

# Create the Pivot Table on the new sheet using the Pivot Cache:

# Add the 'Date' field to Rows and define the date_field variable as
done with name_field in the example above.

# Add the calculated fields
calculated_field = pivot_table.CalculatedFields().Add("Total Sales",
"=SUM(Sales)")

# Group by months
date_field.Subtotals = [False]*12
date_field.NumberFormat = 'MMMM YYYY'

# Sort Rows
date_field.AutoSort(1, "Date")
```

In this example, we created a pivot table and added the Date field to the rows and a calculated field for Total Sales. We then specified that we wanted to format the dates in the month-year format. Finally, the formatted dates were sorted.

To add a grouped field to the pivot table, we will need to know which values belong together (note, the values have been formatted to not display the exact days, but they still differ):

```
# count the unique values for each value of the date column in the
pivot
date_values = pd.DataFrame([[item.Value for item in date_field.
PivotItems()], columns = ['date'])
unique_values = pd.DataFrame(np.transpose(np.unique(date_values,
return_counts=True)), columns=['date', 'count'])
date_values_count = date_values.merge(unique_values).drop_duplicates()


# Group by months
# Set the GroupOn property
date_range = pivot_table_sheet.Range(f"A4:A{starting_row + date_
values_count['count'].iloc[0]}")
date_range.Group()


# You can use the above method to group the other months as well if
you want to
# Note: the pivot is now changed, the second group starts at row
starting_row + 2, instead of starting_row + 32
```

This has created a grouped pivot field, called `Date2`. In the `Date2` field, the days belonging to January are grouped to the `Group1value`, while the other dates are grouped into groups consisting of a single date. Using the preceding example, you can now loop over the other unique values of month-year dates and group the other dates as well. Notice that the calculated field of `Total Sales` is now calculated over the groups.

To finish, we change the format of the new grouped field to the month-year format, change back the raw data in the `Date` field to display the full date, and hide the details of the groups for clarity. Finally, the pivot table is refreshed, and the Excel file is saved and closed:

```
# change the formatting of the grouped column to show only month and
year and change back the original date column to show the full date
# change the formatting of the grouped column to show only month and
year and change back the original date column to show the full date
pivot_table.PivotFields('Date2').NumberFormat = 'MMMM YYYY'
date_field.NumberFormat = 'DD MMMM YYYY'


# hide the details of the grouped values
for item in pivot_table.PivotFields('Date2').PivotItems():
    item.ShowDetail = False


# Refresh data
pivot_table.RefreshTable()


#pivot_table.PivotFields('Date2').Orientation = 2


# Save and close
```

```
workbook.Save()
workbook.Close()
excel.Quit()
```

This is just an example of how you can use groupings in pivot tables to analyze your data more effectively. Depending on your dataset and analysis goals, you can customize the groupings to fit your specific needs.

This section has covered the steps you need to create and manipulate pivot tables directly from Python. We have covered inserting a pivot table into an Excel sheet and adding the various types of fields a pivot table needs as the basics. Then, we went into the more complex areas of calculated fields, formatting, and finally, grouping values. With the skills you learned from this section, you can now create the perfect pivot table for your analysis without opening Excel!

Summary

In this chapter, we embarked on a journey to harness the power of pivot tables through the capabilities of R and Python. Pivot tables – indispensable tools in data analysis – offer a dynamic means of summarizing and exploring vast datasets. By mastering the techniques outlined in this chapter, you've unlocked the full potential of pivot tables, enabling you to automate their creation, manipulation, and enhancement.

We began by introducing the significance of pivot tables in data analysis and established a foundation for our exploration. With a focus on practicality, we guided you through the installation of essential libraries, ensuring that your R or Python environment is well prepared to tackle the intricacies of Excel.

Building pivot tables from scratch was our first venture, providing you with the fundamental knowledge to select data sources, arrange rows and columns, and customize the table's appearance. We left no stone unturned in demystifying the creation process.

Manipulating pivot tables opened a world of possibilities. You learned how to filter, sort, and refresh your data dynamically, which equipped you with the skills to tailor pivot tables to your evolving needs.

Furthermore, we explored advanced pivot table features such as calculated fields and grouping, showcasing the versatility and depth of your newfound expertise. These advanced techniques serve as valuable tools for gaining deeper insights into your data and enhancing your analytical capabilities.

In conclusion, your journey through pivot tables in R and Python has equipped you with a comprehensive skill set to tackle data analysis challenges efficiently and effectively. Armed with this knowledge, you can transform data into actionable insights, streamline your workflow, and make data-driven decisions with confidence. The ability to automate and manipulate pivot tables through R and Python is a valuable asset in today's data-driven world, and you are now well prepared to harness this power to its fullest extent.

In the next chapter, we will understand how **exploratory data analysis** (**EDA**) works for data analysis.

Part 3:
EDA, Statistical Analysis, and Time Series Analysis

Dive into the world of **exploratory data analysis** (**EDA**) with R and Python, uncovering insights and patterns in your Excel data. Explore the fundamentals of statistical analysis, including linear and logistic regression techniques. Delve into the realm of time series analysis, mastering statistics, plots, and forecasting methods to gain valuable insights into temporal data trends and patterns.

This part has the following chapters:

- *Chapter 8, Exploratory Data Analysis with R and Python*
- *Chapter 9, Statistical Analysis: Linear and Logistic Regression*
- *Chapter 10, Time Series Analysis: Statistics, Plots, and Forecasting*

8

Exploratory Data Analysis with R and Python

Exploratory data analysis (EDA) is a crucial initial step in the data analysis process for data scientists. It involves the systematic examination and visualization of a dataset to uncover its underlying patterns, trends, and insights. The primary objectives of EDA are to gain a deeper understanding of the data, identify potential problems or anomalies, and inform subsequent analysis and modeling decisions.

EDA typically starts with a series of data summarization techniques, such as calculating basic statistics (mean, median, and standard deviation), generating frequency distributions, and examining data types and missing values. These preliminary steps provide an overview of the dataset's structure and quality.

Visualization plays a central role in EDA. Data scientists create various charts and graphs, including histograms, box plots, scatter plots, and heat maps, to visualize the distribution and associations within the data. These visualizations help reveal outliers, skewness, correlations, and clusters within the data, aiding in the identification of interesting patterns.

Exploring categorical variables involves generating bar charts, pie charts, or stacked bar plots to understand the distribution of different categories and their relationships. This is valuable for tasks such as customer segmentation or market analysis.

EDA also involves assessing the relationships between variables. Data scientists use correlation matrices, scatter plots, and regression analysis to uncover connections and dependencies. Understanding these associations can guide feature selection for modeling and help identify potential multicollinearity issues.

Data transformation and cleaning are often performed during EDA to address issues such as outliers, missing data, and skewness. Decisions about data imputation, scaling, or encoding categorical variables may be made based on the insights gained during exploration.

Overall, EDA is a critical phase in the data science workflow, as it sets the stage for subsequent data modeling, hypothesis testing, and decision-making. It empowers data scientists to make informed choices about data preprocessing, feature engineering, and modeling techniques by providing a comprehensive understanding of the dataset's characteristics and nuances. EDA helps ensure that data-driven insights and decisions are based on a solid foundation of data understanding and exploration.

In this chapter, we will cover the following topics:

- Exploring data distributions
- Data structure and completeness
- EDA with various packages

Technical requirements

For this chapter, all scripts and files can be found on GitHub at the following link: `https://github.com/PacktPublishing/Extending-Excel-with-Python-and-R/tree/main/Chapter%208`.

For the R section, we will cover the following libraries:

- `skimr 2.1.5`
- `GGally 2.2.0`
- `DataExplorer 0.8.3`

Understanding data with skimr

As an R programmer, the `skimr` package is a useful tool for providing summary statistics about variables that can come in a variety of forms such as data frames and vectors. The package provides a larger set of statistics in order to give the end user a more robust set of information as compared to the base R `summary()` function.

To use the `skimr` package, it must first be installed from CRAN using the `install.packages("skimr")` command. Once installed, the package can be loaded using the `library(skimr)` command. The `skim()` function is then used to summarize a whole dataset. For example, `skim(iris)` would provide summary statistics for the `iris` dataset. The output of `skim()` is printed horizontally, with one section per variable type and one row per variable.

The package also provides the `skim_to_wide()` function, which converts the output of `skim()` to a wide format. This can be useful for exporting the summary statistics to a spreadsheet or other external tool.

Overall, the `skimr` package is a useful tool for quickly and easily obtaining summary statistics about variables in R. It provides a larger set of statistics than the `summary()` R base function and is easy to use and customize. The package is particularly useful for data exploration and data cleaning tasks, as it allows the user to quickly identify potential issues with the data. Now that we have a basic understanding of the `skimr` package, let's see it in use.

This R code is used to generate a summary of the `iris` dataset using the `skimr` package. The `skimr` package provides a convenient way to quickly summarize and visualize key statistics for a dataset.

Here's an explanation of each line of code along with the expected output:

- `if(!require(skimr)){install.packages("skimr")}`: This line checks whether the `skimr` package is already installed. If it is not installed, it installs the package using `install.packages("skimr")`. This ensures that the `skimr` package is available for use in the subsequent code.

- `library(skimr)`: This line loads the `skimr` package into the R session. Once the package is loaded, you can use its functions and features.

- `skim(iris)`: This line calls the `skim()` function from the `skimr` package and applies it to the `iris` dataset. The `skim()` function generates a summary of the dataset, including statistics and information about each variable (column) in the dataset.

Now, let's discuss the expected output. When you run the `skim(iris)` command, you should see a summary of the `iris` dataset displayed in your R console. The output will include statistics and information such as the following:

- **Counts**: The number of non-missing values for each variable

- **Missing**: The number of missing values (if any) for each variable

- **Unique values**: The number of unique values for each variable

- **Mean**: The mean (average) value for each numeric variable

- **Min**: The minimum value for each numeric variable

- **Max**: The maximum value for each numeric variable

- **Standard deviation**: The standard deviation for each numeric variable

- Other summary statistics

The output will look something like the following but with more detailed statistics:

```
> skim(iris)
── Data Summary ─────────────────────────────
                         Values
Name                     iris
Number of rows           150
Number of columns        5

Column type frequency:
  factor                 1
  numeric                4
```

```
Group variables              None

── Variable type: factor ──────────────────────────────────

  skim_variable n_missing complete_rate ordered n_unique top_counts
1 Species                 0              1 FALSE          3 set: 50, ver:
50, vir: 50

── Variable type: numeric ─────────────────────────────────

  skim_variable n_missing complete_rate mean     sd  p0 p25  p50 p75
p100 hist
1 Sepal.Length           0              1
5.84  0.828  4.3   5.1   5.8   6.4   7.9 ▃▃▆▅
2 Sepal.Width            0              1
3.06  0.436  2    2.8   3    3.3   4.4 ▁▆█▂
3 Petal.Length           0              1
3.76  1.77   1    1.6   4.35  5.1   6.9 █▂▆▃
4 Petal.Width            0              1 1.20  0.762 0.1
0.3   1.3   1.8   2.5 █▂▆▅
```

This output provides a comprehensive summary of the `iris` dataset, helping you quickly understand its structure and key statistics. You can also pass off a grouped `tibble` to the `skim()` function and obtain results that way as well.

Now that we have gone over a simple example of using the `skimr` package to explore our data, we can now move on to the `GGally` package.

Using the GGally package in R

At its core, `GGally` is an extension of the immensely popular `ggplot2` package in R. It takes the elegance and flexibility of `ggplot2` and supercharges it with a dazzling array of functions, unleashing your creativity to visualize data in stunning ways.

With `GGally`, you can effortlessly create beautiful scatter plots, histograms, bar plots, and more. What makes it stand out? `GGally` simplifies the process of creating complex multivariate plots, saving you time and effort. Want to explore correlations, visualize regression models, or craft splendid survival curves? `GGally` has your back.

But `GGally` is not just about aesthetics; it's about insights. It empowers you to uncover hidden relationships within your data through visual exploration. The intuitive syntax and user-friendly interface make it accessible to both novices and seasoned data scientists.

What's even better is that GGally encourages collaboration. Its easy-to-share visualizations can be a powerful tool for communicating your findings to a wider audience, from colleagues to clients.

So, if you're looking to elevate your data visualization game, give GGally a try. It's your trusted ally in the world of data visualization, helping you turn numbers into captivating stories. Unlock the true potential of your data and let GGally be your creative partner in crime. Your data has never looked this good! Now, let's get into using it with what is a simple use case:

```
if(!require(GGally)){install.packages("GGally")}
If(!require(TidyDensity)){install.packages("TidyDensity")}
library(GGally)
library(TidyDensity)
tidy_normal(.n = 200) |>
  ggpairs(columns = c("y","p","q","dx","dy"))
```

Let's break it down step by step:

- `if(!require(GGally)){install.packages("GGally")}`: This line checks whether the GGally package is already installed in your R environment. If it's not installed, it proceeds to install it using `install.packages("GGally")`.

- `library(GGally)`: After ensuring that Ggally is installed, the code loads the GGally package into the current R session. This package provides tools for creating various types of plots and visualizations, including scatter plot matrices.

- `library(TidyDensity)`: Similarly, this line loads the TidyDensity package, which is used for creating tidy density plots. Tidy density plots are a way to visualize the distribution of data in a neat and organized manner.

- `tidy_normal(.n = 200)`: Here, the code generates a dataset with 200 random data points. These data points are assumed to follow a normal distribution (a bell-shaped curve). The `tidy_normal` function is used to create this dataset.

- `ggpairs(columns = c("y","p","q","dx","dy"))`: This is where the magic happens. The ggpairs function from the GGally package is called with the dataset generated earlier. It creates a scatter plot matrix where each combination of variables is plotted against each other. The y, p, q, dx, and dy variables are the columns of the dataset to be used for creating the scatter plots.

In summary, this code first installs and loads the necessary R packages (GGally and TidyDensity). Then, it generates a dataset of 200 random points following a normal distribution and creates a scatter plot matrix using the ggpairs function. The scatter plot matrix visualizes the relationships between the specified columns of the dataset, allowing you to explore the data's patterns and correlations. Let's take a look at the resulting plot:

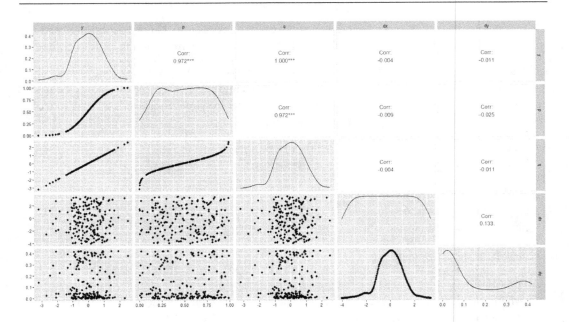

Figure 8.1 – Using GGally on 200 points generated from tidy_normal()

The data here was randomly generated so you will most likely not get the exact same results. Now that we have covered the GGally package with a simple example, we can move on to the DataExplorer package and see how it compares.

Using the DataExplorer package

The DataExplorer R package is created to streamline the majority of data management and visualization responsibilities during the EDA process. EDA is a critical and primary stage in data analysis, during which analysts take their initial glimpse at the data to formulate meaningful hypotheses and determine subsequent action.

DataExplorer provides a variety of functions to do the following:

- **Scan and analyze data variables**: The package can automatically scan and analyze each variable in a dataset, identifying its type, data distribution, outliers, and missing values.

- **Visualize data**: DataExplorer provides a variety of visualization functions to help analysts understand the relationships between variables and identify patterns in the data. These functions include histograms, scatter plots, box plots, heat maps, and correlation matrices.

- **Transform data**: DataExplorer also provides functions to transform data, such as converting categorical variables to numerical variables, imputing missing values, and scaling numerical variables.

`DataExplorer` can be used for a variety of EDA tasks, such as the following:

- **Understanding the overall structure of a dataset**: `DataExplorer` can be used to identify the different types of variables in a dataset, their distributions, and their relationships with each other
- **Identifying outliers and missing values**: `DataExplorer` can help analysts identify outliers and missing values in their data, which can be important to address before building predictive models
- **Generating hypotheses**: `DataExplorer` can help analysts generate hypotheses about the data by identifying patterns and relationships between variables

Here are some examples of how to use the package:

```
install.packages("DataExplorer")
library(DataExplorer)
library(TidyDensity)
library(dplyr)

df <- tidy_normal(.n = 200)
df |>
  introduce() |>
  glimpse()
```

First, we check to see whether the `DataExplorer` package is installed. If it's not, we install it. Then, we load the `DataExplorer` package, as well as the `TidyDensity` and `dplyr` packages.

Next, we create a normally distributed dataset with 200 observations. We use the `tidy_normal()` function for this because it's a convenient way to create normally distributed datasets in R. Typically, one will most likely use the *y* column only from the `tidy_normal()` output.

Once we have our dataset, we use the `introduce()` function from the `DataExplorer` package to generate a summary of the data. This summary includes information about the number of observations and the types of variables.

Finally, we use the `glimpse()` function from the `dplyr` package to display the data transposed. This is a helpful way to get a quick overview of the data and to make sure that it looks like we expect it to.

In other words, this code is a quick and easy way to explore a normally distributed dataset in R. It's great for students and beginners, as well as for experienced data scientists who need to get up and running quickly. Now, let's see the output:

```
> df |>
+   introduce() |>
+   glimpse()
Rows: 1
```

```
Columns: 9
$ rows                  <int> 200
$ columns               <int> 7
$ discrete_columns      <int> 1
$ continuous_columns    <int> 6
$ all_missing_columns   <int> 0
$ total_missing_values  <int> 0
$ complete_rows         <int> 200
$ total_observations    <int> 1400
$ memory_usage          <dbl> 12344
```

Next, let's take a look at the `plot_intro()` function and see its output on the same data with a simple call of `df |> plot_intro()`:

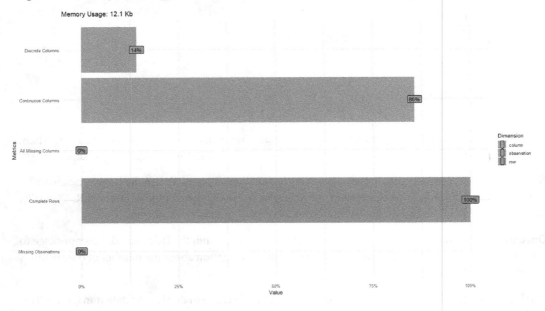

Figure 8.2 – The plot_intro() function

Lastly, we will view the output of the `plot_qq()` function:

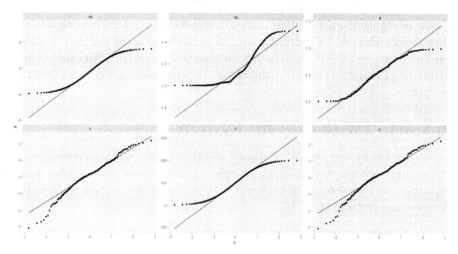

Figure 8.3 – The plot_qq() function with all data

We will now see a **quantile-quantile (Q-Q)** plot with only two variables, both the q and the y columns. Here is the code:

```
df[c("q","y")] |>
  plot_qq()
```

Here is the plot for it:

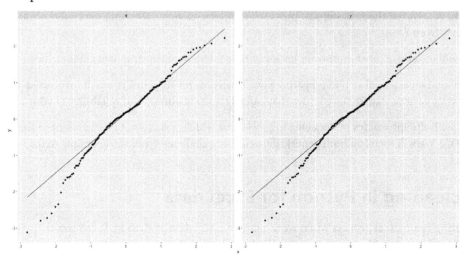

Figure 8.4 – The plot_qq() function with only the y and q columns

It is our intention for you to understand the Q-Q plot, but if that is not the case, a simple search on Google will yield many good results. Another item that was never discussed was how to handle missing data in R. There are a great many functions that can be used in capturing, cleaning, and otherwise understanding them such as `all()`, `any()`, `is.na()`, and `na.omit()`. Here, I advise you to explore these on the internet, all of which have been discussed extensively. Now that we have gone over several different examples of some functions from different packages in R, it's time to explore the same for Python.

Getting started with EDA for Python

As explained earlier, EDA is the process of visually and statistically exploring datasets to uncover patterns, relationships, and insights. It's a critical step before diving into more complex data analysis tasks. In this section, we'll introduce you to the fundamentals of EDA and show you how to prepare your Python environment for EDA.

EDA is the initial phase of data analysis where you examine and summarize your dataset. The primary objectives of EDA are as follows:

- **Understand the data**: Gain insights into the structure, content, and quality of your data
- **Identify patterns**: Discover patterns, trends, and relationships within the data
- **Detect anomalies**: Find outliers and anomalies that may require special attention
- **Generate hypotheses**: Formulate initial hypotheses about your data
- **Prepare for modeling**: Preprocess data for advanced modeling and analysis

Before you can perform EDA, you'll need to set up your Python environment to work with Excel data. We have covered the first steps in previous chapters: namely, installing necessary libraries and loading data from Excel.

Next, we will cover the most important basics of EDA: data cleaning and data exploration.

Data cleaning is an essential step in preparing your Excel data for EDA in Python. It involves identifying and rectifying various data quality issues that can affect the accuracy and reliability of your analysis.

Let's start with the intricacies of data cleaning, without which you cannot be confident in the results of your EDA. We will focus on both generic data cleaning challenges and those unique to data coming from Excel.

Data cleaning in Python for Excel data

Data cleaning is a critical process when working with Excel data in Python. It ensures that your data is in the right format and free of errors, enabling you to perform accurate EDA.

We will start with generating some dirty data as an example:

```python
import pandas as pd
import numpy as np
# Create a DataFrame with missing data, duplicates, and mixed data
types
data = {
    'ID': [1, 2, 3, 4, 5, 6],
    'Name': ['Alice', 'Bob', 'Charlie', 'Alice', 'Eva', 'Eva'],
    'Age': [25, np.nan, 30, 28, 22, 23],
    'Salary': ['$50,000', '$60,000', 'Missing', '$65,000', '$55,000',
    '$75,000']
}
df = pd.DataFrame(data)
# Introduce some missing data
df.loc[1, 'Age'] = np.nan
df.loc[3, 'Salary'] = np.nan
# Introduce duplicates
df = pd.concat([df, df.iloc[1:3]], ignore_index=True)
# Save the sample data in present working directory
df.to_excel('dirty_data.xlsx')
```

The data frame created looks like this:

```
>>> df
   ID     Name   Age    Salary
0   1    Alice  25.0   $50,000
1   2      Bob   NaN   $60,000
2   3  Charlie  30.0   Missing
3   4    Alice  28.0       NaN
4   5      Eva  22.0   $55,000
5   6      Eva  23.0   $75,000
6   2      Bob   NaN   $60,000
7   3  Charlie  30.0   Missing
>>> []
```

Figure 8.5 – Using GGally on 200 points generated from tidy_normal()

With the dirty data ready, we can start cleaning it, which includes handling missing data, duplicates, and data type conversion when cleaning Excel data. Let's see how to do this.

Handling missing data

Begin by identifying cells or columns with missing data. In Python, missing values are typically represented as **NaN** (short for **Not a Number**) or **None**.

Depending on the context, you can choose to replace missing values. Common techniques include the following:

- Filling missing numeric values with the mean, median, or mode. Do note that this will artificially reduce standard error measurements if, for example, a regression is performed. Keep this in mind when cleaning data for modeling purposes!

- Replacing missing categorical data with the mode (most frequent category).

- Using forward-fill or backward-fill to propagate the previous or next valid value.

- Interpolating missing values based on trends in the data.

Python offers several solutions to do this efficiently and statistically robustly, ranging from basic `pandas` methods to dedicated packages with much more robust imputation methods such as `fancyimpute`. Imputation should never be applied blindly, though, as missing data can be information in its own right as well, and imputed values may lead to incorrect analysis results. Domain knowledge, as always, for the win.

It is important to distinguish between the three types of missing data:

- **Missing completely at random (MCAR):**

  - In this scenario, the missingness of data is completely random and unrelated to any observed or unobserved variables.

  - The probability of a data point being missing is the same for all observations.

  - There are no systematic differences between missing and non-missing values.

  - Here is an example: a survey where respondents accidentally skip some questions.

- **Missing at random (MAR):**

  - Missingness depends on observed data but not on unobserved data.

  - The probability of a data point being missing is related to other observed variables in the dataset.

  - Once other observed variables are accounted for, the missingness of data is random.

  - Here is an example: in a survey, men may be less likely to disclose their income compared to women. In this case, income data is missing at random conditional on gender.

- **Missing not at random (MNAR):**

  - Missingness depends on unobserved data or the missing values themselves.

  - The probability of a data point being missing is related to the missing values or other unobserved variables.

- Missingness is not random even after accounting for observed variables.

- Here is an example: in a survey about income, high-income earners may be less likely to disclose their income.

If a significant portion of a row or column contains missing data, you might consider removing that row or column entirely. Be cautious when doing this, as it should not result in a substantial loss of information:

```python
import pandas as pd
import numpy as np
# Load Excel data into a pandas DataFrame
df = pd.read_excel('dirty_data.xlsx', index_col=0)
# Handling Missing Data
# Identify missing values
missing_values = df.isnull().sum()
# Replace missing values with the mean (for numeric columns)
df['Age'].fillna(df['Age'].mean(), inplace=True)
# Replace missing values with the mode (for categorical columns)
df['Salary'].fillna(df['Salary'].mode()[0], inplace=True)
# Forward-fill or backward-fill missing values
# This line is a placeholder to show you what's possible
# df['ColumnWithMissingValues'].fillna(method='ffill', inplace=True)
# Interpolate missing values based on trends
# This line is a placeholder to show you what's possible
# df['NumericColumn'].interpolate(method='linear', inplace=True)
# Remove rows or columns with missing data
df.dropna(axis=0, inplace=True)   # Remove rows with missing data
df.dropna(axis=1, inplace=True)   # Remove columns with missing data

df.to_excel('cleaned_data.xlsx')
```

Dealing with duplicates

Start with detecting duplicate rows. Python libraries such as pandas provide functions to detect and handle duplicate rows. To identify duplicates, you can use the duplicated() method. If applicable, continue with removing duplicate rows: after detecting duplicates, you can choose to remove them using the drop_duplicates() method. Be cautious when removing duplicates, especially in cases where duplicates are expected:

```python
# Handling Duplicates

# Detect and display duplicate rows
duplicate_rows = df[df.duplicated()]
print("Duplicate Rows:")
```

```
print(duplicate_rows)

# Remove duplicate rows
df.drop_duplicates(inplace=True)
```

Handling data type conversion

Reading data from Excel, while highly automated, can lead to incorrectly identified data types. In Python, data types are often automatically assigned when you read Excel data using libraries such as pandas. However, it's essential to verify that each column is assigned the correct data type (e.g., numeric, text, date, etc.).

The effect of that ranges from a too-large memory footprint to actual semantic errors. If, for example, Boolean values are stored as floats, they will be handled correctly but will take up a lot more memory (instead of a single bit with 64 bytes), while trying to convert a string into a float may well break your code. To mitigate this risk, first identify data types in the loaded data. Then, convert data types to the appropriate types. To convert data types in Python, you can use the astype() method in pandas. For example, to convert a column to a numeric data type, you can use df['Column Name'] = df['Column Name'].astype(float).

Here is an example of how that can be done:

```
# Handling Data Type Conversion

# Check data types
print(df.dtypes)

# Convert a column to a different data type (e.g., float)
df.loc[df['Salary']=='Missing', 'Salary'] = np.NaN
df.loc[:, 'Salary'] = df['Salary'].str.replace("$", "")
df.loc[:, 'Salary'] = df['Salary'].str.replace(",", "")
df['Salary'] = df['Salary'].astype(float)
print(df)

# Now that Salary is a numeric column, we can fill the missing values
with mean
df['Salary'].fillna(df['Salary'].mean(), inplace=True)
```

Excel-specific data issues

Let's have a look at data issues that are specific to data loaded from Excel:

- **Merged cells**: Merged cells in Excel files can cause irregularities in your dataset when imported into Python. It's advisable to unmerge cells in Excel before importing. If unmerging isn't feasible, consider preprocessing these cells within Python.

- **Empty cells shifting data**: Empty cells in Excel can disrupt data alignment when importing into Python. You can address this by doing the following:

  - Using the `pandas na_values` parameter when reading Excel files to specify values that should be treated as missing (NaN) during import

  - Manually adjusting the Excel file to remove unnecessary empty cells before import

By addressing these common data cleaning issues within Python for Excel data, you'll ensure that your data is in a clean and usable format for your EDA. Clean data leads to more accurate and meaningful insights during the exploration phase, which we will cover next.

Performing EDA in Python

With your data loaded and cleaned, you can embark on your initial data exploration journey. This phase is crucial for gaining a deep understanding of your dataset, revealing its underlying patterns, and identifying potential areas of interest or concern.

These preliminary steps not only provide a solid foundation for your EDA but also help you uncover hidden patterns and relationships within your data. Armed with this initial understanding, you can proceed to more advanced data exploration techniques and dive deeper into the Excel dataset.

In the subsequent sections, we'll delve into specific data exploration and visualization techniques to further enhance your insights into the dataset. With this knowledge, let's move on to the next section, where we'll explore techniques for understanding data distributions and relationships in greater detail.

Summary statistics

Begin by generating summary statistics for your dataset. This includes basic metrics such as mean, median, standard deviation, and percentiles for numerical features. For categorical features, you can calculate frequency counts and percentages. These statistics provide an initial overview of the central tendency and spread of your data.

Summary statistics provide a concise and informative overview of your data's central tendency, spread, and distribution. This step is essential for understanding the basic characteristics of your dataset, whether it contains numerical or categorical features. The following sections provide a closer look at generating summary statistics.

Numerical features

For numerical features, the following statistics are a good starting point:

- **Mean**: The mean (average) is a measure of central tendency that represents the sum of all numerical values divided by the total number of data points. It provides insight into the data's typical value.

- **Median:** The median is the middle value when all data points are sorted in ascending or descending order. It's a robust measure of central tendency, less affected by extreme values (outliers).

- **Standard deviation:** The standard deviation quantifies the degree of variation or dispersion in your data. A higher standard deviation indicates a greater data spread.

- **Percentiles:** Percentiles represent specific data values below which a given percentage of observations fall. For example, the 25th percentile (Q1) marks the value below which 25% of the data points lie. Percentiles help identify data distribution characteristics.

Categorical features

Categorical features have their own set of summary statistics that will give you insights:

- **Frequency:** For categorical features, calculate the frequency count for each unique category. This shows how often each category appears in the dataset.

- **Percentages:** Expressing frequency counts as percentages relative to the total number of observations provides insights into the relative prevalence of each category.

Generating summary statistics serves several purposes:

- **Understanding your data:** Summary statistics help you understand the typical values and spread of your numerical data. For categorical data, it shows the distribution of categories.

- **Identifying outliers:** Outliers, which are data points significantly different from the norm, can often be detected through summary statistics. Unusually high or low mean values may indicate outliers.

- **Data quality assessment:** Summary statistics can reveal missing values, which may appear as NaN in your dataset. Identifying missing data is crucial for data cleaning.

- **Initial insights:** These statistics offer preliminary insights into your data's structure, which can guide subsequent analysis and visualization choices.

In Python, libraries such as `pandas` make it straightforward to calculate summary statistics. For numerical data, you can use functions such as `.mean()`, `.median()`, `.std()`, and `.describe()`. For categorical data, `.value_counts()` and custom functions can compute frequency counts and percentages.

Here's an example of how you can generate summary statistics for both numerical and categorical data using Python and `pandas`. We'll create sample data for demonstration purposes:

```
import pandas as pd
import random

# Create a sample DataFrame
data = {
```

```
      'Age': [random.randint(18, 60) for _ in range(100)],
      'Gender': ['Male', 'Female'] * 50,
      'Income': [random.randint(20000, 100000) for _ in range(100)],
      'Region': ['North', 'South', 'East', 'West'] * 25
}


df = pd.DataFrame(data)


# Calculate summary statistics for numerical features
numerical_summary = df.describe()


# Calculate frequency counts and percentages for categorical features
categorical_summary = df['Gender'].value_counts(normalize=True)


print("Summary Statistics for Numerical Features:")
print(numerical_summary)


print("\nFrequency Counts and Percentages for Categorical Features
(Gender):")
print(categorical_summary)
```

In this example, we created a sample `DataFrame`, df, with columns for Age, Gender, Income, and Region. We used `df.describe()` to calculate summary statistics (mean, standard deviation, min, max, quartiles, and so on) for numerical features (Age and Income). We then used `df['Gender'].value_counts(normalize=True)` to calculate frequency counts and percentages for the Gender categorical feature. The `normalize=True` parameter expresses the counts as percentages. If it is set to `False`, the `value_counts()` command returns a series containing the raw counts of each unique value in the Gender column.

You can adapt this code to your Excel dataset by loading your data into a `pandas DataFrame` and then applying these summary statistics functions.

Once you've generated summary statistics, you'll have a solid foundation for your data exploration journey. These statistics provide a starting point for further analysis and visualization, helping you uncover valuable insights within your Excel dataset.

Data distribution

Understanding the distribution of your data is fundamental. Is it normally distributed or skewed, or does it follow another distribution? Identifying the data's distribution informs subsequent statistical analysis and model selection.

Before delving deeper into your data, it's essential to understand its distribution. The distribution of data refers to the way data values are spread or arranged. Knowing the data distribution helps you make better decisions regarding statistical analysis and modeling. Here are some key concepts related to data distribution:

- **Normal distribution**: In a normal distribution, data is symmetrically distributed around the mean, forming a bell-shaped curve. Many statistical techniques are simple to apply when the data follows a normal distribution. You can check for normality using visualizations such as histograms and Q-Q plots or statistical tests such as the Shapiro-Wilk test.

- **Skewness**: Skewness measures the asymmetry of the data distribution. A positive skew indicates that the tail of the distribution extends to the right, while a negative skew means it extends to the left. Identifying skewness is important because it can affect the validity of some statistical tests.

- **Kurtosis**: Kurtosis measures the "heavy-tailedness" or "peakedness" of a distribution. A high kurtosis value indicates heavy tails, while a low value suggests light tails. Understanding kurtosis helps in selecting appropriate statistical models.

- **Other distributions**: Data can follow various distributions, such as exponential, log-normal, Poisson, or uniform. Counts often follow Poisson distribution, rainfall amounts are log-normal distributed, and these distributions are everywhere around us! Identifying the correct distribution is essential when choosing statistical models and making predictions.

To analyze data distributions using Python, you can create visualizations such as histograms, kernel density plots, and box plots. Additionally, statistical tests and libraries such as SciPy can help you identify and quantify departures from normality.

Let's take a look at a sample code snippet that generates sample data from a `lognormal` distribution, performs the Shapiro-Wilk test, creates Q-Q plots with both a `Normal` and `lognormal` distribution, and calculates skewness and kurtosis statistics!

First, let's generate some sample data:

```
import pandas as pd
import numpy as np
import matplotlib.pyplot as plt
from scipy import stats
import statsmodels.api as sm

# Generate sample data from a lognormal distribution
np.random.seed(0)
data = np.random.lognormal(mean=0, sigma=1, size=1000)

# Create a Pandas DataFrame
df = pd.DataFrame({'Data': data})
# Next, we can plot a histogram of the data to get visual insights
```

```
into the distribution:
# Plot a histogram of the data
plt.hist(data, bins=30, color='skyblue', edgecolor='black')
plt.title('Histogram of Data')
plt.xlabel('Value')
plt.ylabel('Frequency')
plt.show()
```

The resulting histogram shows a very clear skew, making a `Normal` distribution unlikely and a `lognormal` distribution the likely best choice (unsurprisingly, given how the sample data was generated):

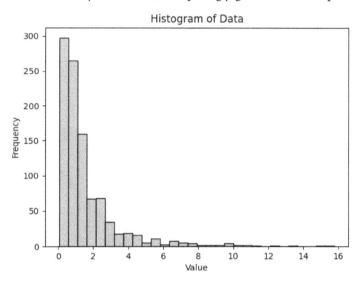

Figure 8.6 – Histogram of the data

Next, we can perform some basic statistical analysis to confirm our suspicions from the histogram – starting with a Shapiro-Wilk test for normality, then plotting a Q-Q plot for the `Normal` distribution, and finally, a Q-Q plot against the suspected distribution of `lognormal`:

```
# Perform the Shapiro-Wilk test for normality
shapiro_stat, shapiro_p = stats.shapiro(data)
is_normal = shapiro_p > 0.05  # Check if data is normally distributed
print(f'Shapiro-Wilk p-value: {shapiro_p}')
print(f'Is data normally distributed? {is_normal}')

# Create Q-Q plot with a Normal distribution
sm.qqplot(data, line='s', color='skyblue')
plt.title('Q-Q Plot (Normal)')
plt.xlabel('Theoretical Quantiles')
```

```
plt.ylabel('Sample Quantiles')
plt.show()

# Create Q-Q plot with a lognormal distribution
log_data = np.log(data)
sm.qqplot(log_data, line='s', color='skyblue')
plt.title('Q-Q Plot (Lognormal)')
plt.xlabel('Theoretical Quantiles')
plt.ylabel('Sample Quantiles')
plt.show()
```

The first Q-Q plot shows that the Normal distribution is a very poor fit for the data:

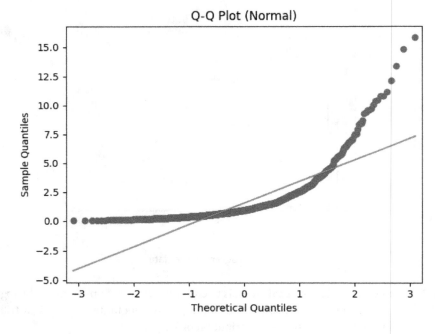

Figure 8.7 – Q-Q plot for the normal distribution

The next Q-Q plot, this time for the lognormal distribution, shows a near-perfect fit, on the other hand:

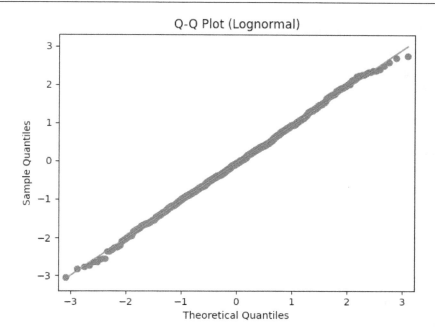

Figure 8.8 – Q-Q plot for the lognormal distribution

Finally, we calculate skewness and kurtosis to be sure we are on the right track and print all the results:

```
# Calculate skewness and kurtosis
skewness = stats.skew(data)
kurtosis = stats.kurtosis(data)

print(f'Skewness: {skewness}')
print(f'Kurtosis: {kurtosis}')
```

From the histogram, the Shapiro-Wilk test rejecting the hypothesis of a `normal` distribution, the two Q-Q plots, and the skewness and kurtosis estimators, we can conclude beyond reasonable doubt that the data was indeed generated from a `lognormal` distribution!

It is now time to move on from single-variable analyses to the relationship between multiple variables.

Associations between variables

Explore relationships between variables through scatter plots and correlation matrices. Identify any strong correlations or dependencies between features. This step can guide feature selection or engineering in later stages of analysis. In this section, we'll delve into methods to investigate these relationships using Python.

We will use the following libraries and sample dataset:

```python
import pandas as pd
import numpy as np
import seaborn as sns
import matplotlib.pyplot as plt
import ppscore as pps

# Generate test data with three variables
np.random.seed(0)
data = {
    'Feature1': np.random.randn(100),
    'Feature2': np.random.randn(100) * 2,
}

# Create a linear Target variable based on Feature1 and a non-linear
function of Feature2
data['Target'] = data['Feature1'] * 2 + np.sin(data['Feature2']) +
np.random.randn(100) * 0.5

# Create a DataFrame
df = pd.DataFrame(data)
```

You can adapt this code to analyze relationships between variables in your Excel data as you have learned in previous chapters.

Correlation heat map

One of the most common ways to assess relationships is by plotting a correlation heat map. This heat map provides a visual representation of the correlations between numerical variables in your dataset. Using libraries such as `Seaborn`, you can create an informative heat map that color-codes correlations, making it easy to identify strong and weak relationships.

Let's take a look at how to do that:

```python
# Calculate and plot the correlation heatmap
corr_matrix = df.corr()
plt.figure(figsize=(8, 6))
sns.heatmap(corr_matrix, annot=True, cmap='coolwarm', fmt=".2f",
    linewidths=.5)
plt.title('Correlation Heatmap')
plt.show()
```

In this code, we create a correlation heat map to visualize the relationships between these variables. The resulting heat map gives nice insights:

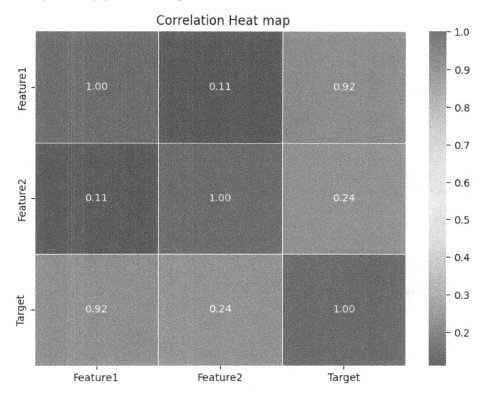

Figure 8.9 – Correlation heat map

Predictive Power Score (PPS)

Beyond traditional correlation measures, the PPS offers insights into non-linear relationships and predictive capabilities between variables. PPS quantifies how well one variable can predict another.

Now, we'll demonstrate how to calculate and visualize PPS matrices using the ppscore library, giving you a deeper understanding of your data's predictive potential:

```
# Calculate the Predictive Power Score (PPS)
plt.figure(figsize=(8, 6))
matrix_df = pps.matrix(df)[['x', 'y', 'ppscore']].pivot(columns='x',
    index='y', values='ppscore')
sns.heatmap(matrix_df, vmin=0, vmax=1, cmap="Blues", linewidths=0.5,
    annot=True)
```

```
plt.title("Predictive Power Score (PPS) Heatmap")
plt.show()

# Additional insights
correlation_target = df['Feature1'].corr(df['Target'])
pps_target = pps.score(df, 'Feature1', 'Target') ['ppscore']

print(f'Correlation between Feature1 and Target: {correlation_
target:.2f}')
print(f'Predictive Power Score (PPS) between Feature1 and Target:
{pps_target:.2f}')
```

In this code snippet, we calculate the PPS matrix, which measures the predictive power of each feature with respect to the Target variable. Finally, we calculate the correlation and PPS specifically between Feature1 and the Target variable. The results of the PPS heat map help gain further insights into the relationship between the variables:

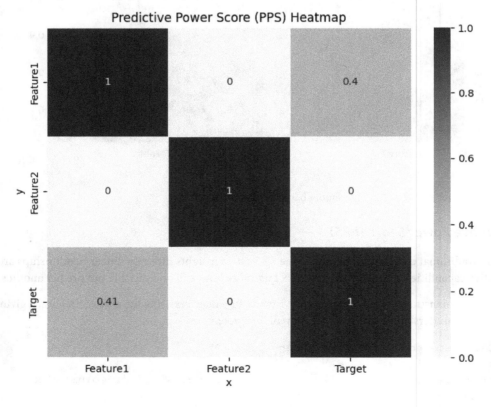

Figure 8.10 – PPS heat map

Scatter plots

Scatter plots are another valuable tool for visualizing relationships. They allow you to explore how two numerical variables interact by plotting data points on a 2D plane. We covered creating scatter plots in *Chapter 6*.

Visualizing key attributes

Visualization is a powerful tool for understanding your data. You can create various plots and charts to visualize key attributes of the dataset. For numerical data, histograms, box plots, and scatter plots can reveal data distributions, outliers, and potential correlations. Categorical data can be explored through bar charts and pie charts, displaying frequency distributions and proportions. These visualizations provide insights that may not be apparent in summary statistics alone. We covered these methods in *Chapter 6*.

Summary

In this chapter, we delved into two pivotal processes: data cleaning and EDA using R and Python, with a specific focus on Excel data.

Data cleaning is a fundamental step. We learned how to address missing data, be it through imputation, removal, or interpolation. Dealing with duplicates was another key focus, as Excel data, often sourced from multiple places, can be plagued with redundancies. Ensuring the correct assignment of data types was emphasized to prevent analysis errors stemming from data type issues.

In the realm of EDA, we started with summary statistics. These metrics, such as mean, median, standard deviation, and percentiles for numerical features, grant an initial grasp of data central tendencies and variability. We then explored data distribution, understanding which is critical for subsequent analysis and modeling decisions. Lastly, we delved into the relationships between variables, employing scatter plots and correlation matrices to unearth correlations and dependencies among features.

By mastering these techniques, you're equipped to navigate Excel data intricacies. You can ensure data quality and harness its potential for informed decision making. Subsequent chapters will build on this foundation, allowing you to perform advanced analysis and visualization to extract actionable insights from your Excel datasets.

In the next chapter, we will put the cleaned and explored data to good use: we will start with **statistical analysis**, in particular, with linear and logistic regression.

## 9

Statistical Analysis: Linear and Logistic Regression

Welcome to our comprehensive guide on linear and logistic regression using R and Python, where we will explore these essential statistical techniques using two popular frameworks: tidymodels and base R and Python. Whether you're a data science enthusiast or a professional looking to sharpen your skills, this tutorial will help you gain a deep understanding of **linear** and **logistic regression** and how to implement them in R and Python. Now, it is possible to perform linear and logistic regression. The issue here is that linear regression can only be performed on a single series of ungrouped data, and performing logistic regression is cumbersome and may require the use of external solver add-ins. Also, the process can only be performed against ungrouped or non-nested data. In R and Python, we do not have such limitations.

In this chapter, we will cover the following topics in both base R and Python and using the tidymodels framework:

- Performing linear regression in both base R and Python and the tidymodels frameworks as well as in Python
- Performing logistic regression in both base R and Python and the tidymodels frameworks as well as in Python

Technical requirements

All code for this chapter can be found on GitHub at this URL: https://github.com/PacktPublishing/Extending-Excel-with-Python-and-R/tree/main/Chapter9. You will need the following R packages installed to follow along:

- readxl 1.4.3
- performance 0.10.8
- tidymodels 1.1.1
- purrr 1.0.2

We will begin by learning about what linear and logistic regression are and then move into the details of everything.

Linear regression

Linear regression is a fundamental statistical method used for modeling the relationship between a dependent variable (usually denoted as "Y") and one or more independent variables (often denoted as "X"). It aims to find the best-fitting linear equation that describes how changes in the independent variables affect the dependent variable. Many of you may know this as the **ordinary least squares** (**OLS**) method.

In simpler terms, linear regression helps us predict a continuous numeric outcome based on one or more input features. For this to work, if you are unaware, many assumptions must be held true. If you would like to understand these more, then a simple search will bring you a lot of good information on them. In this tutorial, we will delve into both simple linear regression (one independent variable) and multiple linear regression (multiple independent variables).

Logistic regression

Logistic regression is another crucial statistical technique, which is primarily used for binary classification problems. Instead of predicting continuous outcomes, logistic regression predicts the probability of an event occurring, typically expressed as a "yes" or "no" outcome. This method is particularly useful for scenarios where we need to model the likelihood of an event, such as whether a customer will churn or not or whether an email is spam or not. Logistic regression models the relationship between the independent variables and the log odds of the binary outcome.

Frameworks

We will explore two approaches to implementing linear and logistic regression in R. First, we will use the base R framework, which is an excellent starting point to understand the underlying concepts and functions. Then, we will dive into `tidymodels`, a modern and tidy approach to modeling and machine learning in R. `tidymodels` provides a consistent and efficient way to build, tune, and evaluate models, making it a valuable tool for data scientists. In Python, we will parallel this exploration with two prominent libraries: `sklearn` and `statsmodels`. `sklearn`, or Scikit-learn, offers a wide array of simple and efficient tools for predictive data analysis that are accessible to everybody and reusable in various contexts. `statsmodels` is more focused on statistical models and hypothesis tests. Together, these Python libraries offer a robust framework for implementing linear and logistic regression, catering to both machine learning and statistical needs.

Throughout this chapter, we will provide step-by-step instructions, code examples, and practical insights to ensure that you can confidently apply linear and logistic regression techniques to your own data analysis projects.

Let's embark on this learning journey and unlock the power of regression analysis in R! With this in place, we move to the first example in base R using the `iris` dataset we saved in *Chapter 1*.

Performing linear regression in R

For this section, we are going to perform linear regression in R, both in base R and by way of the `tidymodels` framework. In this section, you will learn how to do this on a dataset that has different groups in it. We will do this because if you can learn to do it this way, then doing it in a single group becomes simpler as there is no need to group data and perform actions by group. The thought process here is that by doing it on grouped data, we hope you can learn an extra skill.

Linear regression in base R

The first example we are going to show is using the `lm()` function to perform a linear regression in base R. Let's dive right into it with the `iris` dataset.

We will break the code down into chunks and discuss what is happening at each step. The first step for us is to use the `library` command to bring in the necessary packages into our development environment:

```
library(readxl)
```

In this section, we're loading a library called `readxl`. Libraries are collections of pre-written R functions and code that we can use in our own R scripts. In this case, we're loading the `readxl` library, which is commonly used for reading data from Excel files. The path assumes you have a `chapter1` folder and a data file in it called `iris_data.xlsx`:

```
df <- read_xlsx(
    path = "chapter1/iris_data.xlsx",
    sheet = "iris"
)
head(df)
```

Here, we're reading data from an Excel file named `iris_data.xlsx`, located in the `chapter1` folder. We're specifically reading the `iris` sheet from that Excel file. The `read_xlsx` function is used for this purpose. The resulting data is stored in a variable called `df`. The `head(df)` function displays the first few rows of this data frame (`df`) so we can see what it looks like:

```
iris_split <- split(df, df$species)
```

This code splits the `df` dataset into multiple subsets based on the unique values in the `species` column. The result is a list of data frames where each data frame contains only the rows that correspond to a specific species of `iris`.

Now, we are going to define what will be the dependent and independent variables along with the `formula` object:

```
dependent_variable <- "petal_length"
independent_variables <- c("petal_width", "sepal_length", "sepal_
width")
f_x <- formula(
  paste(
dependent_variable,
"~",
paste(independent_variables, collapse = " + ")
)
)
```

Here, we're defining the variables needed for linear regression. `dependent_variable` is `petal_length`, which is the variable we want to predict. `independent_variables` are `petal_width`, `sepal_length`, and `sepal_width`, which are the variables we'll use to predict the dependent variable.

The code then creates an `f_x` formula that represents the linear regression model. It essentially says that we want to predict `petal_length` using the other variables listed, separated by a plus sign:

```
perform_linear_regression <- function(data) {
  lm_model <- lm(f_x, data = data)
  return(lm_model)
}
```

In this part, we're defining a custom R function called `perform_linear_regression`. This function takes one `data` argument, which is a data frame. Inside the function, we use the `lm` function to perform linear regression, using the `f_x` formula we defined earlier and the provided data frame. The resulting linear model is stored in `lm_model`, and we return it as the output of the function:

```
results <- lapply(iris_split, perform_linear_regression)
```

Here, we're applying the `perform_linear_regression` function to each subset of the `iris` dataset using the `lapply` function. This means that we're running linear regression separately for each species of iris, and the results are stored in the `results` list:

```
lapply(results, summary)
```

This code uses `lapply` again, but this time we're applying the `summary` function to each linear regression model in the `results` list. The `summary` function provides statistical information about the linear regression model, such as coefficients and R-squared values:

```
par(mfrow = c(2,2))
lapply(results, plot)
par(mfrow = c(1, 1))
```

These lines of code are used to create a set of four plots to visualize the model performance. We first set the layout of the plots to be a 2x2 grid using `par(mfrow = c(2,2))`, so that 4 plots will be displayed in a 2x2 grid. Then, we use `lapply` to plot each linear regression model in the `results` list. Finally, we reset the plot layout to the default with `par(mfrow = c(1, 1))`:

```
lm_models <- lapply(
iris_split,
function(df) lm(f_x, data = df)
)
```

This part accomplishes the same linear regression analysis as before but combines the linear model creation and summarization into a more concise form using anonymous functions. It first applies the `lm` function to each species subset within `iris_split`, creating a list of linear models stored in `lm_models`. Then, it uses `lapply` to obtain summaries for each of these linear models.

In summary, this R code reads iris data from an Excel file, performs linear regression for each species of `iris`, summarizes the results, and creates visualizations to assess the model's performance. It provides a detailed analysis of how the dependent variable (`petal_length`) is influenced by independent variables (`petal_width`, `sepal_length`, and `sepal_width`) for each species of `iris`.

Linear regression with tidymodels and purrr

Now that we have gone over how to perform a simple linear regression in R on the `iris` dataset, we will do the same with the `tidymodels` framework. Let's dive right into it:

```
f_x <- formula(paste("petal_width", "~", "petal_length + sepal_width +
sepal_length"))
```

This block defines a formula for the linear regression model. The `formula()` function takes two arguments: the response variable and the predictor variables. The response variable is the variable that we want to predict, and the predictor variables are the variables that we think can help us predict the response variable. In this case, the response variable is `petal_width` and the predictor variables are `petal_length`, `sepal_width`, and `sepal_length`:

```
library(dplyr)
library(tidyr)
library(purrr)
library(tidymodels)
nested_lm <- df |>
 nest(data = -species) |>
 mutate(split = map(data, ~ initial_split(., prop = 8/10)),
        train = map(split, ~ training(.)),
        test = map(split, ~ testing(.)),
        fit  = map(train, ~ lm(f_x, data = .)),
        pred = map2(.x = fit, .y = test, ~ predict(object = .x,
newdata = .y)))
```

This block creates a nested linear regression model using the `nest()` function from the `tidyr` package. The `nest()` function groups the data by a specified variable, in this case, the `species` variable.

For each group, the `nest()` function creates a list containing the data for that group. The `mutate()` function is then used to add new columns to the nested data frame.

The `split()` function is used to randomly split the data in each group into a training set and a test set. The `training()` and `testing()` functions are then used to select the training and test sets, respectively. With `map()` and `map2()`, we can iterate over a vector or list or two vectors or lists and apply a function to them.

The `lm()` function is used to fit a linear regression model to the training data in each group. The `predict()` function is then used to predict the response variable for the test data in each group using the fitted linear regression model:

```
nested_lm |>
  select(species, pred) |>
  unnest(pred)
```

This block selects the `species` and `pred` columns from the nested data frame and unnests the `pred` column. The `unnest()` function converts the nested data frame to a regular data frame, with one row for each observation.

The resulting data frame is a nested linear regression model, with one fitted linear regression model for each species.

Let's take a look at an example. We are going to use the `f_x` formula that was created earlier along with the `df` tibble variable we created at the beginning. The following code shows an example of how to use the nested linear regression model to predict the petal width for a new iris flower:

```
library(dplyr)
library(tidyr)
library(purrr)
library(tidymodels)
# Create a nested linear regression model
nested_lm <- df |>
 nest(data = -species) |>
 mutate(split = map(data, ~ initial_split(., prop = 8/10)),
        train = map(split, ~ training(.)),
        test = map(split, ~ testing(.)),
        fit  = map(train, ~ lm(f_x, data = .)),
        pred = map2(.x = fit, .y = test, ~ predict(object = .x,
newdata = .y)))
# Predict the petal width for a new iris flower
new_iris <- data.frame(sepal_length = 5.2, sepal_width = 2.7,
    petal_length = 3.5)
```

```
# Predict the petal width
predicted_petal_width <- predict(nested_lm[[1]]$fit,
    newdata = new_iris))
# Print the predicted petal width
print(predicted_petal_width)
```

Here's the output:

```
1.45
```

The predicted petal width is 1.45 cm. We have now finished going over linear regression in R with a basic example. We will now continue the chapter in the next section on performing logistic regression in R.

Performing logistic regression in R

As we did in the section on linear regression, in this section, we will also perform logistic regression in base R and with the `tidymodels` framework. We are going to only perform a simple binary classification regression problem using the `Titanic` dataset, where we will be deciding if someone is going to survive or not. Let's dive right into it.

Logistic regression with base R

In order to get going, we are going to start with a base R implementation of logistic regression on the `Titanic` dataset where we will be modeling the response of `Survived`. So, let's get straight into it.

The following is the code that will perform the data modeling along with explanations of what is happening:

```
library(tidyverse)
df <- Titanic |>
      as.data.frame() |>
      uncount(Freq)
```

This block of code starts by loading a library called `tidyverse`, which contains various data manipulation and visualization tools. It then creates a data frame called `df` by taking the `Titanic` dataset (assuming it's available in your environment) and performing three operations on it using the `|>` operator, where we then use `as.data.frame()`, which converts the dataset into a data frame, followed by `uncount(Freq)`, which repeats each row in the dataset according to the value in the `Freq` column. This is often done to expand summarized data:

```
set.seed(123)
train_index <- sample(nrow(df), floor(nrow(df) * 0.8), replace =
FALSE)
train <- df[train_index, ]
test <- df[-train_index, ]
```

This section is about splitting the data into a training set and a test set, which is a common practice in machine learning:

- `set.seed(123)`: This sets a random seed for reproducibility, ensuring that random operations produce the same results each time.

- `sample(nrow(df), floor(nrow(df) * 0.8), replace = FALSE)`: This randomly selects 80% of the rows in the `df` data frame (the training set) without replacement and stores their indices in `train_index`.

- `train <- df[train_index, ]`: This creates the training set by selecting the rows from `df` using the `train_index` indices.

- `test <- df[-train_index, ]`: This creates the test set by selecting the rows from `df` that are not in the training set. We next create the model.

    ```
    model <- glm(Survived ~ Sex + Age + Class, data = train, family
    = "binomial")
    ```

Now let's discuss the model code as follows:

- This block trains a logistic regression model using the `glm` function.

- The model is trained to predict the `Survived` variable based on the `Sex`, `Age`, and `Class` variables in the training data. Here, `Age` is actually discrete.

- The `family = "binomial"` argument specifies that this is a binary classification problem, where the outcome is either `Yes` or `No`. The following link helps in choosing an appropriate family: `https://stats.stackexchange.com/a/303592/35448`.

Now, let's set up the model predictions and response variable:

```
predictions <- predict(model, newdata = test, type = "response")
pred_resp <- ifelse(predictions <= 0.5, "No", "Yes")
```

Now, let's go over what we just did:

- Here, we use the trained model to make predictions on the test set.

- `predict(model, newdata = test, type = "response")` calculates the predicted probabilities of survival for each passenger in the test set.

- `ifelse(predictions <= 0.5, "No", "Yes")` converts these probabilities into binary predictions: `"No"` if the probability is less than or equal to `0.5`, and `"Yes"` otherwise. This is common practice, but you must know your project first in order to determine if this is correct or not. Now, onto the `accuracy` variable:

    ```
    accuracy <- mean(pred_resp == test$Survived)
    ```

We created the `accuracy` variable by doing the following:

- This line calculates the accuracy of the model's predictions by comparing `pred_resp` (the model's predictions) to the actual survival status in the test set (`test$Survived`).

- It computes the mean of the resulting logical values, where `TRUE` represents a correct prediction, and `FALSE` represents an incorrect prediction. Let's now go over the rest of the code:

```
print(accuracy)
table(pred_resp, test$Survived)
```

The code prints two things:

- The accuracy of the model on the test set.

- A confusion matrix that shows how many predictions were correct and how many were incorrect. If you would like to understand confusion matrices more, here is a good link: `https://www.v7labs.com/blog/confusion-matrix-guide`.

In summary, this code loads a dataset, splits it into a training and test set, trains a logistic regression model to predict survival, evaluates the model's accuracy, and displays the results. It's a basic example of a binary classification machine learning workflow. Now that we have covered performing logistic regression for a classification problem in base R, we will try our hand at the same but this time using the `tidymodels` framework.

Performing logistic regression using tidymodels

In this section, we will use the `tidymodels` framework to perform the logistic regression on the `Titanic` dataset. Since we have done this in base R already, let's get right into it:

```
library(tidymodels)
library(healthyR.ai)
```

This code loads the two libraries that we will need for our analysis: `tidymodels` and `healthyR.ai`. `tidymodels` is a library that provides a common interface for many machine learning algorithms, while `healthyR.ai` provides a set of tools for evaluating the performance of machine learning models:

```
df <- Titanic |>
    as_tibble() |>
    uncount(n) |>
    mutate(across(where(is.character), as.factor))
```

This code converts the `Titanic` dataset to a `tibble`, which is a data structure that is compatible with `tidymodels`. It also uncounts the n column, which is a column that contains the number of times each row appears in the dataset and is created by the `uncount()` function. Finally, it converts all the character variables in the dataset to factors:

```
# Set seed for reproducibility
set.seed(123)
# Split the data into training and test sets
split <- initial_split(df, prop = 0.8)
train <- training(split)
test <- testing(split)
```

This code splits the `df` dataset into training and test sets. The training set is used to train the model, while the test set is used to evaluate the performance of the model on unseen data. The `initial_split()` function from `tidymodels` is used to perform the split. The `prop` argument specifies the proportion of the data that should be used for training. In this case, we are using 80% of the data for training and 20% of the data for testing:

```
# Create a recipe for pre-processing
recipe <- recipe(Survived ~ Sex + Age + Class, data = train)
# Specify logistic regression as the model
log_reg <- logistic_reg() |> set_engine("glm", family = "binomial")
# Combine the recipe and model into a workflow
workflow <- workflow() %>% add_recipe(recipe) %>% add_model(log_reg)
# Train the logistic regression model
fit <- fit(workflow, data = train)
```

This code trains a logistic regression model to predict survival on the Titanic. The `recipe()` function from `tidymodels` is used to pre-process the data. The `logistic_reg()` function from `tidymodels` is used to specify the logistic regression model. The `workflow()` function from `tidymodels` is used to combine the recipe and model into a workflow. Finally, the `fit()` function from `tidymodels` is used to train the model on the training data:

```
# Predict on the test set
predictions <- predict(fit, new_data = test) |> bind_cols(test) |>
select(Class:Survived, .pred_class)
# Better method
pred_fit_tbl <- fit |> augment(new_data = test)
```

This code predicts the survival probability for each passenger in the test set. The `predict()` function from `tidymodels` is used to make the predictions. The `new_data` argument specifies the data that we want to make predictions on. In this case, we are making predictions on the test set. The `bind_cols()` function is used to bind the predictions to the test set data. The `select()` function is used to select the columns that we want to keep. The `pred_fit_tbl` object is a `tibble` instance that contains the predictions from the model, as well as the ground truth survival labels. This object will be used to evaluate the performance of the model:

```
# Accuracy metrics for the model to be scored against from the
healthyR.ai package
perf <- hai_default_classification_metric_set()
# Calculate the accuracy metrics
perf(pred_fit_tbl, truth = Survived, estimate = .pred_class)
# Print the confusion matrix
predictions |> conf_mat(truth = Survived, estimate = .pred_class)
```

The accuracy check code block evaluates the performance of the model on the test set. It does this by using the `hai_default_classification_metric_set()` function from the healthyR. ai package to create a set of default classification metrics. These metrics include accuracy, precision, recall, and F1 score.

The `perf()` function is then used to calculate the accuracy metrics on the test set. The `pred_fit_tbl` object is the data frame that contains the predictions from the model, as well as the ground truth survival labels. The `truth` and `estimate` arguments specify the columns in the data frame that contain the ground truth and predicted labels, respectively.

The `conf_mat()` function is then used to print the confusion matrix for the model. The confusion matrix is a table that shows how many observations were correctly and incorrectly predicted by the model.

Finally, the `tidy()` and `glance()` functions from the `broom` package can be used to tidy and summarize the fitted model. The `tidy()` function converts the model object to a `tibble` instance, which is a data structure that is easy to work with. The `glance()` function prints a summary of the model, including the coefficients, standard errors, and p-values for all of the variables in the model.

Here is a simple explanation of each of the accuracy metrics that are calculated in the accuracy check code block:

- **Accuracy**: The accuracy of a model is the proportion of observations that are correctly predicted by the model.
- **Precision**: The precision of a model is the proportion of positive predictions that are correct.
- **Recall**: The recall of a model is the proportion of actual positive observations that are correctly predicted by the model.
- **F1 score**: The F1 score is a harmonic mean of the precision and recall metrics. It is a good overall measure of the performance of a model.

The confusion matrix is a helpful tool for understanding how the model is performing. The ideal confusion matrix would have all of the observations on the diagonal, indicating that all of the observations were correctly predicted. However, in practice, no model is perfect and there will be some observations that are incorrectly predicted.

Lastly, we will visualize the model with a **receiver operating characteristic (ROC)** curve. To read more about this type of curve, you can see the following link: `https://www.tmwr.org/performance`. Here is the code that creates the ROC curve:

```
roc_curve(
    pred_fit_tbl, truth = Survived, .pred_Yes,
    event_level = "second"
) |>
    autoplot()
```

Here is the output:

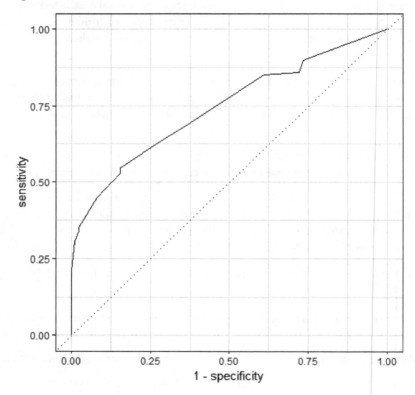

Figure 9.1 – ROC curve for the logistic regression model

Now, we have learned how to perform both linear and logistic regression in both base R and via the `tidymodels` modeling framework. We did this with the `Titanic` and `iris` datasets. Now, it's time to do the same in Python!

Performing linear regression in Python using Excel data

Linear regression in Python can be carried out with the help of libraries such as `pandas`, `scikit-learn`, `statsmodels`, and `matplotlib`. The following is a step-by-step code example:

1. First, import the necessary libraries:

```
# Import necessary libraries
import pandas as pd
import numpy as np
import matplotlib.pyplot as plt
from sklearn.model_selection import train_test_split
import statsmodels.api as sm
from statsmodels.graphics.regressionplots import plot_regress_
exog
from statsmodels.graphics.gofplots import qqplot
```

2. Then, we create an Excel file with test data. Of course, in a real-life scenario, you would not need the mock data – you would skip this step and load the data from Excel (see the next step) after loading the necessary libraries:

```
# Step 0: Generate sample data and save as Excel file
np.random.seed(0)
n_samples = 100
X = np.random.rand(n_samples, 2)   # Two features
y = 2 * X[:, 0] + 3 * X[:, 1] + np.random.randn(n_samples)
# Linear relationship with noise

# Create a pandas DataFrame
data = {'Feature1': X[:, 0], 'Feature2': X[:, 1], 'Target': y}
df = pd.DataFrame(data)

# Save the data to Excel
df.to_excel("linear_regression_input.xlsx")
```

3. Next, import the data from the Excel file with test data and prepare it for analysis using tools you have learned in the previous chapter:

```
# Step 1: Import Excel data into a pandas DataFrame
excel_file = "linear_regression_input.xlsx"
df = pd.read_excel(excel_file)

# Step 2: Explore the data
```

```
# Use the tools learned in the previous chapter on EDA

# Step 3: Data Preparation (if needed)
# Use the tools learned in the previous chapter on data cleaning
```

4. Now, we are ready to carry out the actual analysis. Split the data into training and test data so we can evaluate the model on a dedicated data (sub)set, then fit the **Ordinary Least Squares (OLS)** linear model on the training data:

```
# Step 4: Split data into training and testing sets
X = df[['Feature1', 'Feature2']] # Independent variables
y = df['Target'] # Dependent variable

# Split the data into training and test set using a fixed random
seed for reproducibility
X_train, X_test, y_train, y_test = train_test_split(X, y,
    test_size=0.2, random_state=42)

# Step 5: Fit the Linear Regression model
# Add a constant (intercept) to the independent variables
X_train = sm.add_constant(X_train)
X_test = sm.add_constant(X_test)

# Fit the linear model
model = sm.OLS(y_train, X_train).fit()
```

Note that doing imputation as part of the data cleaning process before splitting the test and training sets may lead to pollution of the test set from the training set. Be conscious of this when performing the data cleaning and preparation steps!

5. Next, evaluate the trained model on the test data:

```
# Step 6: Model Evaluation
y_pred = model.predict(X_test)

# Print the model summary
print(model.summary())
```

This will create summary statistics as the output that provides valuable insights into the relationships within your dataset:

```
>>> # Print the model summary
>>> print(model.summary())
                            OLS Regression Results
==============================================================================
Dep. Variable:                 Target   R-squared:                       0.521
Model:                            OLS   Adj. R-squared:                  0.508
Method:                 Least Squares   F-statistic:                     41.84
Date:                Wed, 14 Feb 2024   Prob (F-statistic):           5.02e-13
Time:                        10:19:13   Log-Likelihood:                 -108.46
No. Observations:                  80   AIC:                             222.9
Df Residuals:                      77   BIC:                             230.1
Df Model:                           2
Covariance Type:            nonrobust
==============================================================================
                 coef    std err          t      P>|t|      [0.025      0.975]
------------------------------------------------------------------------------
const          0.0449      0.296      0.152      0.880     -0.544       0.634
Feature1       1.5628      0.392      3.988      0.000      0.783       2.343
Feature2       3.0963      0.369      8.395      0.000      2.362       3.831
==============================================================================
Omnibus:                        0.261   Durbin-Watson:                   2.275
Prob(Omnibus):                  0.878   Jarque-Bera (JB):                0.319
Skew:                           0.130   Prob(JB):                        0.853
Kurtosis:                       2.833   Cond. No.                         5.57
==============================================================================

Notes:
[1] Standard Errors assume that the covariance matrix of the errors is correctly specified.
>>> []
```

Figure 9.2 – Summary statistics of the model fitted

Actual interpretation of model results is a topic that is beyond the scope of this book, but here are some hints to get you started:

- **Coefficients**: The coefficients associated with each independent variable (predictor) in the model tell you about the strength and direction of the relationship. A positive coefficient indicates a positive correlation, meaning that as the predictor increases, the target variable tends to increase as well. Conversely, a negative coefficient signifies a negative correlation.

- **Intercept**: The intercept represents the predicted value of the target variable when all predictor variables are set to zero. It's essential to consider the intercept's value in the context of your analysis.

- **R-squared (R^2)**: The R-squared value measures the goodness of fit of the model. It tells you the proportion of variance in the target variable that can be explained by the predictors. Higher R-squared values (closer to 1) indicate a better fit. Note that adding more variables will always increase this measure. A "better" fit might result in "overfitting," which is something we don't want. You may want to check model-fit selection criteria such as Mallow's Cp, AIC, BIC, and adjusted R-squared, which penalizes the number of parameters used to fit the model.

- **P-values**: P-values associated with coefficients help determine the statistical significance of each predictor. Lower p-values suggest greater significance (in the sense that it is stronger evidence to reject the null hypothesis). If a p-value is less than a chosen significance level (for example, 0.05), you can conclude that the predictor has a statistically significant effect on the target variable. Please be aware that there are good reasons to not rely on p-values alone; see the ongoing debate on p-hacking and related topics in statistical science.

- **Residuals**: Examining the residuals (the differences between the observed and predicted values) is crucial for assessing model performance. Ideally, residuals should be random, with no apparent patterns. Patterns in residuals may indicate model misspecification.

- **Confidence intervals**: Confidence intervals around coefficients provide a range within which the true population parameter is likely to lie. Wider intervals indicate greater uncertainty.

- **F-statistic**: The F-statistic tests the overall significance of the model. A small F-statistic suggests that the model doesn't explain much variance in the target variable, while a large value indicates a better overall fit.

- **Adjusted R-squared**: Adjusted R-squared adjusts the R-squared value for the number of predictors in the model. It helps you determine whether adding more predictors improves the model's fit.

By carefully examining these elements, you can gain insights into how well the linear model fits your data, the significance of predictor variables, and the overall quality of the model. This information is invaluable for making informed decisions and drawing meaningful conclusions from your analysis.

With the model trained and the fit evaluated, we can visualize the results to help with interpretation. The following code creates a scatterplot of predicted versus observed values:

```python
plt.scatter(X_test['Feature1'], y_test, color='blue', label='Actual')
plt.scatter(X_test['Feature1'], y_pred, color='red',
    label='Predicted')
plt.xlabel('Feature1')
plt.ylabel('Target')
plt.title('Linear Regression Prediction')
plt.legend()
plt.show()
```

Here is the scatterplot for it:

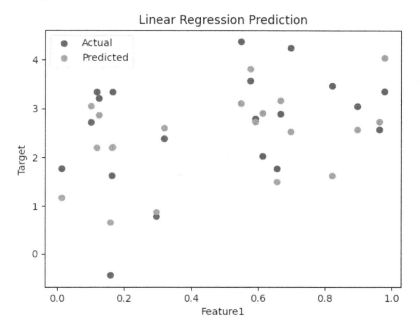

Figure 9.3 – Linear regression prediction plot

In addition, we can create diagnostic plots and visualizations such as residual plots and Q-Q plots, which can help you identify potential issues with the model, such as heteroscedasticity or outliers:

```
# Set the backend to 'TkAgg' before generating the plots if needed -
comment out this line if in WSL or other non-interactive environment
plt.switch_backend('TkAgg')
# Residuals
fig, ax = plt.subplots(figsize=(12, 8))
plot_regress_exog(model, "Feature1", fig=fig)
plt.show()


# Q-Q plot:
qqplot(model.resid, line="s")
plt.show()
```

The two preceding plots look like this:

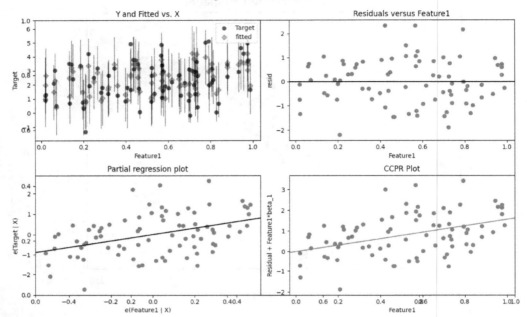

Figure 9.4 – Residuals plot

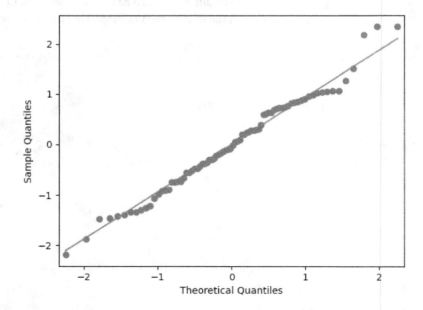

Figure 9.5 – Residuals Q-Q plot

Finally, we can export the results to Excel. This will be covered in detail in the next subsection.

As a side note, `scikit-learn` also has an in-built linear model but that does not come with the handy summary statistics we have used in the preceding code.

This code demonstrated a basic linear regression workflow using Python and Excel data. Let's move on to logistic regression!

Logistic regression in Python using Excel data

In the following code, we generate random sample data with two features (`Feature1` and `Feature2`) and a binary target variable (`Target`) based on a simple condition. We perform logistic regression, evaluate the model using accuracy, the confusion matrix, and a classification report, visualize the results for binary classification, and interpret the coefficients.

The following is a step-by-step code example:

1. Again, we start with importing the necessary libraries:

    ```
    # Import necessary libraries
    import pandas as pd
    import numpy as np
    import matplotlib.pyplot as plt
    from sklearn.model_selection import train_test_split
    from sklearn.linear_model import LogisticRegression
    from sklearn.metrics import accuracy_score, confusion_matrix,
    classification_report
    ```

    For this example, we will use a different sample dataset:

    ```
    # Step 0: Generate sample data
    np.random.seed(0)
    n_samples = 100
    X = np.random.rand(n_samples, 2)  # Two features
    y = (X[:, 0] + X[:, 1] > 1).astype(int)  # Binary classification
    based on a condition

    # Create a pandas DataFrame
    data = {'Feature1': X[:, 0], 'Feature2': X[:, 1], 'Target': y}
    df = pd.DataFrame(data)

    df.to_excel("logistic_regression_input.xlsx")
    ```

2. With your data available in Excel, we can read it and prepare it for the modeling step:

```
# Step 1: Import Excel data into a pandas DataFrame
excel_file = "logistic_regression_input.xlsx"
df = pd.read_excel(excel_file)

# Step 2: Split data into training and testing sets
X_train, X_test, y_train, y_test = train_test_split(X, y,
    test_size=0.2, random_state=42)
```

3. Now, we can create and fit a model. We will use the `scikit-learn` library this time:

```
# Step 3: Create and train the logistic regression model
model = LogisticRegression()
model.fit(X_train, y_train)
```

4. With a model fit, we can now visualize the results:

```
# Step 4: Visualization

# Visualization for binary classification
plt.scatter(X_test[y_test == 1][:, 0],
    X_test[y_test == 1][:, 1], color='blue',
    label='Class 1 (Actual)')
plt.scatter(X_test[y_test == 0][:, 0],
    X_test[y_test == 0][:, 1], color='red',
    label='Class 0 (Actual)')
plt.xlabel('Feature1')
plt.ylabel('Feature2')
plt.title('Logistic Regression Prediction')
plt.legend()
plt.show()
```

5. Unlike with linear regression, we need different goodness-of-fit metrics because we are using logistic regression for a binary classification:

```
# Step 5: Model Evaluation and Interpretation
y_pred = model.predict(X_test)

accuracy = accuracy_score(y_test, y_pred)
conf_matrix = confusion_matrix(y_test, y_pred)
class_report = classification_report(y_test, y_pred)

print("Accuracy:", accuracy)
print("Confusion Matrix:\n", conf_matrix)
print("Classification Report:\n", class_report)
```

The result looks like this:

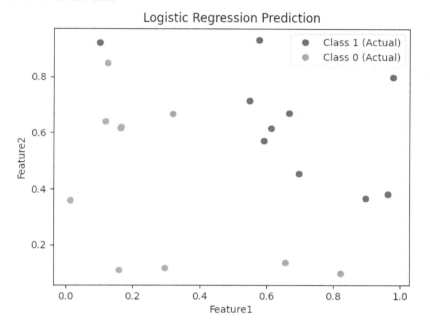

Figure 9.6 – Logistic regression prediction plot

This is the code result:

```
>>> print("Accuracy:", accuracy)
Accuracy: 0.9
>>> print("Confusion Matrix:\n", conf_matrix)
Confusion Matrix:
 [[ 8  2]
 [ 0 10]]
>>> print("Classification Report:\n", class_report)
Classification Report:
               precision    recall  f1-score   support

           0       1.00      0.80      0.89        10
           1       0.83      1.00      0.91        10

    accuracy                           0.90        20
   macro avg       0.92      0.90      0.90        20
weighted avg       0.92      0.90      0.90        20

>>> []
```

Figure 9.7 – Model summary statistics

To interpret the preceding results, you can start with the following:

- `Accuracy` is a fundamental metric, representing the ratio of correctly predicted instances to the total number of instances. While easy to understand, accuracy can be misleading if there's an imbalance between the classes.

- `Confusion Matrix` offers a more detailed view. It breaks down predictions into four categories: true positives, true negatives, false positives, and false negatives. This matrix provides a clear understanding of how well the model performs in terms of correctly classifying positive and negative instances.

- `Classification Report` provides a comprehensive summary. It includes metrics such as `precision`, `recall`, `f1-score`, and `support` for both classes. `Precision` measures how many predicted positives were actually positive, while `recall` quantifies how many actual positives were correctly predicted. The `F1-score` balances `precision` and `recall`. `Support` denotes the number of instances for each class. Together, these metrics offer a more nuanced evaluation of the model's performance in binary classification tasks.

You can use this sample data and code for testing and experimenting with logistic regression.

Please note that contrary to the popular (but incorrect) assertion, logistic regression can be used as a regression as well – what makes it a classifier is an arbitrary cut-off point for the predicted probability. For some use cases, you might want to use the raw regression output (if, for example, you are interested in the predicted probability of the data point belonging to a class, and not the more likely class only) and for others, you might want to play with the cut-off point (if, for example, there is pre-existing domain information that implies that 50% is not the right cut-off point).

That's it! Logistic regression is a relatively simple model with lots of benefits. It's performant, easy to fit, easy to interpret, and very versatile. It's most often used for classification with a domain-knowledge-driven cut-off point, but under the hood, it remains a regression method that can be used for predicting class probabilities.

Summary

In this chapter, we explored the powerful world of linear and logistic regression using Excel data. Linear regression, a fundamental statistical technique, allows us to model relationships between dependent and independent variables. We discussed its assumptions and applications, and walked through the entire process of loading data from Excel, preparing it for analysis, and fitting linear regression models using both R (using base R and `tidymodels`) and Python (with the `scikit-learn` and `statsmodels` libraries).

Through comprehensive code examples, you learned how to perform regression analysis, assess model accuracy, and generate valuable statistics and metrics to interpret model results. We gained insights into creating diagnostic plots, such as residual plots and Q-Q plots, which aid in identifying issues such as heteroscedasticity and outliers.

Additionally, we delved into logistic regression, a powerful tool for class probability prediction and binary classification tasks. We established its importance and applications and outlined the process of data preparation, model fitting, and metrics evaluation. With practical code examples, we observed how logistic regression models can be constructed using `tidymodels` in R and the `scikit-learn` library in Python.

By the end of this chapter, you should have a strong grasp of linear and logistic regression, from theory to practical application, and the ability to harness these techniques to analyze your data efficiently.

With these skills, you are well-equipped to conduct regression analyses and extract valuable insights from your data in Python.

On to the next chapter, where you will learn about time series analysis and its applications to Excel data.

10
Time Series Analysis: Statistics, Plots, and Forecasting

In the realm of mathematical analysis, particularly in the study of data and trends, time series charts play a pivotal role. A time series chart is a graphical representation that displays data points collected over a sequence of time intervals. This tool is indispensable in various fields, including economics, finance, environmental science, and social sciences, for analyzing patterns, trends, and fluctuations in data over time.

A typical time series chart comprises two essential components: the time axis and the data axis. The time axis represents the progression of time, which can be measured in various units, such as seconds, minutes, hours, days, months, or years. The data axis displays the values of the variable being studied, which can be anything from stock prices and temperature readings to population counts and sales figures.

To construct a time series chart, you must do the following:

- **Data collection**: Gather data points at regular time intervals or time stamps. These intervals should be consistent to accurately capture temporal patterns.

- **Data representation**: Plot the collected data points on the graph, aligning each point with its corresponding time stamp on the time axis.

- **Axis scaling**: Choose appropriate scaling for both the time axis and the data axis. This ensures that the patterns are visible and accurately represented.

- **Connect data points**: Depending on the context, data points can be connected with lines, curves, or bars. Connecting points can reveal trends more effectively.

A time series chart's primary function is to enable the analysis of trends, patterns, and anomalies in the data. Several insights can be gained from such analysis:

- **Trend identification**: Time series charts help identify long-term trends, such as gradual increases or decreases in values over time. These trends can provide valuable information for decision-making.

- **Seasonal variations**: Seasonal patterns, such as spikes in sales during holiday seasons, can be identified by observing regular fluctuations in the data over specific periods.

- **Cyclic patterns**: In addition to seasonal variations, cyclic patterns – repeating but irregular fluctuations – can be observed. These might be influenced by factors such as economic cycles or environmental changes.

- **Volatility and outliers**: Sudden spikes or dips in the data can indicate volatility or outliers, drawing attention to events or factors affecting the variable being measured.

Time series charts also serve as a foundation for forecasting and predictive analysis. Mathematical models can be applied to historical data to make predictions about future trends and values. It is important to note that when I say make predictions, I do mean that we are making inferences about what could be likely to happen if all things remain the same. Techniques such as moving averages, exponential smoothing, and **autoregressive integrated moving average** (**ARIMA**) models are commonly used for this purpose.

In the realm of mathematical analysis, a time series chart is a powerful tool that aids in understanding the dynamics of data over time. By visually representing data points and trends, it allows researchers, analysts, and decision-makers to extract valuable insights, identify patterns, and make informed predictions. Through the lens of mathematical analysis, time series charts provide a structured approach to comprehending temporal data, thereby contributing significantly to fields that rely on data-driven decision-making.

In this chapter, we'll cover the following topics:

- Generating random time series objects in R
- Time series plotting with R
- Auto ARIMA modeling with `healthyR.ts`
- Creating a Brownian motion with `healthyR.ts`
- Time series plotting – basic plots and ACF/PACF plots
- Time series statistics and statistical forecasting
- Time series forecasting with deep learning – LSTM

Technical requirements

There are a few technical requirements for this chapter. Note that the code for this chapter can be found at `https://github.com/PacktPublishing/Extending-Excel-with-Python-and-R/tree/main/Chapter%2010`.

Some of the packages that we will be using in this chapter are as follows:

- `healthyR.ts`
- `forecast`
- `timetk`
- `Modeltime`
- `prophet (for Python)`
- `keras`
- `tensorflow`

We will start by creating time series objects in base R. The basic object class for a time series object in R is `ts` and objects can be coerced to that object by either using the `ts()` function directly or calling `as.ts()` on an object such as a vector.

Generating random time series objects in R

We are going to generate some random time series objects in base R. Doing this is very simple as base R comes with some distribution functions already packed in. We will make use of the random normal distribution by making calls to the `rnorm()` function. This function has three parameters to provide arguments to:

- n: The number of points to be generated
- mean: The mean of the distribution, with a default of 0
- sd: The standard deviation of the distribution, with the default being 1

Let's go ahead and generate our first random vector. We will call it `x`:

```
# Generate a Random Time Series
# Set seed to make results reproducible
set.seed(123)
# Generate Random Points using a gaussian distribution with mean 0 and
sd = 1
n <- 25
x <- rnorm(n)
head(x)
```

```
[1] -0.56047565
-0.23017749  1.55870831  0.07050839  0.12928774  1.71506499
```

In the preceding code, we did the following:

- `set.seed(123)`: This line is all about ensuring that the random numbers that are generated in your code are consistent each time you run it. By setting a seed value (in this case, `123`), you ensure that the random numbers that are generated by your code will be the same every time you run it. This is useful for reproducibility in your analysis.

- `n <- 25`: Here, you're defining a variable called n and setting its value to 25. This variable represents the number of data points you want to generate in your random time series.

- `x <- rnorm(n)`: This is where the actual data generation happens. You're creating a new variable, x, and using the `rnorm()` function to generate random numbers. These numbers are drawn from a Gaussian (or normal) distribution, which is often called a bell curve. n specifies the number of random data points to generate, which in this case is 25.

- `head(x)`: Finally, you're using the `head()` function to display the first few values of the x variable. This helps you quickly inspect what the generated data looks like. It's a handy way to get a glimpse of your data without printing the entire dataset.

To summarize, this code sets a random seed for reproducibility, specifies the number of data points you want (25), and generates these data points from a Gaussian distribution, storing them in the x variable. Then, it shows the first few values of x using the `head()` function. This code is often used in data analysis and statistics when you need random data to work with or simulate real-world scenarios.

Now, let's convert this vector, x, into a time series object using the `ts()` function:

```
# Make x a ts object
ts_obj <- ts(x)
```

Let's check the class of the newly created object:

```
class(ts_obj)
[1] "ts"
```

We must do the same for its structure and attributes:

```
str(ts_obj)
 Time-Series [1:25] from 1 to 25: -0.5605 -0.2302 1.5587 0.0705 0.1293
...
attributes(ts_obj)
$tsp
[1]  1 25  1
$class
[1] "ts"
```

So, what happened exactly? Let's go over it in a simple yet concise manner.

This R code does the following:

- `ts_obj <- ts(x)`: This creates a time series object (`ts_obj`) from a vector or data series, x. This step converts x into a time series format.
- `class(ts_obj)`: This checks and displays the class of `ts_obj`. This should return `ts`, indicating that `ts_obj` is indeed a time series.
- `str(ts_obj)`: This line displays the structure of `ts_obj`, providing information about the time series. In this case, it shows that the time series has 25 data points ranging from 1 to 25, along with the values themselves.
- `attributes(ts_obj)`: This shows the attributes of the time series object. In this case, it displays the time span (`tsp`) with values of `1 25 1`, which means that the time series starts from period 1 and ends at period 25 with a frequency of 1.

So, this code essentially takes a vector, x, converts it into a time series object, and then provides information about the class and structure of the resulting time series. Now, let's visualize the time series by using the `plot` function. We can do this with `plot(ts_obj)`:

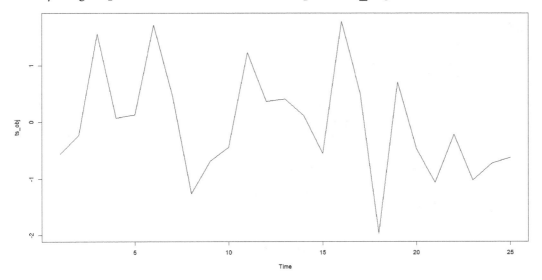

Figure 10.1 – Plot of a time series object from rnorm(25)

Now that we have covered how to coerce a vector into a time series object, we can discuss how to change the start, end, and frequency parameters.

Manipulating the time series parameters

Now, we are going to use the previous vector we created from `rnorm()` and convert it into different time series objects with different starts, ends, and frequencies. This sort of thing is very simple to do in base R.

Let's see some code manipulation first; then, we will go through and explain the examples:

```
# Change Start
ts(x, start = 1980)
ts(x, start = c(1980, 05))
ts(x, start = 1980, frequency = 12)
ts(x, start = 1980, frequency = 12/3)
# Change End
ts(x, end = 2023)
ts(x, end = 2023, frequency = 12)
ts(x, end = 2023, frequency = 12/3)
        Qtr1        Qtr2          Qtr3         Qtr4
2017 -0.56047565  -0.23017749   1.55870831   0.07050839
2018  0.12928774   1.71506499   0.46091621  -1.26506123
2019 -0.68685285  -0.44566197   1.22408180   0.35981383
2020  0.40077145   0.11068272  -0.55584113   1.78691314
2021  0.49785048  -1.96661716   0.70135590  -0.47279141
2022 -1.06782371  -0.21797491  -1.02600445  -0.72889123
2023 -0.62503927
```

Here are the explanations for each of the preceding examples. The last one in the preceding code block shows the output of the last manipulation:

- `ts(x, start = 1980)`: This creates a time series with a start date in 1980. The exact month and day are not specified, so the default is January 1, 1980.

- `ts(x, start = c(1980, 05))`: This sets the start date to May 1980 (year and month) explicitly.

- `ts(x, start = 1980, frequency = 12)`: This line creates a time series with a start date in 1980 and a monthly frequency, indicating that each data point represents one month.

- `ts(x, start = 1980, frequency = 12/3)`: This sets the start year to 1980 and specifies a frequency of 4, which means each data point is a quarter (three months) apart.

- `ts(x, end = 2023)`: This creates a time series with an end date in 2023. The start date is not specified here, so it defaults to the beginning of the series.

- `ts(x, end = 2023, frequency = 12)`: This line indicates that the end date is 2023 with a monthly frequency, assuming each data point represents one month.

- `ts(x, end = 2023, frequency = 12/3)`: This sets the end year to 2023 and specifies a frequency of 4, meaning each data point is a quarter (three months) apart.

These variations allow you to control the temporal characteristics of your time series data, such as the start and end points and the frequency of observations. Now that we have generated some data, let's plot it out.

Time series plotting

In this section, we will cover plotting time series objects, along with plotting some diagnostics such as decomposition. These plots include time series plots themselves, **autocorrelation function (ACF)** plots, and **partial autocorrelation function (PACF)** plots. We will start by using the AirPassengers dataset, which we will read in via the `readxl` package:

```
# Read the airpassengers.xlsx file in and convert to a ts object
starting at 1949
ap_ts <- read_xlsx("./Chapter 10/airpassengers.xlsx")  |>
  ts(start = 1949, frequency = 12)
# Plot the ts object
plot(ap_ts)
```

This produces the following chart:

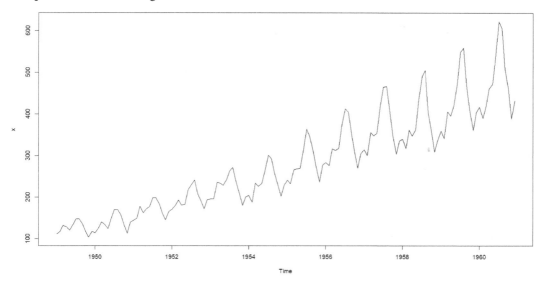

Figure 10.2 – Visualizing the AirPassengers time series dataset

From here, it is easy to see that the data has a trend and a seasonal cycle component. This observation will lead us to our next visual. We will decompose the data into its parts and visualize the decomposition. The decomposition of the time series breaks the data down into the following parts:

- The observed data
- The trend of the data
- The seasonal cycle of the data
- The remaining "randomness" or "residual/remainder"

Let's go ahead and see what it looks like. First, we have the code:

```
plot(decompose(ap_ts))
```

Here's the plot:

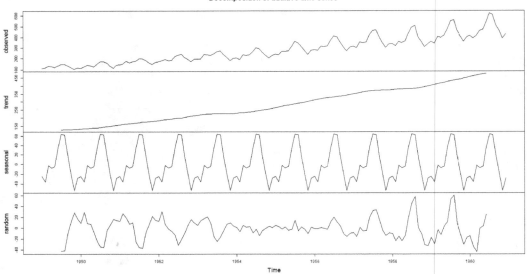

Figure 10.3 – Plot of a decomposed time series

Now that we have visualized the decomposition, we can start analyzing the ACF and PACF plots.

Creating ACF and PACF plots in R

In this section, we are going to cover ACF and PACF plots. An ACF plot is an autocorrelation function plot. An autocorrelation function is the relationship between a current observation in time against a previous observation in time. It tells you how correlated a current observation is compared to different lags of the same time series. So, if there is a strong seasonal demand for beer, you will see a strong correlation for them at the same seasonal period before it.

First, let's look at the output of the `acf()` function:

```
acf(ap_ts)
```

Here's the plot for it:

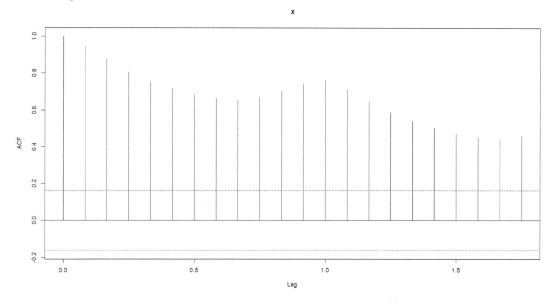

Figure 10.4 – ACF plot of the AirPassengers data

Here, we can see that all of the points are significantly related to their previous points because the data itself is trending upward. However, we can also see that there are peaks and valleys in the data, which is representative of the seasonal correlations.

Now, let's take a look at the PACF plot, which is also generated by the `acf()` function where the type is set to "partial."

The partial autocorrelation is the relationship between an observation, *t*, and some observation, *t-n*. With a relationship between *t* and the previous observations through *t-n* removed, the partial autocorrelation is the result of removing the effects of the terms at shorter lags. Now, let's look at the PACF of the same time series, `acf(ap_ts, type = "partial")`:

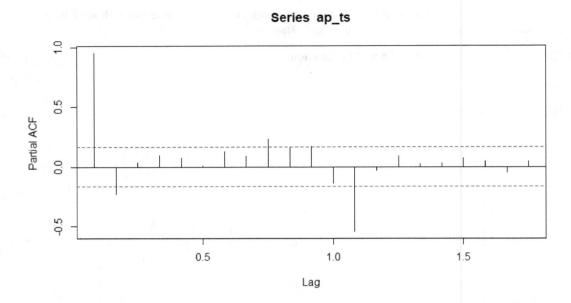

Figure 10.5 – PACF of the AirPassengers data

With that, we've gone over how to quickly create ACF and PACF plots in R. We have also provided a very quick overview of what they are. Now, let's learn how to model the time series with the `healthyR.ts` library.

Auto ARIMA modeling with healthyR.ts

Time series, just like any other set of data, can be modeled. The methods are vast, both old and new. In this section, we are going to discuss ARIMA modeling, and more specifically building an automatic ARIMA model with the `healthyR.ts` library in R. ARIMA models themselves attempt to describe the autocorrelations in the data.

In this section, we will use a workflow that ends with the `ts_auto_arima()` function creating and fitting a tuned model. This model requires our data to be in tibble format. So, to do this, we will use the AirPassengers dataset and make sure it is a tibble.

Let's get started with the dataset we have already brought in and coerce it into a tibble:

```
library(healthyR.ts)
library(dplyr)
library(timetk)
ap_tbl <- ts_to_tbl(ap_ts) |>
  select(-index)
> class(ap_tbl)
[1] "tbl_df"        "tbl"           "data.frame"
```

In the preceding code, we loaded the `healthyR.ts` and `dplyr` libraries and then took the already existing `ap_ts` time series object and converted it into a tibble using the `ts_to_tbl()` function from the `healthyR.ts` library. The next thing we have to do is create a train/test split using the `time_series_split()` function from the `timetk` library:

```
# Time Series Split
splits <- time_series_split(
   data = ap_tbl
   , date_var = date_col
   , assess = 12
   , skip = 3
   , cumulative = TRUE
)
> splits
<Analysis/Assess/Total>
<132/12/144>
```

Now that we have created the analysis/assess data splits, we are ready to run the main function. This function is intended to be a boilerplate function in that it will do most things automatically. However, you can always take the model and do what you wish with it. These boilerplate functions from `healthyR.ts` are not meant to be the end-all-be-all.

Let's run the function now and then take a look at the outputs:

```
Library(modeltime)
ts_auto_arima <- ts_auto_arima(
   .data = ap_tbl,
   .num_cores = 10,
   .date_col = date_col,
   .value_col = x,
   .rsamp_obj = splits,
   .formula = x ~ .,
   .grid_size = 20,
   .cv_slice_limit = 5,
   .tune = TRUE
)
```

In the preceding, we have provided the tibble that holds the data and the number of cores that we want to use – in our case, 10. Next, we supplied the column that holds the date – in this case, `date_col` – with the value column being x from our supplied tibble. Next up was our resampling object, splits, and then our formula, which gets passed to the recipe function internally to the `ts_auto_arima()` function. In this case, it is x against the date. We supply a grid size of 20 to make the tuning grid and a slice limit of 5 so that no more than five slices of data are generated. Most importantly, we set the `.tune` parameter to `TRUE`. This instructs the function to go ahead with model tuning. Model tuning can result in it taking a few seconds/minutes for data to be returned.

Let's look at the output. The first thing that we will look at is the recipe information:

```
> ts_auto_arima$recipe_info
$recipe_call
recipe(.data = ap_tbl, .date_col = date_col, .value_col = x,
    .formula = x ~ ., .rsamp_obj = splits, .tune = TRUE, .grid_size =
20,
    .num_cores = 10, .cv_slice_limit = 5)

$recipe_syntax
[1] "ts_arima_recipe <-"
[2] "\n  recipe(.data = ap_tbl, .date_col = date_col, .value_col = x,
.formula = x ~ \n       ., .rsamp_obj = splits, .tune = TRUE, .grid_size
= 20, .num_cores = 10, \n     .cv_slice_limit = 5)"

$rec_obj

── Recipe ──────────────────────────────────────────────


── Inputs
Number of variables by role
outcome:   1
predictor: 1
```

So, from the preceding output, we can see that we have both a single outcome and a predictor variable. This is all we need for an auto ARIMA model with no exogenous regressors.

Now, let's look at the model information:

```
ts_auto_arima
> ts_auto_arima$model_info
$model_spec
ARIMA Regression Model Specification (regression)

Main Arguments:
  seasonal_period = tune::tune()
  non_seasonal_ar = tune::tune()
  non_seasonal_differences = tune::tune()
  non_seasonal_ma = tune::tune()
  seasonal_ar = tune::tune()
  seasonal_differences = tune::tune()
  seasonal_ma = tune::tune()

Computational engine: arima
```

In the preceding code, we can see that all the parameters of the model are set to `tune::tune()`. This will allow the model to be run through the tuning grid:

```
$wflw
══ Workflow
Preprocessor: Recipe
Model: arima_reg()

── Preprocessor
0 Recipe Steps

── Model
ARIMA Regression Model Specification (regression)

Main Arguments:
  seasonal_period = tune::tune()
  non_seasonal_ar = tune::tune()
  non_seasonal_differences = tune::tune()
  non_seasonal_ma = tune::tune()
  seasonal_ar = tune::tune()
  seasonal_differences = tune::tune()
  seasonal_ma = tune::tune()

Computational engine: arima
```

The following workflow object that's created shows that the recipe has no steps to it as no transformations of any type are being performed:

```
$fitted_wflw
…
── Model
Series: outcome
ARIMA(4,1,2)(1,0,1)[12]

Coefficients:
         ar1      ar2      ar3      ar4      ma1      ma2     sar1     sma1
      -0.221   0.9020   0.0894  -0.2144   0.0477  -0.9523   0.9695  -0.0869
s.e.   0.092   0.0996   0.0958   0.0875   0.0367   0.0365   0.0143   0.0927

sigma^2 = 99.46:  log likelihood = -497.36
AIC=1012.72    AICc=1014.21    BIC=1038.6

$was_tuned
[1] "tuned"
```

The fitted workflow object shows that the best model that was selected was the `ARIMA(4,1,2)` `(1,0,1)[12]` model. It also gives us our coefficients and model AIC.

Next, we will take a look at the `model_calibration` object of the return output:

```
> ts_auto_arima$model_calibration
$plot

$calibration_tbl
# Modeltime Table
# A tibble: 1 × 5
  .model_id .model.model_desc.type .calibration_data
       <int> <list>        <chr>                          <chr> <list>
1            1 <workflow> ARIMA(4,1,2)(1,0,1)[12] Test  <tibble [12 ×
4]>

$model_accuracy
# A tibble: 1 × 9
  .model_id .model_desc.type    mae  mape  mase smape  rmse   rsq
       <int> <chr>                          <chr> <dbl> <dbl> <dbl>
<dbl> <dbl> <dbl>
1            1 ARIMA(4,1,2)(1,0,1)[12] Test    16.2  3.35
0.335   3.35  19.5 0.960
```

Here's the resulting plot:

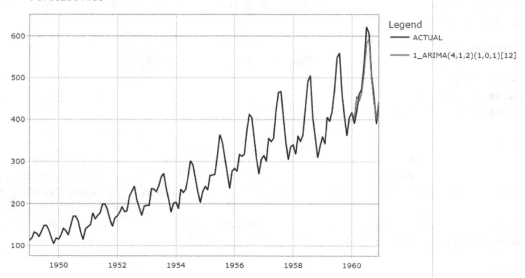

Figure 10.6 – Auto ARIMA calibration plot

Lastly, we are going to go over the `tuned_model` object of the return:

```
> ts_auto_arima$tuned_info
$tuning_grid
# A tibble: 20 × 7
   seasonal_period non_seasonal_ar non_seasonal_differences non_
seasonal_ma seasonal_ar
   <chr>            <int>            <int>                    <int>        <int>
 1 weekly              3                0                        1            2
 2 yearly              5                1                        4            0
# i 2 more variables: seasonal_differences <int>, seasonal_ma <int>


$tscv
# Time Series Cross Validation Plan
# A tibble: 5 × 2
  splits              id
  <list>              <chr>
1 <split [120/12]> Slice1
2 <split [117/12]> Slice2
3 <split [114/12]> Slice3
4 <split [111/12]> Slice4
5 <split [108/12]> Slice5


$tuned_results
# Tuning results
# NA
# A tibble: 5 × 4
  splits              id       .metrics                 .notes
  <list>              <chr>    <list>                   <list>
1 <split [120/12]> Slice1 <tibble [120 × 11]> <tibble [1 × 3]>
2 …
$grid_size
[1] 20
$best_metric
[1] "rmse"


$best_result_set
# A tibble: 1 × 13
   seasonal_period non_seasonal_ar non_seasonal_differences non_
seasonal_ma seasonal_ar
   <chr>            <int>            <int>                    <int>        <int>
1 yearly              4                1                        2            1
# i 8 more variables: seasonal_differences <int>, seasonal_ma <int>,
.metric <chr>,
```

```
#    .estimator <chr>, mean <dbl>, n <int>, std_err <dbl>, .config
<chr>
$tuning_grid_plot
`geom_smooth()` using method = 'loess' and formula = 'y ~ x'
$plotly_grid_plot
```

From the preceding code, we can see that there is a great deal of information that comes from this portion of what is returned from the function. This should contain everything you need to make an informed decision about whether you should keep tinkering or move on.

Let's look at the last plot, which is returned as both a static ggplot2 object and a plotly object:

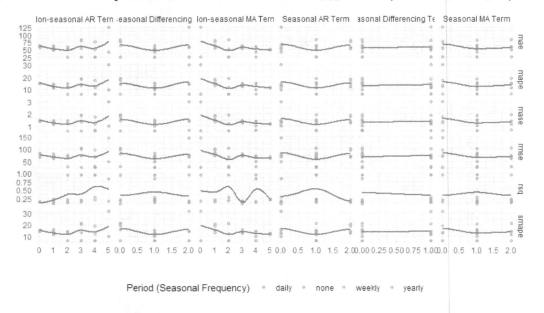

Figure 10.7 – The tuning grid of the auto ARIMA model

With this done, let us now see how Brownian motion concept works.

Creating a Brownian motion with healthyR.ts

The final time series plot that we are going to showcase is the **Brownian motion**. Brownian motion, also known as the *Wiener process*, is a fundamental concept in finance and mathematics that describes the random movement of particles in a fluid. In the context of finance, it is often used to model the price movement of financial instruments such as stocks, commodities, and currencies.

Here are some of the key characteristics of Brownian motion:

- **Randomness**: Brownian motion is inherently random. The future direction and magnitude of movement at any point in time cannot be predicted with certainty.

- **Continuous path**: The path of a Brownian motion is continuous, meaning that the asset's price can move smoothly without sudden jumps or gaps.

- **Independent increments**: The changes in the asset's price over non-overlapping time intervals are independent of each other. In other words, the price movement in one interval does not affect the price movement in another.

- **Gaussian distribution**: The increments of a Brownian motion (that is, the changes in price) are normally distributed, following a Gaussian or normal distribution. This is in line with the notion that in financial markets, small price changes are more common than large ones.

- **Constant variance**: The variance of the price increments remains constant over time. This is sometimes referred to as the **homoscedastic** property.

Mathematically, the movement of an asset's price, $S(t)$, over time, t, can be described using the stochastic differential equation:

Here, we have the following:

- $dS(t)$ is the infinitesimal change in the asset's price over a small time interval, dt

- μ is the drift or expected average rate of return of the asset over time

- σ is the volatility of the asset, representing the standard deviation of its price changes

- $dW(t)$ is the Wiener process, representing a random increment

The Brownian motion is a cornerstone of financial models such as the Black-Scholes option pricing model and the Vasicek interest rate model, among others. It helps in understanding and estimating the behavior of financial instruments by capturing their inherent randomness and volatility. However, it's important to note that real financial markets can deviate from a perfect Brownian motion due to factors such as market sentiment, news, and other external influences.

We can quickly generate a Brownian motion and plot its output with the `healthyR.ts` library. Here's the code:

```
library(healthyR.ts)
ts_brownian_motion() |>
  ts_brownian_motion_plot(t, y)
```

Here's the output of the preceding code. This is a random process, so your output will likely not match:

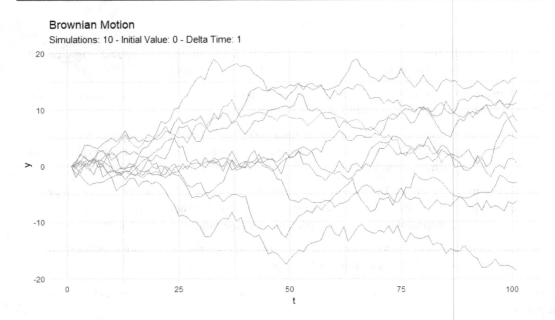

Figure 10.8 – Creating and viewing a Brownian motion with the healthyR.ts library

Now that we have gone over time series data in R, let's go over to Python and see how it is done there.

Time series analysis in Python – statistics, plots, and forecasting

Before diving into time series analysis, it's crucial to have data to work with. In this section, we'll walk through the process of creating mock time series data, saving it to an Excel file, and then reading it back into pandas. This will serve as our foundation for the upcoming time series analysis.

As always, we'll start by loading the relevant libraries:

```
import pandas as pd
import numpy as np
import matplotlib.pyplot as plt
```

Then, we must create the sample data and save it to Excel so that it can be used in the rest of this chapter:

```
# Create a date range
date_rng = pd.date_range(start='2022-01-01', end='2023-12-31',
    freq='D')

# Create a trend component
```

```
trend = 0.05 * np.arange(len(date_rng))

# Create a seasonal component (cyclicality)
seasonal = 2.5 * np.sin(2 * np.pi * np.arange(len(date_rng)) / 365)

# Add some random noise
noise = np.random.normal(0, 0.5, len(date_rng))

# Combine all components to create the time series
time_series = trend + seasonal + noise

# Create a DataFrame
df = pd.DataFrame({'Date': date_rng, 'Value': time_series})

# Save the data to an Excel file
df.to_excel('time_series_data.xlsx', index=False)
```

Finally, we must load the data from Excel and have a look at the loaded data, as follows:

```
# Read the data back into pandas
loaded_df = pd.read_excel('time_series_data.xlsx')

# Display the first few rows
print(loaded_df.head())
```

In this example, we generate a synthetic time series with a linear trend, sine-wave seasonal component, and random noise. This kind of dataset is more representative of real-world time series data, where patterns often involve a combination of these elements. The dataset is then saved to an Excel file, and you can read it back into Python for analysis as needed.

As we discussed in *Chapter 6*, the first step of analysis is plotting (insert sinister laugh)!

Time series plotting – basic plots and ACF/PACF plots

Visualizing time series data is a crucial step in understanding its underlying patterns and trends. In this section, we'll explore various time series plots and how to create them using Python. These visualizations help us gain insights into seasonality, trends, and autocorrelation within the time series data.

We'll start by loading the required libraries:

```
import pandas as pd
import numpy as np
import matplotlib.pyplot as plt
import statsmodels.api as sm
from statsmodels.graphics.tsaplots import import plot_acf, plot_pacf
```

Then, we must load the data from Excel and ensure the date information is converted correctly:

```
# Load time series data (replace 'time_series_data.xlsx' with your
data file)
data = pd.read_excel('time_series_data.xlsx')

# Convert the 'Date' column to datetime format and set it as the index
data['Date'] = pd.to_datetime(data['Date'])
data.set_index('Date', inplace=True)
```

Now, we can create a basic plot of the time series for a first look:

```
# Plot the time series
plt.figure(figsize=(12, 6))
plt.plot(data['Value'])
plt.title('Time Series Plot')
plt.xlabel('Date')
plt.ylabel('Value')
plt.grid(True)
plt.show()
```

This is what the plot looks like:

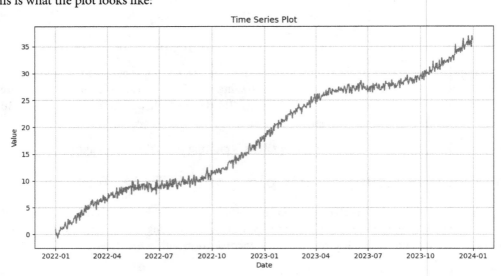

Figure 10.9 - Caption

Next, we must create the more advanced ACF and PACF plots with the following code:

```
# ACF and PACF plots
fig, (ax1, ax2) = plt.subplots(2, 1, figsize=(12, 8))

# ACF plot
plot_acf(data['Value'], lags=10, ax=ax1)
ax1.set_title('Autocorrelation Function (ACF)')

# PACF plot
plot_pacf(data['Value'], lags=40, ax=ax2)
ax2.set_title('Partial Autocorrelation Function (PACF)')

plt.tight_layout()
plt.show()
```

The resulting plots are shown here:

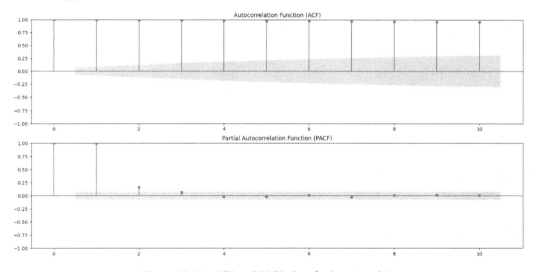

Figure 10.10 – ACF and PACF plots for lags 1 and 2

Here, we started by loading the time series data from an Excel file and converting the **Date** column into a datetime index. Then, we created a time series plot to visualize the data over time. Additionally, we generated ACF and PACF plots to explore autocorrelation patterns within the time series. These plots are valuable for identifying potential lag values for time series models.

Now, let's have a look at how ACF and PACF plots help with gaining insights into time series data. In particular, we'll see how they can be used to understand seasonality, trends, and autocorrelation.

Autocorrelation function (ACF) plot

The ACF plot shows the correlation between a time series and its lagged values. In other words, it quantifies how well the current value of the series is correlated with its past values.

Peaks in the ACF plot at specific lags indicate potential seasonality or periodic patterns in the data. For instance, a significant peak at lag 7 in a daily series suggests a weekly seasonality, while a peak at lag 12 in a monthly series may indicate a yearly seasonality.

By analyzing the ACF plot, you can identify the lag values at which correlations significantly deviate from zero. These lags can provide insights into the seasonality of the data. Additionally, identifying exponential decay in ACF can suggest an autoregressive component in your time series model.

Partial autocorrelation function (PACF) plot

The PACF plot measures the direct relationship between a time series and its lagged values while removing the effects of intermediate lags.

Peaks in the PACF plot at specific lags indicate the number of lagged values that directly impact the current value of the series. For example, a significant peak at lag 1 and no significant peaks beyond that suggest a first-order **autoregressive (AR)** process.

The PACF plot helps in determining the order of autoregressive terms (p) in ARIMA models. It can also reveal abrupt changes in the time series, indicating structural breaks or shifts.

By analyzing these plots in conjunction with your time series data, you can gain valuable insights into the presence of seasonality, trends, and autocorrelation. These insights are instrumental in selecting appropriate time series models and making accurate forecasts.

The plots shown in *Figure 10.9* show that for the PACF plot, only lag 1 has a strong autocorrelation, while the ACF plot is tricked by the way the random data was generated and shows a high autocorrelation across all lags investigated.

With the insights gained from these plots, we can move on to the meat of the matter: statistical analysis and forecasting

Time series statistics and statistical forecasting

Data exploration and statistical analysis are crucial steps in understanding the characteristics of time series data. In this section, we'll walk you through how to perform data exploration and apply statistical analysis techniques in Python to gain valuable insights into your time series.

Statistical analysis for time series data

After exploring the data using the plots in the previous section, let's move on to statistical analysis to gain a deeper understanding. This section focuses on two areas:

- **The Augmented Dickey-Fuller (ADF) test**: This statistical test is used to determine whether the time series data is stationary. Stationary data is easier to model and forecast.

- **Time series decomposition**: Time series decomposition separates the data into its constituent components: trend, seasonality, and residuals. This decomposition aids in isolating patterns for forecasting.

We'll understand both of these in the following sections.

The ADF test

The ADF test is a statistical method that's used to evaluate the *stationarity* of a time series. Stationarity is a fundamental concept in time series analysis as it simplifies the modeling process. A stationary time series has statistical properties, such as constant mean and variance, that do not change over time. Non-stationary data, on the other hand, exhibits trends or seasonality, making it challenging to model and forecast accurately.

In the ADF test, the null hypothesis (H0) assumes that the data is non-stationary. The alternative hypothesis (H1) suggests that the data is stationary. By analyzing the p-value obtained from the test, you can determine whether to reject the null hypothesis. A low p-value (typically less than 0.05) indicates that the data is stationary, while a high p-value suggests non-stationarity. Therefore, when conducting the ADF test, a p-value less than 0.05 is an indicator of a stationary time series.

Here is a code sample that implements the ADF test in Python using our trusty `statsmodels` library:

```python
from statsmodels.tsa.stattools import adfuller
import pandas as pd

# Read the data back into pandas
df = pd.read_excel('time_series_data.xlsx')

# Augmented Dickey-Fuller Test
adf_result = adfuller(df['Value'])
print("\nAugmented Dickey-Fuller Test:")
print(f"ADF Statistic: {adf_result[0]}")
print(f"P-value: {adf_result[1]}")
print("Null Hypothesis (H0): Data is non-stationary")
print("Alternative Hypothesis (H1): Data is stationary")

if adf_result[1] <= 0.05:
    print("Result: Reject the null hypothesis. Data is stationary.")
```

```
else:
    print("Result: Failed to reject the null hypothesis. Data is non-
stationary.")
```

Not surprisingly, we failed to reject the null hypothesis as the time series data we generated earlier has a clear linear trend and hence it is not stationary.

For further insights, we can analyze the detailed output further:

```
>>> # Print ADF test results
>>> print("Test Statistic:", adf_result[0])
Test Statistic: -0.24536819384067887
>>> print("p-value:", adf_result[1])
p-value: 0.9328933413659218
>>> print("Lags Used:", adf_result[2])
Lags Used: 9
>>> print("Number of Observations Used for the ADF Regression:", adf_result[3])
Number of Observations Used for the ADF Regression: 720
>>> print("Critical Values:")
Critical Values:
>>> for key, value in adf_result[4].items():
...     print(f"  {key}: {value}")
...
  1%: -3.439464954327953
  5%: -2.8655625802683473
  10%: -2.5689120852623457
>>> print("Maximized Information Criterion (IC):", adf_result[5])
Maximized Information Criterion (IC): 1208.8292254446185
>>> []
```

Figure 10.11 – ADF test results

As you can see, the result of the ADF test, as returned by `adfuller`, contains several components:

- **Test statistic:** The first value in the result tuple (-0.24536819384067887, in our case) is the test statistic. This statistic is used to assess the null hypothesis that a unit root is present in a time series dataset. The more negative (or less positive) the test statistic, the stronger the evidence against the null hypothesis.

- **p-value:** The second value (0.9328933413659218, in our case) is the p-value associated with the test statistic. It represents the probability of observing the given test statistic if the null hypothesis were true. A small p-value (typically less than 0.05) suggests rejecting the null hypothesis in favor of stationarity.

- **Lags used:** The third value (9, in our case) represents the number of lags used in the regression when estimating the ADF test.

- **Number of observations used for the ADF regression and critical values:** The fourth value (720, in our case) represents the number of observations used in the ADF regression.

- **Dictionary**: The next part of the result is a dictionary containing critical values for different confidence levels (1%, 5%, and 10%). These critical values are used to determine the significance of the test statistic.

- **Maximized information criterion (IC)**: The last value (1208.8292254446185, in our case) is the maximized IC. It represents a measure of the goodness-of-fit of the model. Lower values of the IC indicate a better fit.

In summary, you would typically interpret the ADF test result by focusing on the test statistic and p-value. If the test statistic is more negative (or less positive) and the p-value is small (typically less than 0.05), it suggests rejecting the null hypothesis of a unit root and concluding that the time series is stationary.

Time series decomposition

Time series decomposition is a technique that's used to break down a time series dataset into its key components: trend, seasonality, and residuals. These components provide valuable insights into the underlying patterns of the time series, making it easier to understand and forecast.

Let's understand each of these components:

- **Trend**: The trend component represents the underlying long-term movement or tendency in the data. It captures the overall direction – that is, whether data is increasing or decreasing over time.

- **Seasonality**: Seasonality refers to the repeating patterns in the data at fixed intervals. These could be daily, weekly, monthly, or yearly patterns, depending on the data. Detecting seasonality is crucial for understanding periodic trends and adjusting for them during forecasting.

- **Residuals**: Residuals are the irregular or random components of the time series data. They represent what remains after removing the trend and seasonality. Analyzing residuals helps identify any leftover patterns or unusual events in the data.

In our code, we apply time series decomposition to break down the time series into its constituent components, and we visualize each component. This process allows us to understand the structure of the data, making it easier to identify underlying patterns for forecasting.

Let's have a look at an implementation for time series decomposition in Python:

```
from statsmodels.tsa.seasonal import seasonal_decompose
import matplotlib.pyplot as plt

# Time Series Decomposition
decomposition = seasonal_decompose(df['Value'],
    model='additive',  period=365)
trend = decomposition.trend
seasonal = decomposition.seasonal
```

```
residual = decomposition.resid

# Plot the decomposition components
plt.figure(figsize=(12, 8))
plt.subplot(411)
plt.plot(df['Date'], df['Value'], label='Original')
plt.legend(loc='best')
plt.subplot(412)
plt.plot(df['Date'], trend, label='Trend')
plt.legend(loc='best')
plt.subplot(413)
plt.plot(df['Date'], seasonal, label='Seasonal')
plt.legend(loc='best')
plt.subplot(414)
plt.plot(df['Date'], residual, label='Residual')
plt.legend(loc='best')
plt.suptitle("Time Series Decomposition")
plt.show()
```

The resulting plot is self-explanatory (especially as it reflects how the data was artificially generated):

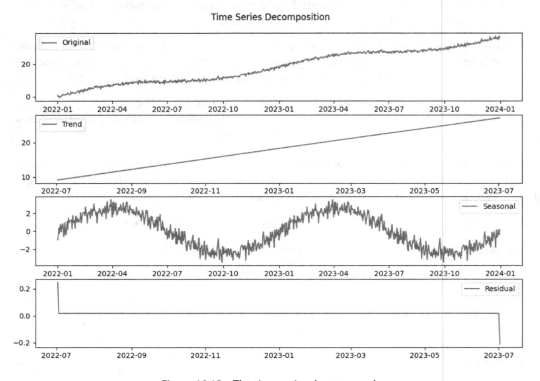

Figure 10.12 – The time series decomposed

In this section, we have covered the basic statistics that can help you understand your time series and the core techniques to handle the most typical challenges to modeling: decomposition and how to interpret the components. With a deeper understanding of our time series thanks to the plots provided and statistical analysis, we can move on to the highest value-added step: prediction.

Understanding predictive modeling approaches

In this section, we'll delve into predictive modeling approaches using two powerful Python libraries – `statsmodels` and `prophet`.

These libraries provide diverse tools to tackle time series forecasting, enabling you to make informed decisions and predictions based on your time series data.

Forecasting with statsmodels

`statsmodels` is a popular library in the Python ecosystem that offers a wide range of statistical tools, including time series analysis. For forecasting, it provides functionality for building ARIMA models. ARIMA models are a staple in time series analysis, allowing you to capture and model complex patterns within your data.

Building an ARIMA model with `statsmodels` involves selecting the appropriate order of differencing, autoregressive components, and moving average components to best represent the underlying patterns of the data. Once the model has been established, you can make forecasts and evaluate its performance.

Finally, it is very important to note that since the time series we have is not stationary, we should be modeling the changes or differences in our time series.

Let's have a look at the workflow in code!

1. First, import the necessary libraries and load the data:

    ```python
    # Import necessary libraries
    import pandas as pd
    import numpy as np
    import statsmodels.api as sm
    from scipy.stats import norm
    import matplotlib.pyplot as plt

    # Load the time series data (replace with your data)
    time_series_data = pd.read_excel('time_series_data.xlsx')
    ['Value']
    ```

2. Then, check for stationarity and decide if we want to model the time series itself or the differences:

```
# Perform the Augmented Dickey-Fuller test to check for
stationarity
result = sm.tsa.adfuller(time_series_data, autolag='AIC')

# If the p-value is greater than a threshold (e.g., 0.05),
perform differencing to make the data stationary
if result[1] > 0.05:
        differenced_data = np.diff(time_series_data, n=1)
else:
        differenced_data = time_series_data
```

3. Now (with the differenced data since our time series is not stationary), we can build the actual model and fit it:

```
# Build an ARIMA model
order = (1, 1, 1)  # Values based on ACF and PACF analysis
model = sm.tsa.ARIMA(differenced_data, order=order)

# Fit the ARIMA model
model_fit = model.fit()
```

4. Optionally, we could perform some hypertuning on the order parameters instead of basing our decision on the graphs only. However, for this example, this will suffice. Hypertuning is the action of tuning the parameters defining the model rather than the parameters fitted to the data, such as the order of the ARIMA model.

5. Now, we can create our forecast with the trained model.

    Note that since we modeled the differenced data, we need to translate the forecasts back into the actual time series:

```
# Make forecasts
forecast_steps = 50  # Adjust the number of forecast steps as
needed
forecast = model_fit.forecast(steps=forecast_steps)

# If the p-value is greater than a threshold (e.g., 0.05),
perform differencing to make the data stationary
if result[1] > 0.05:
        # The model was trained on the differenced data so the
forecasts have to be added to the last data point
        cumsum_forecasts = np.cumsum(forecast)

        # Add this cumulative sum to the last observed value in
your raw data
        real_forecasts = cumsum_forecasts + time_series_
```

```
        data[len(time_series_data)-1]

    else:
            real_forecasts = forecast
```

6. Then, we must calculate the basic statistics and use them to calculate a confidence interval:

```
# Retrieve ARIMA model parameters
params = model_fit.params
p, d, q = order
resid = model_fit.resid

# Compute the standard errors
stderr = np.std(resid)

# Calculate the confidence intervals
z_score = norm.ppf(0.975)  # For a 95% confidence interval
conf_int = np.column_stack((real_forecasts - z_score * stderr,
        real_forecasts + z_score * stderr))

# Separate the forecasts into point forecasts and confidence
intervals
point_forecasts = real_forecasts  # The point forecasts
forecast_stderr = stderr  # The standard errors of the forecasts
lower_bound = conf_int[:, 0]  # Lower confidence interval bounds
upper_bound = conf_int[:, 1]  # Upper confidence interval bounds
```

7. Finally, we must plot the forecast together with the original time series for visual evaluation of the model:

```
# Visualize the original time series and forecasts
plt.figure(figsize=(12, 6))
plt.plot(time_series_data, label='Original Time Series',
color='blue')
plt.plot(range(len(time_series_data),
    len(time_series_data) + forecast_steps),
    real_forecasts, label='Forecast', color='red')
plt.fill_between(range(len(time_series_data),
    len(time_series_data) + forecast_steps),
    lower_bound, upper_bound, color='pink', alpha=0.5)
plt.xlabel('Time Steps')
plt.ylabel('Value')
plt.title('ARIMA Time Series Forecast')
plt.legend()
plt.show()
```

The resulting plot gives us some nice insights:

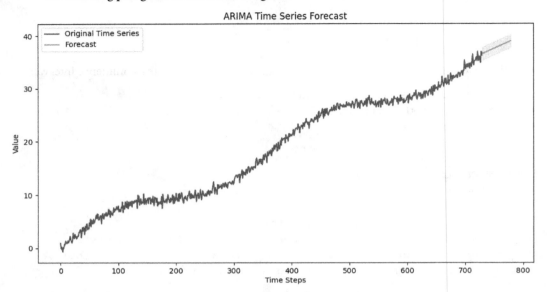

Figure 10.13 – The time series and the statsmodel forecast

We can see that while the trend is nicely captured and some of the seasonality also appears, the model is too simplistic to fully capture the nature of the time series.

To remedy this, we can use a more complex model from a dedicated time series library: `prophet`.

Time series forecasting with Facebook's prophet

The specialized `prophet` library is designed explicitly for time series forecasting tasks. It is known for its ease of use and extensive model selection for a wide variety of forecasting scenarios.

`prophet` provides an intuitive way to model time series data. It also features tools for hyperparameter optimization and forecasting evaluation.

The code we will use is also visibly simpler:

1. First, we must load the necessary libraries, read the Excel data in, and prepare it by creating a DataFrame with the columns `prophet` expects:

    ```
    # Import necessary libraries
    import pandas as pd
    from prophet import Prophet
    from prophet.plot import plot
    # Load the time series data (replace with your data)
    ```

```
time_series_data = pd.read_excel('time_series_data.xlsx')

# Create a DataFrame with 'ds' and 'y' columns
df = pd.DataFrame({'ds': time_series_data['Date'],
    'y': time_series_data['Value']})
```

2. Then, we must customize the model a little using domain knowledge (in this case, coming from the fact that we generated the data this way):

```
# Initialize and fit the Prophet model without weekly
seasonality
model = Prophet(weekly_seasonality=False)

# Add custom seasonality obtained from domain knowledge (in this
case: we generated the data so)
model.add_seasonality(name='custom_season', period=365,
    fourier_order=5)

# Fit the customized model
model.fit(df)
```

3. Finally, we can create our forecast and plot it and its components:

```
# Create a dataframe for future dates
forecast_steps = 150  # Adjust the number of forecast steps as
needed
future = model.make_future_dataframe(periods=forecast_steps,
    freq='D')

# Make predictions
forecast = model.predict(future)

# Plot the forecast
fig = model.plot(forecast)

fig.show()

# Plot components of the forecast (trend, yearly, and weekly
seasonality)
fig2 = model.plot_components(forecast)

fig2.show()
```

The resulting plot shows a much higher quality forecast than statsmodel with a tight confidence interval. The seasonality is captured visibly, along with the trend:

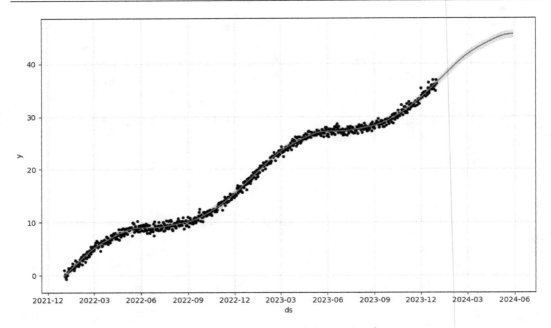

Figure 10.14 – The time series and the prophet forecast

To dig deeper into the model fit, let's have a look at the components of the fitted time series model:

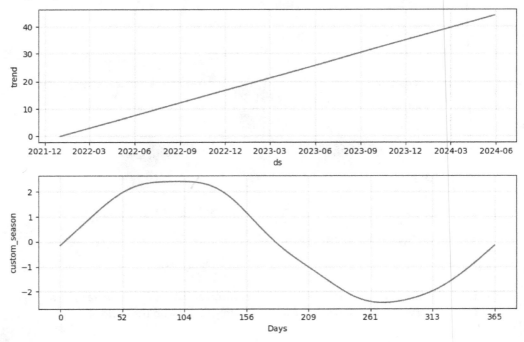

Figure 10.15 – The components of the time series model fitted by prophet

As you can see, `prophet` fits a model in a very simple way without having to guess what the starting parameters are. You can and should use any domain knowledge to improve the initial model.

In the preceding code, we switched off the default weekly seasonality and added a custom annual seasonality. We can do much more if necessary:

- We can add a custom holiday calendar, for example, using the `model.add_country_holidays(country_name='US')` command

- We can play around with change points if we are sure they are present but unsure exactly where

- We can hypertune the Fourier order of the custom seasonality

With the forecasting done with `statsmodel` and `prophet`, it's time to wrap up this section and move on to the next.

In this section, you built a strong foundation in statistical analysis and forecasting for your time series data. These skills are crucial for understanding past trends and making predictions, enabling data-driven decisions and insights.

In the next section, we will have a look at deep learning models for time series analysis.

Time series forecasting with deep learning – LSTM

This section will give you insights into advanced time series forecasting techniques using deep learning models. Whether you're working with traditional time series data or more complex, high-dimensional data, these deep learning models can help you make more accurate predictions. In particular, we will cover the **Long Short-Term Memory** (**LSTM**) method using `keras`.

We will be using `keras` with a `tensorflow` backend, so you need to install both libraries:

1. As always, let's load the necessary libraries and preprocess some time series data:

```
import numpy as np
import pandas as pd
import matplotlib.pyplot as plt
from keras.models import Sequential
from keras.layers import LSTM, Dense
from sklearn.preprocessing import MinMaxScaler

# Load the time series data (replace with your data)
time_series_data = pd.read_excel('time_series_data.xlsx')

# Normalize the data to be in the range [0, 1]
scaler = MinMaxScaler()
data = scaler.fit_transform(
    time_series_data['Value'].to_numpy().reshape(-1, 1))
```

2. With the dataset prepared, we will split it into training and testing sets and reshape them for LSTM input:

```
# Split the data into training and testing sets
train_size = int(len(data) * 0.67)
train, test = data[0:train_size, :], data[train_size:len(data),
:]

# Create sequences and labels for training
def create_dataset(dataset, look_back=1):
    X, Y = [], []
    for i in range(len(dataset) - look_back):
        a = dataset[i:(i + look_back), 0]
        X.append(a)
        Y.append(dataset[i + look_back, 0])
    return np.array(X), np.array(Y)

look_back = 3
X_train, Y_train = create_dataset(train, look_back)
X_test, Y_test = create_dataset(test, look_back)

# Reshape the data for LSTM input
X_train = np.reshape(X_train, (X_train.shape[0], 1,
    X_train.shape[1]))
X_test = np.reshape(X_test, (X_test.shape[0], 1,
    X_test.shape[1]))
```

3. Now that the data has been prepared, let's create and train an LSTM model:

```
model = Sequential()
model.add(LSTM(4, input_shape=(1, look_back)))
model.add(Dense(1))
model.compile(loss='mean_squared_error', optimizer='adam')
model.fit(X_train, Y_train, epochs=100, batch_size=1, verbose=2)
```

This code defines a simple LSTM model, compiles it, and trains it using our training data. You can customize the model architecture and training parameters as needed for your specific time series analysis. Note that the training time is significantly longer than with the simpler models we used in the previous section.

4. Once the model has been trained, we can make predictions and scale them back so that we can compare them with the original dataset:

```
# Make predictions:
trainPredict = model.predict(X_train)
testPredict = model.predict(X_test)

# Inverse transform the predictions to the original scale
trainPredict = scaler.inverse_transform(trainPredict)
testPredict = scaler.inverse_transform(testPredict)
```

5. Finally, visualize the actual dataset and the prediction for the test set:

```
# Plot the training predictions
trainPredictPlot = np.empty_like(data)
trainPredictPlot[:, :] = np.nan
trainPredictPlot[look_back:len(trainPredict) + look_back, :] =\
    trainPredict

# Plot the test predictions
testPredictPlot = np.empty_like(data)
testPredictPlot[:, :] = np.nan
testPredictPlot[len(trainPredict) + (look_back * 2):len(data),
    :] = testPredict

# Plot the training data in blue
plt.plot(time_series_data['Value'], color='blue', label=
    'Actual Data')

# Create shaded regions for the training and test data

plt.fill_between(range(len(data)), 0,
    trainPredictPlot.reshape(-1),
    color='lightgray', label='Training Data')
plt.fill_between(range(len(data)), 0,
    testPredictPlot.reshape(-1),
    color='lightcoral', label='Test Data')

# Overlay the predictions in green
plt.plot(testPredictPlot, color='green', label='Predictions')

plt.title('Time Series Analysis with LSTM')
plt.legend()
plt.show()
```

The resulting image is quite impressive for such a small dataset and simple model:

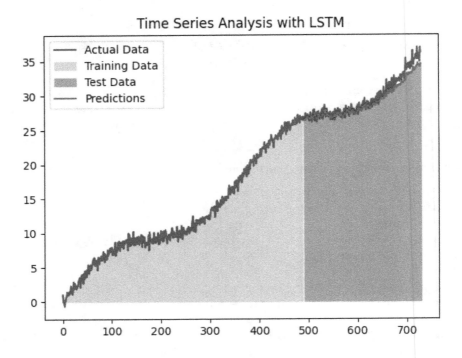

Figure 10.16 – The actual data (in blue) and the prediction for the test set (in green)

Remember that this is a basic example. LSTM models can be significantly more complex, and you might need to explore techniques such as stacked LSTMs, hyperparameter tuning, and more, depending on your specific time series data.

This concludes our journey into time series analysis with Python. Let's recap what you have learned in this chapter!

Summary

In this chapter, we delved into the fascinating world of time series analysis. We began by exploring time series plotting, mastering essential plots, and understanding the significance of ACF/PACF plots.

Moving forward, we ventured into time series statistics, including the ADF test, time series decomposition, and statistical forecasting with tools such as `statsmodels` and `prophet`.

To elevate our forecasting game, we embraced deep learning, employing LSTM networks using Python's `keras` library. We learned to develop accurate time series forecasts and create insightful visualizations for data-driven insights.

This chapter equipped us with a comprehensive set of skills for time series analysis, enabling us to unravel the hidden patterns and insights within time-based data, from plotting to statistical analysis and deep learning forecasting.

In the next chapter, we will discuss a different integration method – that is, calling R and Python from Excel directly.

Part 4:
The Other Way Around – Calling R and Python from Excel

In this part, you willl unlock the power of R and Python within Excel with comprehensive solutions designed for seamless integration. You will discover how to leverage BERT and `xlwings` for streamlined communication between Excel and your preferred programming language locally. You will explore open source API solutions such as Plumber and FastAPI, along with commercial offerings such as Posit Connect and ownR, to expand the capabilities of your Excel workflow with API-based integration.

This part has the following chapter:

- *Chapter 11, Calling R/Python Locally from Excel Directly or via an API*

11

Calling R/Python Locally from Excel Directly or via an API

In this chapter, we are going to discuss calling R and Python from within Excel. You may ask yourself why you would want to do that when there are many functions inside of Excel that one can use or, if so desired, can write with the VBA portion of the application. One reason why you might want to call R or Python from Excel is to leverage the power and flexibility of these programming languages for data analysis and visualization. Excel is a widely used spreadsheet application that can handle large datasets and perform basic calculations and functions. However, Excel has some limitations when it comes to more advanced or customized tasks, such as statistical modeling, machine learning, web scraping, natural language processing, and so on. By calling R or Python from Excel, you can access the rich libraries and packages that these languages offer and use them to manipulate, transform, and visualize your data in more sophisticated ways. You can also automate your workflows and create reproducible reports and dashboards. Calling R or Python from Excel can enhance your productivity and efficiency, as well as expand your analytical capabilities.

We will be a bit different here. In this chapter, we will cover two (very) different methods for calling R and Python from Excel: local calls, where R or Python is installed on the same machine, and running and using API calls, where the R or Python functionality is deployed to a server as an API endpoint. For the latter, we will have a look at open-source tools and some of the most popular commercial solutions.

Technical requirements

In this chapter, you can find all the code on GitHub at the following link: `https://github.com/PacktPublishing/Extending-Excel-with-Python-and-R/tree/main/Chapter%2011`.

You will need to install the following external software:

- BERT, which can be found here: `http://bert-toolkit.com/download-bert`
- Python and `xlwings` (refer to the *Setting up an environment* section)
- `plumber` for R
- FastAPI for Python

Let's begin with the first part.

Calling R and Python from Excel locally

In this first part of the chapter, we are going to learn about using the +or Excel that can interface with R directly, along with `xlwings` to interact with Python from Excel. We will also quickly show how one can use a VBA script to call R from Excel. In this chapter, we're going to cover the following main topics:

- Why you would want to call R/Python from Excel locally
- Setting up an environment
- Calling R/Python directly from Excel

Let's begin!

Why you would want to call R/Python from Excel locally

As we discussed in the opening, it is possible to do a wide variety of analysis and programming in Excel via the use of VBA. However, this can be tedious to write and difficult to implement. By harnessing the power of `BERT` and `xlwings`, you can use an already rich landscape of functions that are ready to go or write your own in those languages and use them in Excel.

With `BERT`, you get the power of R in Excel: R is a powerful statistical programming language with a wide range of capabilities. `BERT` allows you to use these capabilities directly in Excel without having to switch to a separate R environment. This can be very convenient if you are already working in Excel and don't want to leave the application.

`BERT` allows you to write R functions that can be used as custom Excel functions. This can be useful for creating functions that are not available in Excel or for improving the performance of existing Excel functions. For example, you can create a Brownian motion by using `BERT` to call a function built inside of R, which is going to be much easier to code in R than it would in Excel.

What BERT is for R, xlwings is for Python. The benefits are analogous as well: create your solution in Python and call it from Excel directly.

Let's start with setting up your environment so you can get your hands dirty!

Setting up an environment

Since setting up an environment for BERT and xlwings is non-trivial, we will walk you through the process in detail in the coming subsections.

Steps to set up BERT for R

In this section, we will cover the installation of BERT for Windows so that we can utilize BERT to manipulate Excel from inside of R. The first thing that we will have to do is download the BERT installer, which can be obtained from here: https://bert-toolkit.com/download-bert.

Once this is downloaded, you can then install it as you would any other program. Once installed, you can then use the **Add-ins** ribbon from Excel to open the **BERT Console**, as shown here:

Figure 11.1 – BERT Console from the Add-ins ribbon in Excel

Once you see it, click the button, and the console will open, as shown here:

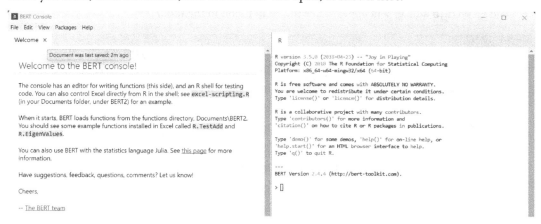

Figure 11.2 – The BERT Console

Now, let's move to Python.

Steps to set up xlwings for Python

In this subsection, we will cover the steps required to set up `xlwings`:

Installing Python

Ensure that Python is installed on your machine. You can download the latest version from the official Python website (`https://www.python.org/downloads/`). During installation, you can check the box that says **Add Python to PATH** for easier access.

Installing Excel add-ins:

Follow these simple steps to get started with `xlwings`:

1. Open a command prompt and run the following:

    ```
    pip install xlwings
    ```

    You may receive a warning along the lines of this: `WARNING: The script xlwings.exe is installed in '<folder>' which is not on PATH`. If you do, you will have to specify the full path to be able to call `xlwings` in the next step.

2. To install the add-in, use the command-line client:

    ```
    xlwings addin install (Re)start Excel
    ```

3. In Excel, open the VBA editor, then go to the **Tools** menu, open **References** and click the checkbox for **xlwings**. Click **OK** and head back to Excel. This step is not necessary for every user; first, check if the ribbon is already available after restarting Excel!

    The `xlwings` add-in will appear after the **Help** menu in the toolbar:

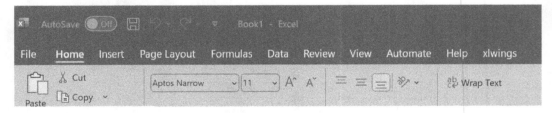

Figure 11.3 – xlwings in the ribbon in Excel

Configuring the Excel and Python environment

Configure xlwings by specifying the Python interpreter path in the Excel add-ins settings. However, this is typically done automatically by xlwings.

To verify the setup, run any of the examples given in the next section.

Troubleshooting

If you encounter issues, refer to the documentation for xlwings (https://docs.xlwings. org/en/stable/). Check for common troubleshooting tips and solutions.

This step-by-step guide ensures a smooth setup of your local environment, enabling Excel and Python to work seamlessly together. Following these instructions will provide a solid foundation for the subsequent chapters, allowing you to harness the combined power of Excel and Python.

Now that you have set up, let's get to the meat of how to actually use these tools!

Calling R/Python directly from Excel

In this section, we will dig into the ways you can call R and Python from Excel using the tools set up in the previous section. We will cover several ways of achieving this and give examples so that you can try them out as well.

Executing R with VBA and BERT

Another great way of calling R from Excel is via the VBA macro. This requires that a workbook be saved as a macro-enabled workbook. Since BERT is designed to work from Excel to R, the syntax of an R expression can be written in the VBA console and called with the following in VBA:

```
Application.Run "BERT.Exec", r
```

Let's look at an easy example:

```
Sub PlotNormalDensity()
    r = "plot(density(rnorm(1000)))"
    Application.Run "BERT.Exec", r
End Sub
```

This will end up producing a plot of the density of a random normal distribution. Let's see the output:

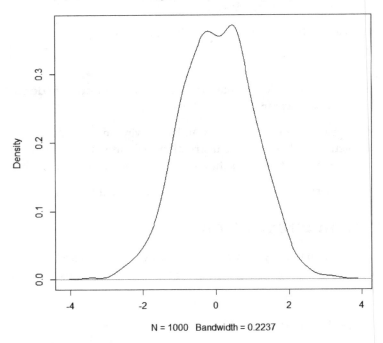

Figure 11.4 – Using BERT to call R from VBA

Interacting with Excel via BERT

It is possible to manipulate Excel with BERT using the **Excel Scripting Interface**. You may ask yourself, "Why would I want to do such a thing"? Well, remember, with BERT, you have access to not only Excel but R as well. This means that you can use R functions that may not exist in Excel to generate data; let's see an example. This was done in the left pane.

First, we will define a range:

```
rng <- EXCEL$Application$get_Range( "A1:B4" )
```

This will define a range in R for the cells A1 : B4 and will place it in the global environment as a variable called rng. This was typed into BERT's R interface. Now that this range is defined, it is possible to see how many range commands are at your fingertips and what some of them are:

```
> length(ls(rng))
[1] 234
```

```
> head(ls(rng))
[1] "Activate"                           "AddComment"
                   "AddCommentThreaded"
[4] "AdvancedFilter"      "AllocateChanges"      "ApplyNames"
```

So, we see that there are 234 range commands available. By calling `ls(rng)`, the R console will print out all of the commands; here, we use `head()` so that only the first few are shown. Here, we are going to use the `RAND()` Excel command to place random numbers into the defined range:

```
rng$put_Formula("=RAND()");
```

Let's take a look at the output in the Excel file:

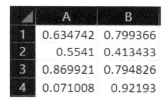

◢	A	B
1	0.634742	0.799366
2	0.5541	0.413433
3	0.869921	0.794826
4	0.071008	0.92193

Figure 11.5 – Using the RAND() function from BERT in Excel

If we want to stay inside of BERT and see the values that were sent to Excel, we can do the following:

```
> rng$get_Value()
                    [,1]                 [,2]
[1,]  0.63474248  0.7993663
[2,]  0.55409965  0.4134328
[3,]  0.86992109  0.7948257
[4,]  0.07100827  0.9219299
```

Now that we have gone over some basics of how to work with Excel via R, it is time to see how we can achieve similar things in Python.

Calling Python from Excel using xlwings

You have three options to call Python from Excel using `xlwings`:

- The Run button under the `xlwings` tab of the ribbon
- Macros: These call Python from Excel
- **User Defined Functions (UDFs)** (Windows only)

Let's have a look at the pros and cons of all three, as well as an example!

The Run button

The Run button expects a function called `main` in a Python module with the same name as your workbook. This is a quote from the documentation and a hard prerequisite. The main benefit of this method is that there is no VBA and no macros; you can use a normal XLSX file, which can be very useful in security-restricted situations where XLSM files are not allowed.

To try out the Run button, follow these steps:

1. Create a Python module called `sumitup.py` with the following code:

```python
import xlwings as xw

def main():
            wb = xw.Book.caller()
            a = wb.sheets[0]['A1'].value
            b = wb.sheets[0]['A2'].value
            wb.sheets[0]['A3'].value = a + b
            pass
```

2. Open Excel and fill cell A1 with 2 and cell A2 with 3.

3. Save the Excel sheet as `sumitup.xlsx` in the same folder where `sumitup.py` is saved.

4. Click the Run button in the `xlwings` menu in the Ribbon.

The cons of this method are the strict naming convention and file placement, and the lack of flexibility; only the function `main()` will be called, and the Python code needs to encode which fields will be used as input and where the output will go, meaning you cannot pass on inputs to the function from the Excel side.

Macros

If you require more flexibility, and you can use a macro (and save your file as XLSM), you can use RunPython from VBA.

In this example, RunPython will import the `world` module and run the `helloworld()` function from that module. To run this example, try the following steps:

1. Create a `.xlsm` file and save it as `world.xlsm`.

2. Open the VBA editor and try the following:

    I.   Open **References** from the **Tools** menu and make sure `xlwings` is checked:

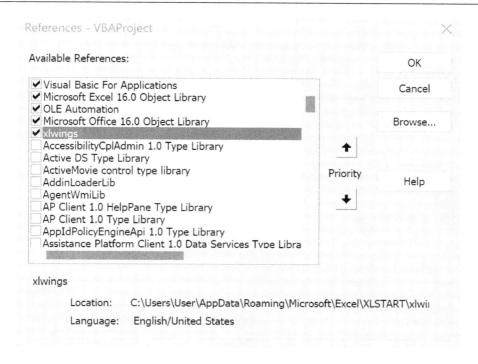

Figure 11.6 – Adding the xlwings reference to the VBA project

II.   Create a new macro in the file with Sub as follows:

```
Sub HelloWorld()
            RunPython "import world; world.helloworld()"
End Sub
```

3. Create the hello.py module in the same folder where you saved the .xlsm file with the following content:

```
import xlwings as xw

def helloworld():
    wb = xw.Book.caller()
    wb.sheets[0]['A1'].value = 'Hello World!'
```

4. Now, you can run the macro in world.xlsm and see the results!

As you can see, using macros addresses one of the cons of the Run button, namely the location and name of the Python module(s) and function(s) used. However, you still cannot pass on inputs directly from the Excel file; the inputs have to be in pre-determined cells in the Excel file, and the output cell(s) have to be pre-determined as well.

Note that you can change both the name of the module (to not match the name of the Excel file) and the location of the module (i.e., have it saved in a different folder than the .xlsm file). From the xlwings documentation, it reads that *"Per default, RunPython expects world.py in the same directory as the Excel file with the same name, but you can change both of these things: if your Python file is in a different folder, add that folder to the PYTHONPATH in the config. If the file has a different name, change the RunPython command accordingly."*

UDFs

User-defined functions allow the user to extend Excel to add custom functions that can be used in the same way as SUM() and IF().

Writing a UDF in Python with xlwings is as easy, as seen here:

```python
import xlwings as xw
import numpy as np

@xw.func
@xw.arg('x', np.array, ndim=2)
@xw.arg('y', np.array, ndim=2)
def matrix_add(x, y):
    return x + y
```

In the preceding example, we specify that the inputs are both numpy array instances and define the function for matrix addition.

To integrate Python functions into Excel using xlwings, you'll need to set up your Python source file in a specific way. By default, xlwings expects a Python source file to be located in the same directory as your Excel file and to have the same name as the Excel file but with a .py extension instead of .xlsm.

Alternatively, you can specify a specific module via the **UDF Modules** feature in the xlwings ribbon.

Once you've prepared your Python source file, you can import the functions into Excel by following these steps:

1. Save an Excel file with the same name as your Python module and save it as a .xlsm file in the same folder where the Python module is located.

2. In Excel, go to the xlwings tab and click on **Import Python UDFs** to pick up the changes made to your Python module.

3. Enter the data into two ranges in your Excel sheet (ensure that the dimensions of the ranges are appropriate for matrix multiplication).

4. In a cell, enter the formula =matrix_add([range1], [range2]), where [range1] and [range2] are the ranges where you have entered data.

You should see the correct result displayed in the cell:

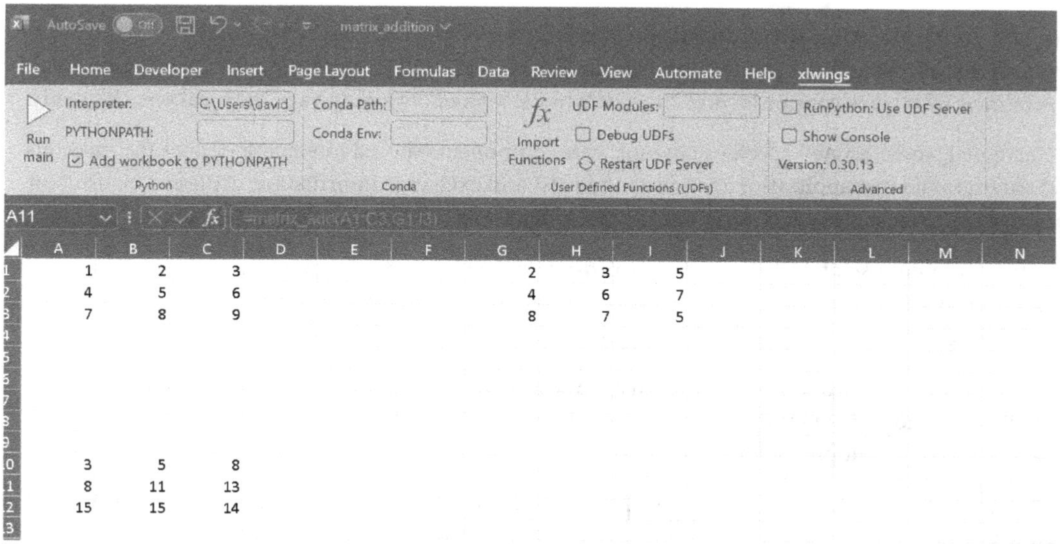

Figure 11.7 – Using the matrix_add function from xlwings to Excel

The pro of this method is self-evident: the Excel user can determine what inputs to use and where the output should go without actually interacting with Python (or you, the Python developer).

The con of the method is the generic one for xlwings and all similar solutions; for a local Python (or R) installation, all the dependencies must be correctly set up and the correct version must be made available to all users.

Please be aware that UDFs do not work with Python, which is available from the Microsoft Store.

It is noteworthy that alternatives exist, particularly PyXLL, which is a popular alternative to xlwings. It provides similar functionality with similar restrictions (including but not limited to not working with Python installed from the Microsoft Store).

In this chapter, you have learned about why and how to call R and Python directly from Excel using the tools BERT and xlwings.

In the next part of the chapter, we will look at another way of enacting such integration without the need for a local installation and staying in full control of the code and its version (which can be handy in enterprise settings) but with a need for a server environment instead.

Calling R and Python from Excel via an API

An **API**, or **Application Programming Interface**, serves as a bridge between different software applications, allowing them to communicate and share data in a standardized way. It's like a waiter at a restaurant who takes your order and conveys it to the kitchen, bringing back the meal once it's ready.

In the digital world, an API specifies how software components should interact. It defines the methods and data formats that applications can use to request and exchange information. APIs can be used for various purposes, such as accessing web services, databases, or even hardware devices.

One fundamental use of APIs is enabling third-party developers to integrate their applications with existing services or platforms. In the context of your coding interests in R and Python, APIs can be utilized for data retrieval and for exposing your models to other software, including Excel.

The beauty of APIs lies in their versatility. They abstract the complexity of underlying systems, providing a standardized way for developers to interact with them. This abstraction allows for more straightforward development and integration processes, fostering collaboration and innovation.

In essence, APIs are the unsung heroes of the digital world, facilitating seamless communication between diverse software components and enabling the creation of more powerful and interconnected applications. Whether you're working with data, web services, or other software, understanding and effectively using APIs can significantly enhance your capabilities as a programmer.

In this section, we're going to cover the following main topics:

- An introduction to APIs
- Open-source solutions for exposing R and Python as API endpoints
- Calling APIs from Excel for integration

An introduction to APIs

You can think of APIs as a set of rules that will allow one piece of software to interact with another. A quick example of the usage of an API would be the weather app on a smartphone connecting with the weather system to get the current weather or a forecast of the weather.

An easy way to think of an API, besides a mechanism for different systems to communicate, is to think of a contract. The documentation of an API will specify how a system can connect with and talk with the system, what it is allowed to do, and how often.

Systems that maintain an API will often act as a sort of client and server type arrangement. A REST API is one of the most popular types of API today. **REST** stands for **representational state transfer**. The major pro of this type of API is that it is stateless. Statelessness means that servers do not save client data between requests. The requests that are sent to the server will remind you of a URL. A generic REST API call might look like the following:

```
GET https://example.com/api/v1/users
```

You could think of the preceding as obtaining a list of users, and you might think that you would obtain a list because this was a GET request. Here is a generic POST request:

```
POST https://example.com/api/v1/users
Content-Type: application/json
{
   "name": "John Doe",
   "email": "john.doe@example.com"
}
```

Here, you have posted (POST) data to the server. So, with a REST API, think of posting and getting information from and to the server.

Now that we understand what an API is and some of the types and use cases they have, we can now move on to taking a look at open-source solutions for exposing R/Python as an API endpoint.

Open source solutions for exposing R as API endpoints

We are going to start off by first showing how to expose R as an API endpoint via the plumber package. The plumber package and its associated documentation can be found at the following URL: https://www.rplumber.io/index.html.

The first thing we will do is build out a very simple single-argument API to obtain the histogram of a standard normal distribution. Let's take a look at the code; we will then discuss what is happening inside of it:

```
#* Plot out data from a random normal distribution
#* @param .mean The mean of the standard normal distribution
#* @get /plot
#* @serializer png
function(.mean) {
   mu <- as.numeric(.mean)
   hist(rnorm(n = 1000, mean = mu, sd = 1))
}
```

The lines starting with #* are comments. In the plumber API, these comments are special and are used for documentation. They describe what the API endpoint does and provide information about the parameters. The first comment introduces the purpose of the API endpoint. It states that the API will generate a plot based on data from a random normal distribution. The line #* @param .mean The mean of the standard normal deviation describes a parameter called .mean, representing the mean of the standard normal distribution. Parameters in plumber APIs are like inputs that can be passed to the API when making a request.

The following `#* @get /plot` comment specifies that this API endpoint can be accessed using an `HTTP GET` request, and the endpoint path is `/plot`. In simpler terms, if you want to use this API, you'd request something like `http://your-api-url/plot`. The function is defined as follows: `function(.mean)`; here, the actual R function starts. It takes a parameter, `.mean`, which is the mean of the standard normal distribution. In order for the argument to be passed to the `rnorm()` function itself, we must make sure that we declare it as a numeric data type. We do this internally as follows: `mu <- as.numeric(.mean)`, where the parameter `.mean` is converted to a numeric value and stored in a variable called mu. After we convert the argument into a numeric, we can pass it off to `rnorm()` and `hist()` in order to create the plot.

Finally, we are at the point where we generate and plot the data. This is done with the following bit of code: `hist(rnorm(n = 1000, mean = mu, sd = 1))`: This line generates 1000 random numbers from a normal distribution with the specified mean (mu) and standard deviation (`sd = 1`). Then, it creates a histogram of these numbers. Essentially, it's generating random data and plotting a histogram.

In summary, this plumber API, when deployed, creates an endpoint (`/plot`) that, when accessed with a mean value, generates a histogram plot based on random data from a normal distribution. The mean is a parameter that you provide when making a request to this API. It's a simple yet powerful example of how you can use R and plumber to expose data processing capabilities over the web.

Now that we have generated the code that will produce the API, let's look at the output once the code is run. To do so, let's see the following script:

```
# Library Load
library(plumber)

# Set dir and file path
wd <- getwd()
sub_dir <- paste0("/Chapter 11/")
full_dir <- paste0(wd, sub_dir)
f <- "plumber_api.R"
f_path <- paste0(full_dir, f)

# Initiate root
root <- pr(f_path)
root
# Plumber router with 1 endpoint, 4 filters, and 0 sub-routers.
# Use `pr_run()` on this object to start the API.
├──[queryString]
├──[body]
├──[cookieParser]
├──[sharedSecret]
└──/plot (GET)
```

Let's give a line-by-line explanation:

```
# Library Load
library(plumber)
```

This line loads the `plumber` package, which is required to create plumber APIs:

```
# Set dir and file path
wd <- getwd()
sub_dir <- paste0("/Chapter 11/")
full_dir <- paste0(wd, sub_dir)
f <- "plumber_api.R"
f_path <- paste0(full_dir, f)
```

These lines set the directory and file path of the `plumber` API file. The `getwd()` function returns the working directory, which is the current directory that R is using. The `paste0()` function is used to concatenate strings, so the `sub_dir` variable contains the string `/Chapter11/`, and the `full_dir` variable contains the path to the `/Chapter12/` directory. The `f` variable contains the filename of the plumber API file, which is `plumber_api.R`. The `f_path` variable contains the full path to the plumber API file, which is the combination of the `full_dir` and `f` variables:

```
# Initiate root
root <- pr(f_path)
```

This line initiates the plumber API by calling the `pr()` function with the `f_path` variable as the argument. The `pr()` function reads the plumber API file and creates a plumber API object:

```
root
```

This line simply returns the `root` variable, which is the plumber API object. The R code provided creates a plumber API from a file called `plumber_api.R`. The plumber API can then be used to expose R functions as web endpoints.

Let's use a simple analogy: Imagine that you have a restaurant and want to offer a delivery service. You could create a simple website that allows customers to order food online. The website would need to be able to communicate with your restaurant's kitchen to place orders. In this analogy, the plumber API is like the website, and the R functions are like the restaurant's kitchen. The plumber API allows you to expose R functions to the outside world so that other applications can communicate with them. Now let's run the API and see what happens; we do this with the following code: `pr_run(root)`:

Figure 11.8 – plumber GET API

We see that when we run the preceding code, we get a screen back that will allow us to test out the API; so, let's do just that.

To do that, we can click on the **GET** button, as this is a GET API call. When we do that, we get the following screen:

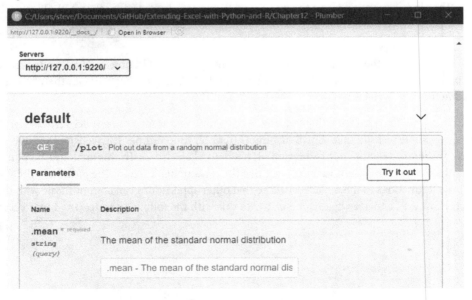

Figure 11.9 – Enter arguments for API

We see that we can enter an argument to the parameter of .mean; let's enter 10. First, click the **Try it out** button, and then you can enter a value; then, you can hit **Execute**, as shown in the following screenshot:

Figure 11.10 – Enter the argument and click Execute

Now, let's hit that **Execute** button and check out the output. We get a couple of things; one is the curl request:

```
curl -X GET "http://127.0.0.1:9220/plot?.mean=10" -H "accept: image/
png"
```

Next, we get the request URL:

```
http://127.0.0.1:9220/plot?.mean=10
```

Last but not least, we get the histogram:

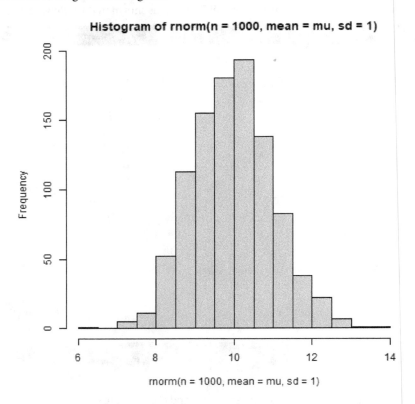

Figure 11.11 – The histogram generated by the API call

Now that we have learned how to build and use the API for R, we will learn how to do the same for Python in the next section.

Open-source solutions for exposing Python as an API endpoint

FastAPI is a modern, fast (high-performance) web framework for building APIs with Python 3.7+ based on standard Python-type hints. It's easy to use and allows you to create robust APIs quickly.

You can install FastAPI using pip:

```
pip install fastapi
```

The following is a simplified example of creating a `FastAPI` endpoint to expose a Python function:

```
from fastapi import FastAPI, Query

app = FastAPI()

@app.get("/api/add")
def add_numbers(
    num1: int = Query(..., description="First number"),
    num2: int = Query(..., description="Second number"),
):
    result = num1 + num2
    return {"result": result}
```

In this example, the `add_numbers` function available at the `/api/add` endpoint takes two query parameters (`num1` and `num2`), representing the numbers to be added. The `Query` function from FastAPI is used to define these parameters with optional descriptions. The result is then calculated, and a JSON response containing the result is returned.

With this example, you can now send a `GET` request to `/api/add?num1=3&num2=4` to get the result. The `num1` and `num2` parameters are specified in the query string of the URL.

`FastAPI` automatically generates OpenAPI and JSON Schema documentation, making it convenient for users to understand and interact with your API.

To run the development server, run the following from the command line:

```
uvicorn your_app_name:app --reload
```

Replace `your_app_name` with the name of your Python file, keeping in mind that the python file name should be different than `fastapi` or similar to the previously installed module.

> **Important note**
> Ensure that your API is secured, especially if it's accessible over the internet. `FastAPI` provides features for handling authentication and authorization.

We have covered creating an API for both R and Python. It is time to call the API we have created from Excel!

Calling APIs from Excel VBA

Now, we are going to go over the code that will allow us to use a `curl` request to obtain the image from the API that was generated from the `plumber_api.R` file. In order to do this, you will have to run the code from the previous section: `root |> pr_run()`; this is the portion that will open up the swagger dialogue and give you the URL that is running from `plumber`. For me, at the time of this writing, it is as follows: `http://127.0.0.1:6855`.

In this section, we are going to specifically execute the `GET` request via a `curl` command in VBA. Here is the code that will run, and the explanation will follow:

```
Sub MakeCurlRequestAndInsertImage()
        ' Define the curl command
        Dim curlCommand As String
        curlCommand = "curl -X GET ""http://127.0.0.1:6855/plot?.
mean=0"" -H ""accept: image/png"" -o " & Environ("TEMP") & "\temp_
image.png"

        ' Run the curl command using Shell
        Shell "cmd /c " & curlCommand, vbHide

        ' Create a new worksheet or refer to an existing one (Sheet1)
        Dim ws As Worksheet
        Set ws = ActiveWorkbook.Worksheets("Sheet1")

        ' Clear previous content in Sheet1
        ws.Cells.Clear

        ' Insert the image into the worksheet
        ws.Pictures.Insert(Environ("TEMP") & "\temp_image.png").Select
End Sub
```

Let's break down the code step by step in simple terms:

Define the `curl` command:

```
Dim curlCommand As String
curlCommand = "curl -X GET ""http://127.0.0.1:6855/plot?.mean=0"" -H
""accept: image/png"" -o " & Environ("TEMP") & "\temp_image.png"
```

This part creates a variable (curlCommand) to store a command-line instruction. The command is essentially telling the computer to use curl (a command-line tool for making HTTP requests) to get an image from the specified web address (http://127.0.0.1:6855/plot?.mean=0). All of this goes on a single line in the VBA editor. The -H flag specifies an HTTP header, in this case, telling the server that we accept an image in PNG format. The -o flag specifies the output file, and it's set to save the image in the temporary folder with the name temp_image.png.

Run the curl command using Shell:

```
Shell "cmd /c " & curlCommand, vbHide
```

This line executes the curlCommand using the Windows Command Prompt (cmd /c). The vbHide at the end means that the command prompt window will not be visible while executing:

```
Create or refer to a worksheet (Sheet1):
Dim ws As Worksheet
Set ws = ActiveWorkbook.Worksheets("Sheet1")
```

This part creates a variable (ws) to represent a worksheet in Excel. It either creates a new worksheet named "Sheet1" or refers to an existing one in the active workbook.

Clear the previous content in Sheet1:

```
ws.Cells.Clear
```

This line removes any existing content in the specified worksheet ("Sheet1").

Insert the image into the worksheet:

```
ws.Pictures.Insert(Environ("TEMP") & "\temp_image.png").Select
```

This line inserts the image downloaded by the curl command into the specified worksheet ("Sheet1"). Environ("TEMP") refers to the system's temporary folder. "\temp_image.png" is the name of the image file downloaded by the curl command.

In summary, this VBA code automates the process of using the curl command to download an image from a web address and then inserts that image into an Excel worksheet named Sheet1. The worksheet is cleared first to ensure no previous content remains.

Now, let's see the output from the VBA script:

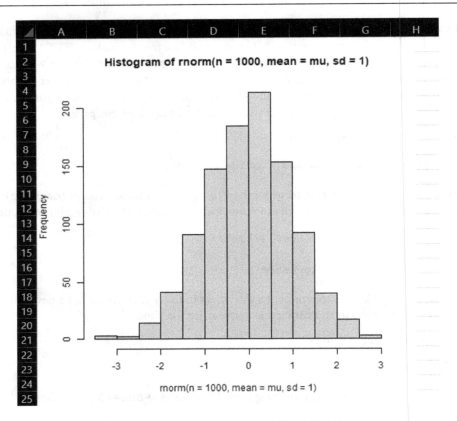

Figure 11.12 – Histogram generated by R from VBA

In this section, you have learned how to create an API via the plumber package in R. You have also learned how to call this API via a curl request inside of an Excel VBA macro.

The beauty of an API-based solution is that Excel (and, in turn, your end-user) does not have to know that the code behind the API is written in R. The same macro could call an API written in Python without any changes!

So, what are the pros and cons of this approach?

The pros have been spelled out previously: no local installation, no need to maintain the R/Python environment for every user, and full control over the code running behind the API. Should you need to update anything, from the R/Python version via the package dependencies to the code itself, you can do this on the server side without involving your end user.

One con is general to all API-based solutions: it requires a server to be set up and maintained, which usually is both too difficult and not allowed for data analysts and data scientists. This means dedicated IT resources are needed.

A con specific to open source solutions for API hosting is one general to all open source solutions: what you save on license fees you pay in having to do more yourself. Open-source API solutions expect you to handle security (see the note at the end of the FastAPI section), the integration with the enterprise landscape (such as user management), and, generally, do everything yourself.

Finally, a con of both `plumber` and `FastAPI` is the need to write custom code to define your API endpoints and functionality. In a single-person team, this is not a big issue other than the hours needed, but in larger teams, this often leads to a fractured landscape where it is difficult to enforce naming conventions and standardization.

In the next section of this chapter, we will have a look at some of the most commonly used commercial solutions for hosting R and Python API endpoints and see how they address these questions.

Commercial API solutions for R and Python

In this section, we will cover some of the most commonly used commercial API solutions for R and Python.

Azure Functions (and similar solutions from the other large cloud providers)

Azure Functions is a serverless computing service offered by Microsoft Azure. It allows you to run event-triggered code without explicitly provisioning or managing infrastructure. You can build APIs, respond to events, and perform various tasks using a wide range of supported languages, including Python and JavaScript:

- **Use cases**: Ideal for building lightweight, event-driven APIs or microservices. Integration with other Azure services provides scalability and flexibility.

- **Pro**: A "serverless" infrastructure means minimal need for IT involvement.

- **Con**: Limited flexibility (e.g., choice of R/Python version) and difficulty in migrating to other cloud providers.

Posit Connect

Posit Connect is a commercial solution designed to connect R and Python to Excel. It facilitates the integration of analytics and data science directly into Excel workbooks, allowing users to leverage the power of R and Python within the familiar Excel interface.

- **Use cases**: Particularly suitable for organizations where Excel is a primary tool for data analysis, providing a seamless way to enhance Excel's capabilities with advanced analytics.

- **Pro**: A deeply integrated ecosystem for Posit solutions, including RStudio, Quarto, and Shiny Pro.

- **Con**: It utilizes plumber and FastAPI/Flask, so you will need to write custom code to define your API, leading to the drawbacks discussed under the open source API solutions. Only Linux servers are supported, both on-premise and in-cloud.

ownR Infinity platform

ownR Infinity is a versatile platform designed to empower R and Python functionalities within a user-friendly environment. Enabling the creation of personalized functions and models transforms them into accessible APIs, with a particular focus on seamless integration within Excel.

- **Use cases**: Suited for organizations heavily reliant on R and Python for advanced data analytics. Perfect for users seeking to augment Excel's capabilities with statistical and data analysis features.

- **Pros**: Provides a user-friendly interface for leveraging the capabilities of R and Python without extensive programming knowledge. Enables seamless integration of R and Python functionalities across various environments.

- **Con**: Only Linux servers are supported, both on-premises and in-cloud.

For an example of how to use an ownR API from Excel, you can download an example workbook from here: `https://bitbucket.org/functionalanalytics/examples/src/master/ccy%20converter%20Excel%20demo%20button.xlsm`.

The example uses a hosted API for the following code base: `https://bitbucket.org/functionalanalytics/converter/src/master/`

Note that there is no need to write custom code beyond the pure Python code (or R code) and no need to add security, deployment, and other considerations manually, as these are automatically added by ownR.

These commercial solutions provide high levels of integration and features for connecting Python and R with Excel and other frontends, catering to diverse use cases and preferences within the analytics and data science community.

The pros of commercial solutions compared to open source ones boil down to the level of support and handholding with things such as out-of-the-box security, deeper and easier integration with the wider enterprise landscape, and a dedicated support organization in case of problems.

The con is an obvious one: these solutions have license fees that require a dedicated budget. While all these companies aim at pricing in a way that the reduction of manual work and increased added value justify the price tag, a discussion with the budget holders is never easy.

Summary

In this chapter, you have learned ways to call R and Python from Excel instead of the other way around to empower your end users even further. We have covered the reasons for doing so and two very different approaches: calling R and Python locally and via an API endpoint.

For locally calling R and Python, we covered `BERT` and `xlwings` in detail, from setting up and testing the environment via creating R and Python solutions up to and including how to call those solutions from Excel using the various methods provided by `BERT` and `xlwings`, such as VBA code and UDFs.

Next, you learned about API endpoints and the benefits of using an API endpoint to connect Python and R to Excel. We discussed the pros and cons of such a setup and then delved into the two flavors of API hosting: open source tools and commercial solutions. We have covered the two most used open source setups: plumber for R and FastAPI for Python. Finally, we had a look at commercial solutions for hosting R and Python API endpoints.

The next (and last) chapter will cover a more domain-oriented topic: data analysis and visualization with Python and R in Excel.

Part 5:
Data Analysis and Visualization with R and Python for Excel Data – A Case Study

Delve into the world of data analysis and visualization within Excel using the power of Python and R. Through a captivating case study, you will discover how to leverage these versatile programming languages to uncover insights, visualize data, and drive informed decision-making directly within Excel.

This part has the following chapter:

- *Chapter 12, Data Analysis and Visualization with R and Python in Excel – A Case Study*

12

Data Analysis and Visualization with R and Python in Excel – A Case Study

In this final chapter, we are going to perform an analysis—**visualization** and a simple model—built with data from Excel and place all those outcomes back into it. This can be useful when there is a lot of data, or the calculations themselves are best suited to being done outside of Excel.

First, we will start with importing our data and then performing some data exploration via visualizations. For this chapter, we are going to use the `diamonds` dataset from the R package called `ggplot2`. We will view the data where the price is the outcome and look at it via different facets of the diamond's characteristics. After the visualizations are done, we will perform some simple modeling to predict the price of a diamond based on its characteristics.

In this chapter, we're going to cover the following main topics:

- Getting a visualization
- Performing a simple **machine learning** (ML) model

Technical requirements

For this chapter, we will be using the following packages/libraries:

- `ggplot2 3.4.4`
- `dplyr 1.1.4`
- `healthyR 0.2.1`
- `readxl 1.4.3`
- `tidyverse 2.0.0`
- `janitor 2.2.0`
- `writexl 1.5.0`
- `healthyR.ai 0.0.13`

Getting visualizations with R

In this section, we are going to go over getting some visualizations of the data. We will create several visualizations and give short interpretations of the outcomes in them. For this, we will create two histograms in base R and a few different visuals using the `ggplot2` library.

Getting the data

The first thing we need to do is load the libraries and get the data. I am working in a directory specific to this book so I can source the function directly from the chapter I wrote the `read_excel_sheets()`? function in; your path might be different. Let's look at the code up to this point:

```
# Library Load
library(ggplot2)
library(dplyr)
library(healthyR)
library(readxl)
# Source Functions
source(paste0(getwd(),"/Chapter1/excel_sheet_reader.R"))
# Read data
file_path <- paste0(getwd(), "/Chapter12/")
df <- read_excel_sheets(
    filename = paste0(file_path, "diamonds_split.xlsx"),"),
    single_tbl = TRUE
)
```

What we have done here is to simply call in a few libraries into our environment, pull in the sheet reading function, and read in our data. We loaded the `read_excel_sheets()` function into our environment using the `source()` command. You might be wondering how the data was created for this section, and it is important because it was exported from the `ggplot2` library. Here is the code if you want to re-create the data so that the preceding code will work, and the following sections will also work:

```
# Library Load
library(tidyverse)
library(writexl)
library(janitor)
# Write File to disk
file_path <- paste0(getwd(), "/Chapter12/")
# Split data by cut and clean names of the list
df_list <- split(diamonds, diamonds$cut) |>
  clean_names()
# Write to xlsx
df_list |>
  write_xlsx(paste0(file_path, "diamonds_split.xlsx"))
```

Now that we have gone over how to produce and read in the data, let's start taking a look at some visuals.

Visualizing the data

We are going to use two different methods of creating graphs in this section, firstly, with base R and secondly with `ggplot2`. With that in mind, let's get started.

Base R visuals

The first thing that we are going to do is to create some histograms of the `price` column in the `diamonds` dataset. The price is the outcome variable we will use as the predictor in our model in the next section. First, we need to create a vector of breaks that will get passed to the histograms. There is much literature available on techniques for optimal binning strategies. The basic crux is that this will help provide the appropriate shape to the histogram that best represents the data. That is a separate topic and not one that we will pursue in this book, as it is a topic that can span a book unto itself. There is a function called `opt_bin()` from the `healthyR` package that will produce a tibble of break points for a `value` column that is passed to it. Let's look at it:

```
breaks <- tibble(x = df$price) |>
  opt_bin(x) |>
  pull(value)
head(breaks)
[1]   326.000 1130.217 1934.435 2738.652 3542.870 4347.087
```

The purpose of doing this is to try and capture the proper density of information in the data. The `hist()` base function does a good job of this already with a standard method. Now, let's go ahead and create the plots and see the methods side by side. We will use `par(mfrow = c(1, 2))` so that we can plot them side by side:

```
par(mfrow = c(1, 2))
hist(df$price, main = "Price Histogram - Default binning",
     xlab = "Price", ylab = "Frequency")
hist(df$price, breaks = breaks, main = "Price Histogram - Optimal
binning",
     xlab = "Price", ylab = "Frequency")
par(mfrow = c(1, 1))
```

Let's take a look at what it produced:

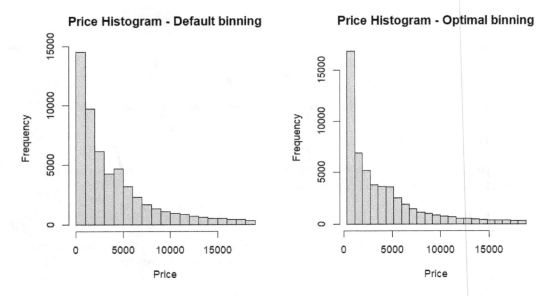

Figure 12.1 – Histogram comparison between default binning and optimal binning

We can see that the shape of the histogram is slightly different, but again, this strategy might not work for you, or you may have another strategy that you employ with regularity; this was simply a way to illustrate that different methods do exist. That is the end of making visuals via base R; we will now move on to using `ggplot2`.

Visuals with ggplot2

We are now going to make the rest of the visuals with `ggplot2` as I find the syntax a bit easier and the graphics one can produce are a bit more sophisticated, aside from the fact that the package is part of the `tidyverse`, which means it is interoperable with the rest of the packages in it such as `dplyr`. You may need to install the `hexbin` package as well. Let's get started:

```
df |>
  ggplot(aes(x = carat, y = price, fill = cut)) +
  geom_hex(bins = length(breaks), alpha = 1/5) +
  facet_wrap(~ clarity, scales = "free") +
  theme_minimal() +
  labs(
      x = "Carat",
      y = "Price",
      title = "Diamonds Data",
      fill = "Cut"
  ) +
  hr_scale_color_colorblind()
```

Here's a breakdown of the code.

For the data and aesthetics, this is how it goes:

- `df |> ggplot(...)`: This starts the visualization using the data in `df`.
- `aes(x = carat, y = price, fill = cut)`: This defines aesthetics for the plot:
  - x: The x-axis represents the carat weight
  - y: The y-axis represents the price
  - `fill`: The color fill represents the diamond cut

For the hexagon geometry, this is what we have:

- `geom_hex(bins = length(breaks), alpha = 1/5)`: This plots hexagons representing data points.
- `bins`: This controls the number of bins for the hexagonal grid. Here, it uses the same number as defined in `breaks` (not shown in the provided code).
- `alpha`: This is the opacity of the hexagons, set to 1/5 for better visibility.

For faceting by clarity, this is what we have:

- `facet_wrap(~ clarity, scales = "free")`: This groups data into subplots based on diamond clarity, with independent color scales for each plot

These are the themes and labels:

- `theme_minimal()`: This applies a minimal theme for cleaner visuals
- `labs(..., title = "Diamonds Data")`: This adds labels for axes and title.

This is the code for the colorblind-friendly color scale:

- `hr_scale_color_colorblind()`: This ensures the color palette is optimized for colorblind viewers

Now, let's check the output.

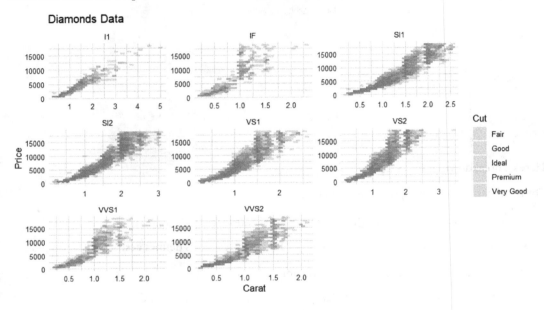

Figure 12.2 – ggplot2 of diamonds data with hex geometry

Overall, this code visualizes the relationship between the carat weight, price, and cut of diamonds, considering clarity groups with a colorblind-friendly color scheme.

The next visual we will see uses a boxplot to check the dispersion of the data:

```
df |>
  ggplot(aes(x = carat, y = price, fill = cut)) +
  geom_boxplot(alpha = 1/5, outlier.color = "lightgrey") +
  facet_wrap(~ clarity, scales = "free") +
  theme_minimal() +
  labs(
    x = "Carat",
    y = "Price",
    title = "Diamonds Data",
    fille = "Cut"
  ) +
```

```
hr_scale_color_colorblind()
```

Again, let's see the output:

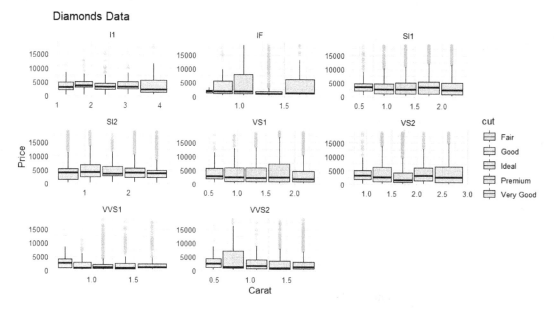

Figure 12.3 – ggplot2 boxplot of price dispersion

We can now look at the mean price with a question to ponder: does it show the information accurately? Let's refer to the following code:

```
df  |>
    summarize(m = mean(price), .by = c(clarity, cut))  |>
    ggplot(aes(x = clarity, y = m, group = cut, color = cut)) +
    geom_point() +
    geom_line() +
    geom_smooth() +
    facet_wrap(~cut, ncol = 2) +
    labs(x= "Clarity",
          y = "Mean Price",
          title = "Mean Price by Clarity and Cut",
          color = "Cut") +
    theme_minimal() +
    hr_scale_color_colorblind()
```

The output of this code is as follows:

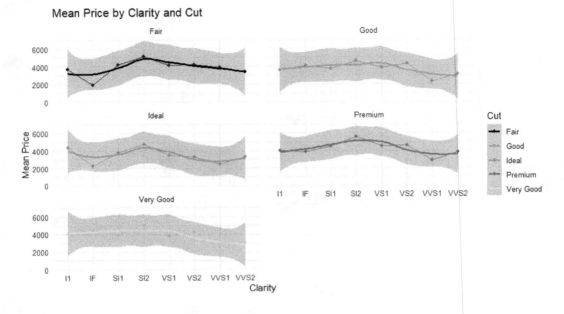

Figure 12.4 – ggplot2 mean price dispersion

Here is another view of the mean price, but this time by looking at the mean price per carat:

```
df |>
  summarize(m = mean(price/carat), .by = c(cut, color, clarity)) |>
  ggplot(aes(x = color, y = m, group = clarity, color = clarity)) +
  geom_point() +
  geom_line() +
  facet_wrap(~ cut, ncol = 2, scales = "free") +
  labs(x= "Clarity",
       y = "Mean Price",
       title = "Mean Price per Carat by Clarity, Color and Cut",
       color = "Cut") +
  theme_minimal() +
  hr_scale_color_colorblind()
```

Let's see what story this tells:

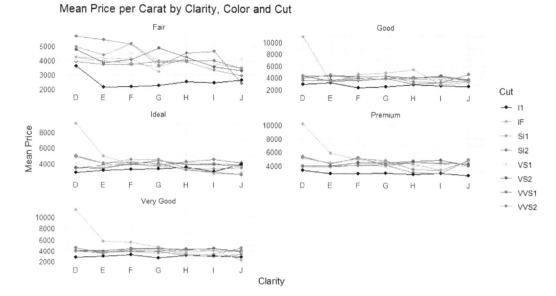

Figure 12.5 – ggplot mean price per carat

These are very good diamonds – does it matter what the cut or color is as long as the clarity is better than fair? Seems like it does not.

Lastly, we will look at a histogram of price faceted by cut rather than colored by it and we are going to use the breaks data we created previously. See the following code:

```
df |>
  ggplot(aes(x = price)) +
  geom_histogram(breaks = breaks, fill = "lightblue",
                          color = "black") +
  theme_minimal() +
  facet_wrap(~ cut, ncol = 2, scales = 'free') +
  labs(x = "Price", y = "Frequency", title = "Price Histogram by Cut")
```

Let's take a last look:

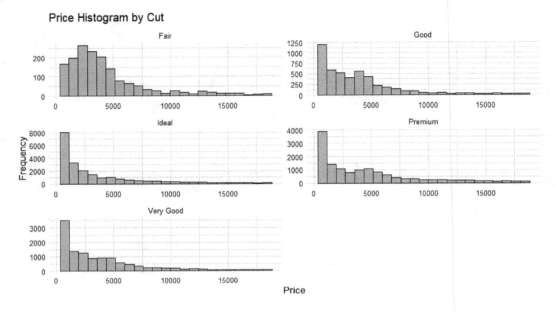

Figure 12.6 – Histogram of price faceted by the cut

Now that we have created all the visuals, we can move on to the modeling phase.

Performing a simple ML model with R

In this section, we are going to go over performing a simple ML model in R. There are so many different ways to do this in R that it would be impossible for me to list them all, however, CRAN has done this so you and I don't have to. If you want to see a task view of ML on CRAN, you can follow this link: https://cran.r-project.org/view=MachineLearning.

For this section, we are going to use the XGBoost algorithm as implemented by the healthyR.ai package. The algorithm is not written differently, the only difference is how data is saved in the output. The healthyR.ai package also contains a preprocessor for the XGBoost algorithm to ensure that the input data matches what the algorithm is expecting before modeling. The two main functions that we will be using are hai_xgboost_data_prepper() and hai_auto_xgboost().

We will not cover loading the data in again as it was covered previously. Let's get started!

Data preprocessing

Before we get started, we are going to preprocess our data so that it meets the needs of the algorithm for modeling. This is made easy by the `hai_xgboost_data_prepper()` function from the `healthyR.ai` library. We are going to see what the data looks like before and after the data is processed. Let's see the following code and then the output:

```
# Lib Load
library(healthyR.ai)
library(dplyr)

glimpse(head(df, 2))
Rows: 2
Columns: 10
$ carat    <dbl> 0.22, 0.86
$ cut      <chr> "Fair", "Fair"
$ color    <chr> "E", "E"
$ clarity  <chr> "VS2", "SI2"
$ depth    <dbl> 65.1, 55.1
$ table    <dbl> 61, 69
$ price    <dbl> 337, 2757
$ x        <dbl> 3.87, 6.45
$ y        <dbl> 3.78, 6.33
$ z        <dbl> 2.49, 3.52
```

This is the data before processing begins. We see that there are 10 columns, and we can see the datatypes of each of those columns clearly in the output. Now, let's create a `recipe` object by passing our data into `hai_xgboost_data_prepper()` and checking the output from there. This function takes two arguments: `.data` and `.recipe_formula`:

```
# Pass data through pre-processor
rec_obj <- hai_xgboost_data_prepper(
  .data = df,
  .recipe_formula = price ~ .
)
rec_obj
— Recipe ——————————
— Inputs
Number of variables by role
outcome:    1
predictor: 9
```

```
—— Operations
• Factor variables from: tidyselect::vars_select_helpers$where(is.
character)
• Novel factor level assignment for: recipes::all_nominal_predictors()
• Dummy variables from: recipes::all_nominal_predictors()
• Zero variance filter on: recipes::all_predictors()
```

Now, let's look at the processed data. We can see in the following that columns have been added and all the datatypes are now <dbl>, which is what was called for in the preprocessor:

```
# Now see the juiced output
get_juiced_data(rec_obj) |>
  head(2) |>
  glimpse()
Rows: 2
Columns: 24
$ carat          <dbl> 0.22, 0.86
$ depth          <dbl> 65.1, 55.1
$ table          <dbl> 61, 69
$ x              <dbl> 3.87, 6.45
$ y              <dbl> 3.78, 6.33
$ z              <dbl> 2.49, 3.52
$ price          <dbl> 337, 2757
$ cut_Good       <dbl> 0, 0
$ cut_Ideal      <dbl> 0, 0
$ cut_Premium    <dbl> 0, 0
$ cut_Very.Good  <dbl> 0, 0
$ color_E        <dbl> 1, 1
$ color_F        <dbl> 0, 0
$ color_G        <dbl> 0, 0
$ color_H        <dbl> 0, 0
$ color_I        <dbl> 0, 0
$ color_J        <dbl> 0, 0
$ clarity_IF     <dbl> 0, 0
$ clarity_SI1    <dbl> 0, 0
$ clarity_SI2    <dbl> 0, 1
$ clarity_VS1    <dbl> 0, 0
$ clarity_VS2    <dbl> 1, 0
$ clarity_VVS1   <dbl> 0, 0
$ clarity_VVS2   <dbl> 0, 0
```

Now that we have seen the data after processing, let's use the `hai_auto_xgboost()` function to perform the modeling. Here is the full function call and documentation on it can be at `https://www.spsanderson.com/healthyR.ai/reference/hai_auto_xgboost.html`:

```
hai_auto_xgboost(
  .data,
  .rec_obj,
  .splits_obj = NULL,
  .rsamp_obj = NULL,
  .tune = TRUE,
  .grid_size = 10,
  .num_cores = 1,
  .best_metric = "f_meas",
  .model_type = "classification"
)
```

We will now create the model and check the output. I am using `.num_cores = 10`, `.best_metric = "rsq"`, and `.model_type = "regression"`, and I do not suggest you run this yourself unless you have plenty of time to spare.

Now, perform modeling using the `hai_auto_xgboost()` function:

```
auto_xgb <- hai_auto_xgboost(
  .data = df,
  .rec_obj = rec_obj,
  .best_metric = "rsq",
  .num_cores = 10,
  .model_type = "regression"
)
```

This produces a rather large object; on my machine, it is 196.1 MB, with the largest portion coming from `$tuned_info` sitting at `169836312 bytes`, which is mainly due to the `plotly` plot and the Monte Carlo cross-validation `tibble`, due to the size of the incoming data. We can now take a look at some of the objects that are exported:

```
xgb_wflw_fit <- auto_xgb$model_info$fitted_wflw
class(xgb_wflw_fit)
[1] "workflow"
mod_spec <- xgb_wflw_fit[["fit"]][["actions"]][["model"]][["spec"]]
mod_spec
Boosted Tree Model Specification (regression)

Main Arguments:
  trees = 817
  min_n = 17
```

```
tree_depth = 9
learn_rate = 0.0205081386887847
loss_reduction = 2.0421383990836e-05
sample_size = 0.762693894910626


Computational engine: xgboost
```

The first thing we did was pull out the fitted workflow object, which can be used to make predictions on data using the generic `predict()` function. We know it is a `workflow` object from when we ran `class(xgb_wflw_fit)`.

The final thing we do is to actually take a look at the specification of the fitted model itself. This will show us what the parameters were set to during the cross-validation process. It is important to remember that I did not use a seed, which means that you can obtain different results. This was meant to be a primer and not an exhaustive write-up of the inputs and outputs, but rather just a showcase of how an XGBoost model can be fitted to data from an Excel file, given one cannot perform such a modeling task with the ease it was done in R.

Now, we can move on to the Python section, where we will follow a similar workflow for the same dataset.

Getting visualizations with Python

In this section, we are going to go over visualizations of the data in Python, analogous to the preceding R section. We will use `plotnine` to have visualizations similar to those created in R using `ggplot2` and provide interpretations of the results.

Getting the data

Like in the earlier chapters, we will load the data using `pandas`. Just like before, the path to the XLSX file may be different for you from what I have, so adjust the `filepath` accordingly:

```python
import pandas as pd

# Define the file path (may be different for you)
file_path = "./Chapter 12/diamonds.xlsx"

# Load the dataset into a pandas DataFrame
df = pd.read_excel(file_path)

# Display the first few rows of the DataFrame
print(df.head())
```

Note that we use the raw `diamonds` dataset without spitting it first and then recombining it, as it was done in the R part of the chapter.

Visualizing the data

Once we have our data loaded, we can use `plotnine` to create visualizations. In this section, we'll demonstrate how to visualize various aspects of the `diamonds` dataset.

Using the dataset loaded before, we can have a first look at the data:

```python
from plotnine import ggplot, aes, geom_bin2d, facet_wrap, theme_
minimal, labs, scale_fill_manual


# Define a colorblind-friendly color palette
color_palette = ["#E69F00", "#56B4E9", "#009E73", "#F0E442",
"#0072B2", "#D55E00", "#CC79A7"]


# Plot using plotnine
(
    ggplot(df, aes(x='carat', y='price', fill='cut')) +
    geom_bin2d(bins=20) +  # Adjust the bins parameter as needed
    facet_wrap('~ clarity', scales='free') +
    theme_minimal() +
    labs(
        x='Carat',
        y='Price',
        title='Diamonds Data',
        fill='Cut'
    ) +
    scale_fill_manual(values=color_palette)
)
```

This Python code replicates the R code used at the beginning of the chapter using `plotnine` for data visualization. The `ggplot()` function initializes the plot, `aes()` defines the aesthetics, `geom_bin2d()` adds the geometry, `facet_wrap()` creates facets, `theme_minimal()` sets the theme, `labs()` adds labels, and `scale_fill_manual(values=color_palette)` ensures the color palette is colorblind friendly using the predefined `color_palette`.

The resulting image will look like this:

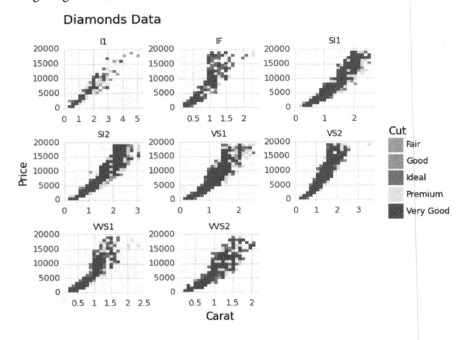

Figure 12.7 – The plotnine scatterplot of the diamonds dataset

As you can see, the plot shows the relationship between carat weight and price by color-coding the cut of diamonds, using a colorblind-friendly color scheme.

Let's have a look at the boxplot of the data (we will not re-import all of the `plotnine` functions again):

```
from plotnine import geom_boxplot
# Plot using plotnine
(
    ggplot(df, aes(x='carat', y='price', fill='cut')) +
    geom_boxplot(alpha=1/5, outlier_color="lightgrey") +
    facet_wrap('~ clarity', scales='free') +
    theme_minimal() +
    labs(
        x='Carat',
        y='Price',
        title='Diamonds Data',
        fill='Cut'
    ) +
    scale_fill_manual(values=color_palette)
)
```

In this code, `geom_boxplot()` is used to create boxplots. The `outlier_color` parameter is set to `lightgrey` to change the color of outliers in the boxplot:

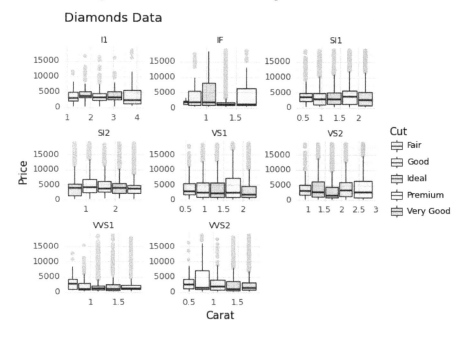

Figure 12.8 – The boxplot of the diamonds dataset

The core purpose of data visualization remains to get insights into the data to better understand it. What if we plot the mean price? Do we see what we need to see?

We can use the `groupby` functionality from `pandas` to aggregate the prices, calculate the mean per group, and create a plot with points, lines, and smoothed lines to visualize the mean price by clarity and cut:

```
from plotnine import geom_point, geom_line, geom_smooth, scale_color_
manual

# Plot the mean price
(
    ggplot(df.groupby(['clarity', 'cut']).mean().reset_index(),
aes(x='clarity', y='price', group='cut', color='cut')) +
    geom_point() +
    geom_line() +
    geom_smooth() +
    facet_wrap('~ cut', ncol=2) +
    labs(
```

```
        x='Clarity',
        y='Mean Price',
        title='Mean Price by Clarity and Cut',
        color='Cut'
    ) +
    theme_minimal() +
    scale_color_manual(values=color_palette)
)
```

Let's have a look at the resulting data vizualization:

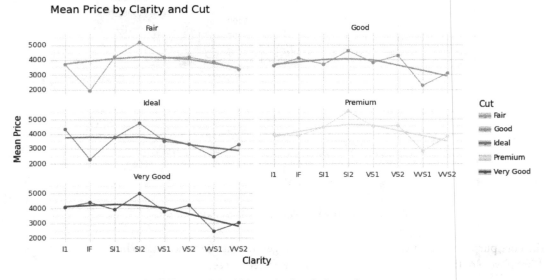

Figure 12.9 – Mean price by clarity and cut

For each cut, a similar curve becomes visible: the mean price first rises by clarity and then drops. Both rise and fall are the least relevant for the **Ideal** clarity while they are the strongest for **Premium** and **Very Good** clarities.

Could we gain more insights from plotting the mean price in a different grouping? Let's take a look at the mean price per carat:

```
# Calculate mean price per carat by clarity, color, and cut
df_mean = df.groupby(['cut', 'color', 'clarity']).apply(lambda x:
(x['price'] / x['carat']).mean()).reset_index(name='m')

# Plot using plotnine
(
        ggplot(df_mean, aes(x='color', y='m', group='clarity',
color='clarity')) +
```

```
geom_point() +
geom_line() +
facet_wrap('~ cut', ncol=2, scales='free') +
labs(
        x='Clarity',
        y='Mean Price',
        title='Mean Price per Carat by Clarity,
        Color and Cut',
        color='Cut'
) +
scale_color_manual(values=color_palette)
)
```

The resulting image indeed shows some interesting things:

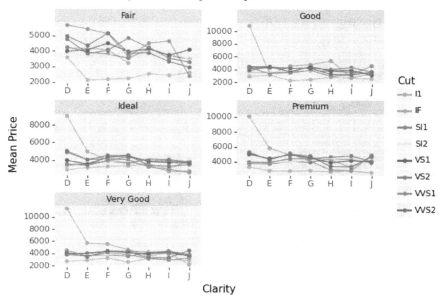

Figure 12.10 – The mean price per carat by clarity, color, and cut

For all clarities but **Fair**, we see that the D color has an extreme price for the IF cut but for the others, the prices remain similar. For **Fair** clarity, however, the prices show a clear downward trend with the only large price difference being between D and other colors for the I1 cut.

Finally, before moving on to modeling, let's have a look at the histogram of prices by cut:

```
from plotnine import geom_histogram


# Create a histogram of price by Cut
(
        ggplot(df, aes(x='price')) +
        geom_histogram(fill='lightblue', color='black') +
        theme_minimal() +
        facet_wrap('~ cut', ncol=2, scales='free') +
        labs(x='Price', y='Frequency', title='Price Histogram by Cut')
)
```

We use default binning because, unfortunately, the great package used for the R version, `healthyR`, is not available for Python (yet).

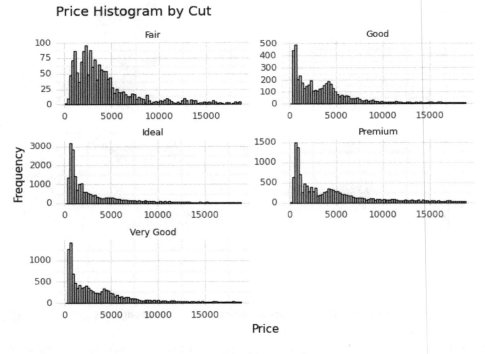

Figure 12.11 – Price histogram by cut

We can see that the price has a very long tail (that is, extremely high prices are relatively typical even though infrequent) and, surprisingly, we can see a second high point for **Good** and **Premium** cuts (and to a lesser extent for **Very Good** cut as well).

With the data better understood thanks to the visualizations, we can start with the modeling!

Performing a simple ML model with Python

In this section, we create a simple ML model in Python. Python has grown to be the primary go-to language for ML work (with R as the obvious alternative) and the number of packages implementing ML algorithms is difficult to overestimate. Having said that, `sklearn` remains the most widely used so we will also choose it for this section. Similarly to the R part of the chapter, we will use the `xgboost` model because it has a great balance between performance and explainability.

We will use the data loaded in the previous section.

Data preprocessing

The first thing to do for the modeling phase is to prepare the data. Fortunately, `sklearn` comes with a preprocessing functionality built-in!

Let's review the steps involved in data preprocessing:

- **Handling missing values**: Before training a model, it's essential to address missing values in the dataset. `sklearn` provides methods for imputing missing values or removing rows/columns with missing data.

- **Feature scaling**: Many ML algorithms perform better when features are on the same scale. `sklearn` offers utilities for scaling features, including standardization (scaling features to have zero mean and unit variance) and normalization (scaling features to a specified range).

- **Encoding categorical variables**: ML algorithms typically require numerical inputs, so categorical variables need to be encoded into numerical representations. `sklearn` provides methods for one-hot encoding categorical variables or encoding them using ordinal labels.

- **Splitting data**: Before training a model, it's essential to split the dataset into training and testing sets to evaluate the model's performance. `sklearn` offers functions for splitting datasets into training and testing sets with specified proportions.

- **Feature engineering**: `sklearn` supports various feature engineering techniques, such as polynomial features generation, interaction terms creation, and dimensionality reduction using techniques such as **principal component analysis** (**PCA**).

> **Note**
>
> It is important to do the feature engineering in a way that doesn't pollute the training data with information from the test data, just like for data cleaning (such as imputation).

We have covered data cleaning to a great extent in the dedicated chapter, so we will make use of the fact that the diamonds dataset is clean already. We will move on to feature scaling and the encoding of categorical variables instead:

```python
from sklearn.preprocessing import StandardScaler, OneHotEncoder
from sklearn.model_selection import train_test_split
import numpy as np

# Encode categorical variables
encoder = OneHotEncoder()
df_encoded = encoder.fit_transform(df[['cut', 'color', 'clarity']])

# Scale numerical features
scaler = StandardScaler()
df_scaled = scaler.fit_transform(df[['carat', 'depth', 'table',
    'x', 'y', 'z']])

# Concatenate encoded categorical features with scaled numerical
features
df_processed = np.concatenate((df_encoded.toarray(), df_scaled),
    axis=1)

# Split data into training and testing sets
X_train, X_test, y_train, y_test = train_test_split(
    df_processed, df["price"], test_size=0.2, random_state=42)
```

This code snippet demonstrates how to encode categorical variables (cut, color, and clarity) using one-hot encoding and scale numerical features using StandardScaler from sklearn. Then, it concatenates the encoded categorical features with scaled numerical features and splits the dataset into training and testing sets using train_test_split().

Let's compare the data before and after the preprocessing.

The original dataset looks like this:

```
>>> print(df)
       carat        cut color clarity  depth  table  price     x     y     z
0       0.23      Ideal     E     SI2   61.5   55.0    326  3.95  3.98  2.43
1       0.21    Premium     E     SI1   59.8   61.0    326  3.89  3.84  2.31
2       0.23       Good     E     VS1   56.9   65.0    327  4.05  4.07  2.31
3       0.29    Premium     I     VS2   62.4   58.0    334  4.20  4.23  2.63
4       0.31       Good     J     SI2   63.3   58.0    335  4.34  4.35  2.75
...      ...        ...   ...     ...    ...    ...    ...   ...   ...   ...
53935   0.72      Ideal     D     SI1   60.8   57.0   2757  5.75  5.76  3.50
53936   0.72       Good     D     SI1   63.1   55.0   2757  5.69  5.75  3.61
53937   0.70  Very Good     D     SI1   62.8   60.0   2757  5.66  5.68  3.56
53938   0.86    Premium     H     SI2   61.0   58.0   2757  6.15  6.12  3.74
53939   0.75      Ideal     D     SI2   62.2   55.0   2757  5.83  5.87  3.64

[53940 rows x 10 columns]
>>> []
```

Figure 12.12 – Raw data as read from Excel

As you can see, the dataset contains a mix of numerical and categorical variables (the latter ones will be encoded using one-hot encoding).

After the preprocessing, the dataset looks like this:

```
>>> pd.DataFrame(X_train)
        0    1    2    3    4    5    6    7    8    9   10   11   12   13   14   15   16   17   18   19        20        21        22        23        24        25
0      0.0  1.0  0.0  0.0  0.0  0.0  0.0  1.0  0.0  0.0  0.0  0.0  0.0  0.0  0.0  0.0  1.0  0.0  0.0  0.0  2.557052 -2.547385  2.928129  2.227628  2.149919  1.744764
1      0.0  0.0  0.0  0.0  1.0  0.0  1.0  0.0  0.0  0.0  0.0  0.0  0.0  0.0  0.0  0.0  1.0  0.0  0.0  0.0  0.447378 -1.221133  1.137995  0.747798  0.661464  0.540273
2      0.0  0.0  0.0  1.0  0.0  0.0  0.0  0.0  0.0  1.0  0.0  0.0  0.0  0.0  0.0  0.0  0.0  0.0  1.0  0.0  0.637249  0.523936  0.242928  0.765627  0.705242  0.795341
3      0.0  1.0  0.0  0.0  0.0  0.0  1.0  0.0  0.0  0.0  0.0  0.0  0.0  0.0  0.0  0.0  1.0  0.0  0.0  0.0  1.481118 -0.174092  3.375663  1.318335  1.256846  1.248797
4      0.0  0.0  0.0  0.0  1.0  0.0  0.0  0.0  0.0  1.0  0.0  0.0  0.0  0.0  0.0  0.0  1.0  0.0  0.0  0.0  1.523312  0.244725 -0.204605  1.371823  1.388180  1.404672
...    ...  ...  ...  ...  ...  ...  ...  ...  ...  ...  ...  ...  ...  ...  ...  ...  ...  ...  ...  ...       ...       ...       ...       ...       ...       ...
43147  0.0  0.0  0.0  0.0  1.0  0.0  0.0  0.0  0.0  0.0  1.0  0.0  0.0  0.0  0.0  0.0  1.0  0.0  0.0  0.0  0.531765  0.454133  0.690462  0.667566  0.678975  0.724489
43148  0.0  0.0  1.0  0.0  0.0  0.0  1.0  0.0  0.0  0.0  0.0  0.0  0.0  0.0  0.0  0.0  0.0  0.0  0.0  0.0 -0.691846 -0.523105 -1.899672 -0.625856 -0.634367 -0.678389
43149  0.0  0.0  0.0  0.0  1.0  0.0  0.0  1.0  0.0  0.0  0.0  0.0  0.0  0.0  1.0  0.0  0.0  0.0  0.0  0.0 -0.987200 -1.011725  0.242928 -1.106447 -1.115926 -1.188526
43150  0.0  0.0  0.0  1.0  0.0  0.0  0.0  0.0  0.0  1.0  0.0  0.0  0.0  1.0  0.0  0.0  0.0  0.0  0.0  0.0  0.215314  0.733344  0.690462  0.355554  0.258706  0.398568
43151  0.0  0.0  1.0  0.0  0.0  0.0  1.0  0.0  0.0  0.0  0.0  0.0  0.0  1.0  0.0  0.0  0.0  0.0  0.0  0.0  0.721636 -0.941922  0.242928  0.970664  0.924133  0.809512

[43152 rows x 26 columns]
```

Figure 12.13 – Preprocessed training data

The preprocessed training data shown earlier has fewer rows (the rest makes up the test data) but more columns: while the price column is not present (it's the variable we want to predict), the categorical variables have been replaced by multiple 0 and 1 values – the result of one-hot encoding. For each unique value of each categorical variable, a new column has been introduced that has 1 if the original dataset had that value and 0 if it had something else.

The y_train variable has the value of the price column for each row in the train data.

With the preprocessed data, we can start the modeling:

```
from sklearn.ensemble import GradientBoostingRegressor
from sklearn.metrics import mean_squared_error

# Instantiate XGBoost regressor
xgb_reg = GradientBoostingRegressor(random_state=42)

# Train the model
xgb_reg.fit(X_train, y_train)

# Predict on the test set
y_pred = xgb_reg.predict(X_test)

# Calculate RMSE
rmse = np.sqrt(mean_squared_error(y_test, y_pred))
print("Root Mean Squared Error:", rmse)
```

In this code, we observe the following:

1. We import `GradientBoostingRegressor` from `sklearn.ensemble`.
2. We instantiate a gradient boosting regressor (`xgb_reg`) from `scikit-learn`'s implementation.
3. We train the model using the `fit` method with the training data (`X_train` and `y_train`).
4. We make predictions on the test set using the `predict` method and calculate the **root mean squared error (RMSE)** (RMSE) between the predicted values (`y_pred`) and the actual target values (`y_test`).

The RMSE is a widely used metric in regression analysis that measures the average magnitude of the errors between predicted values and observed values. It provides a single numerical value to assess the goodness of fit of a regression model. RMSE is on the same scale (units) as the target variable (`price`).

Lower values of RMSE indicate that the model's predictions are closer to the actual values, implying better performance. In other words, a lower RMSE signifies that the model has a smaller average deviation from the true values, which indicates higher accuracy and a better predictive capability.

The RMSE is particularly useful because it considers the magnitude of errors and penalizes larger errors more heavily than smaller ones. Therefore, minimizing the RMSE leads to a model that provides more precise and accurate predictions.

Overall, the RMSE serves as a valuable tool for comparing different regression models and assessing their predictive accuracy in real-world applications.

The model result has an RMSE of around `720`, which is significantly lower than the average price (`3933`) and the standard deviation of the `price` variable (`3989`). This is good news, indeed, as it indicates the model fit was quite good.

Of course, you can consider other ML models (random forests, `lightgbm` or `catgbm`, or even **deep learning models**) and other goodness-of-fit metrics (R^2, MAE, etc.). This section is intended to be a primer on the end-to-end workflow, so exploring those options is beyond the scope of this book.

Summary

In this last chapter, we explored techniques for performing data analysis and visualization using R and Python with data sourced from Excel. We began by loading and visualizing the `diamonds` dataset and the `ggplot2` and `plotnine` libraries for data visualization. Through various plots such as boxplots, mean price visualizations, and histograms, we gained insights into the relationships between different variables in the dataset.

Moving on to ML modeling, we utilized the `healthyR` and the `scikit-learn` libraries to preprocess the data, including encoding categorical variables and splitting the dataset into training and testing sets. We then implemented a regression model using the XGBoost algorithm, assessing its performance using the RMSE metric.

By harnessing the strengths of R, Python, and Excel, users can enhance their analytical capabilities and derive valuable insights from their data.

Thank you for joining us on this journey through the exciting world of data analysis and visualization with R and Python in Excel. We hope you found the content engaging and the examples insightful. As you continue to explore and implement the knowledge gained from this book, we hope you will discover new possibilities and opportunities in your data-driven endeavors. Happy analyzing and visualizing!

Index

packtpub.com

Subscribe to our online digital library for full access to over 7,000 books and videos, as well as industry leading tools to help you plan your personal development and advance your career. For more information, please visit our website.

Why subscribe?

- Spend less time learning and more time coding with practical eBooks and Videos from over 4,000 industry professionals

- Improve your learning with Skill Plans built especially for you

- Get a free eBook or video every month

- Fully searchable for easy access to vital information

- Copy and paste, print, and bookmark content

Did you know that Packt offers eBook versions of every book published, with PDF and ePub files available? You can upgrade to the eBook version at packtpub.com and as a print book customer, you are entitled to a discount on the eBook copy. Get in touch with us at customercare@packtpub.com for more details.

At www.packtpub.com, you can also read a collection of free technical articles, sign up for a range of free newsletters, and receive exclusive discounts and offers on Packt books and eBooks.

Other Books You May Enjoy

If you enjoyed this book, you may be interested in these other books by Packt:

Data Modeling with Microsoft Excel

Bernard Obeng Boateng

ISBN: 978-1-80324-028-2

- Implement the concept of data modeling within and beyond Excel
- Get, transform, model, aggregate, and visualize data with Power Query
- Understand best practices for data structuring in MS Excel
- Build powerful measures using DAX from the Data Model
- Generate flexible calculations using Cube functions
- Design engaging dashboards for your users

Building Interactive Dashboards in Microsoft 365 Excel

Michael Olafusi

ISBN: 978-1-80323-729-9

- Understand the importance of dashboards in today's business analytics environment
- Delve into the various essential formulae in Excel
- Utilize Power Query to shape and transform data to extract insights easily
- Explore the power of the new dynamic array functions in M365
- Employ PivotTable and Power Pivot to automate your dashboards
- Master the setup and optimization of your dashboard canvas
- Discover best practices for visualization, charts, and effective dashboard creation
- Consolidate your knowledge through a hands-on concluding project

Packt is searching for authors like you

If you're interested in becoming an author for Packt, please visit authors.packtpub.com and apply today. We have worked with thousands of developers and tech professionals, just like you, to help them share their insight with the global tech community. You can make a general application, apply for a specific hot topic that we are recruiting an author for, or submit your own idea.

Share Your Thoughts

Now you've finished *Extending Excel with Python and R*, we'd love to hear your thoughts! Scan the QR code below to go straight to the Amazon review page for this book and share your feedback or leave a review on the site that you purchased it from.

https://packt.link/r/1804610690

Your review is important to us and the tech community and will help us make sure we're delivering excellent quality content.

Download a free PDF copy of this book

Thanks for purchasing this book!

Do you like to read on the go but are unable to carry your print books everywhere?

Is your eBook purchase not compatible with the device of your choice?

Don't worry, now with every Packt book you get a DRM-free PDF version of that book at no cost.

Read anywhere, any place, on any device. Search, copy, and paste code from your favorite technical books directly into your application.

The perks don't stop there, you can get exclusive access to discounts, newsletters, and great free content in your inbox daily

Follow these simple steps to get the benefits:

1. Scan the QR code or visit the link below

https://packt.link/free-ebook/9781804610695

2. Submit your proof of purchase
3. That's it! We'll send your free PDF and other benefits to your email directly